PADRE MAC

MURDO EWEN MACDONALD

THE MAN FROM HARRIS

CONTENTS

PREFACE TO AUTOBIOGRAPHY

FOR many years Murdo Ewen Macdonald's many friends and admirers have urged him to record the high points of his remarkable life. We are all very pleased that he has now completed this work.

Murdo Ewen Macdonald has touched the lives of many people over the years. His relatively humble background gave him a humility and a reluctance to discuss his own accomplishments. This has facilitated his admirable success in reaching and influencing many people, especially the young. His scholarly achievements led him early in life to a career in the ministry. Thus his personality, his talent for teaching and his scholarship set the stage for years of outstanding Christian service.

His ability to reach people of all faiths has been a function of his ability to communicate his ideas, his dedication to the fundamentals of faith and his emphasis on basic Christian thinking. His wide and varied experiences have strengthened his appeal to all. He is fluent in Gaelic as well as English. He has served with distinction as a military chaplain and parachuted into combat in North Africa in 1942. He was a prisoner of war in Germany and has lectured in many English-speaking countries.

Murdo Ewen Macdonald came into my life when he volunteered to serve as a chaplain in the American camp at Stalag Luft III in Germany. This was in 1943 when victory seemed far away and American Air Forces were suffering heavy losses over Germany. We survivors found few bright spots in our dirty and crowded existence. The presence of Padre Mac, as we called him, was one of these. He was regarded not only with respect, but with fondness by hundreds of young men to whom he provided guidance and encouragement. To some, this was on an individual basis and to others, he provided an inspiring message of hope, faith and courage each Sunday morning. It was a rare and memorable spectacle to see young men of all faiths crowding into our small theatre on a "standing-room-only" basis to hear him speak.

Half a century later, at each of the reunions of members of this

1

particular camp, listening to Padre Mac on Sunday morning has become an institution. He comes back to us time after time from far away Scotland to re-inspire us with an urgent message, ecumenical in nature, and somehow always touching us in a way that sends us home reassured, thoughtful and confident of God's providence.

Many have wondered at the unique closeness of our group. We are indistinguishable in appearance from other senior citizens. We come together every few years to retell our war stories and simply to enjoy each other. We are told by those who work closely with many veteran's reunions that we are different in some indefinable way. Possibly being all survivors of one of the most dangerous forms of war's catastrophes has something to do with it. I believe that there is at least one other element involved. Murdo Ewen Macdonald entered our lives at a most important time, helped us to mature with a sound sense of values, a renewed faith in our Maker and a clearer understanding of the real meaning of freedom. Indeed, he helped us shape our lives.

A. P. Clark,
Lt. General, US Air Force (Ret.),
August 6, 1992.

PROLOGUE

THERE can be no question that, when we read this book, we find ourselves in the presence of an exceptional man.

I suppose we could attempt to define this extraordinariness in many different ways, but it is best to do so by stating what appear to be paradoxes.

Here is a man of peace who becomes a commando and a para-trooper and a boxer. Here is the son of a crofter who in his time has preached in churches attended by the most brilliant and influential congregations, and yet remains a convinced Socialist. Here is a Gael, who, a lover of freedom, taught Biblical English to a German prison guard and was by means of a joke said to speak perfect Oxford English. Here is a professor who, apparently notorious for his absent-mindedness, has a phenomenal memory for detail, incidents and people, which comes close to total recall. Here is a minister who, coming from one of the most fundamentalist regions in the world, yet makes jokes in church.

It is a quite astonishing life. And perhaps its most extraordinary chapters are those that deal with his period in a Prison of War camp. Surely this is one of the most testing experiences that any man can have, where, as Sartre wrote, it may come to pass that "hell is other people." (Nor does the author himself neglect to quote this state-ment). Nevertheless, Murdo Ewen survives this experience tri-umphantly though he sees some of the bravest of men collapse into breakdown and madness as they come face to face with their own demons and despair in a merciless environment. Indeed these chap-ters are a testimony to the strength and greatness of the human spirit and its endless inventiveness in a world almost without hope. Nor does he surrender to a simplistic anti-German hostility, for among the Germans too he found humanity (though, of course, not among all of them).

I think the reason why Murdo Ewen survived — and what shines through the book as a whole — was because of his love of people, his natural gregariousness. The brilliant and intellectual are here. But here also are men of genius, eccentrics, Highland women and men, saints, theologians, workers, officers (some sadistic, some not) narrow-minded fundamentalists, all seen in the light of a pervading humour, and often irreverence. The book is in fact a summoning up of people seen in all their varying virtues and vices and weaknesses and when one considers how bad most people's memories are for names, over a long period of years it is astonishing how many of them he remembers.

In this book, to qualify for the Kingdom of God one must first and foremost be an authentic human being: and to have the sublime gift of humour seems almost to be essential as well. For Murdo Ewen, God is not the image of a narrow-minded minister: He too has the gift of laughter. He is not opposed to the arts or the sciences: He has created their possibility. Would a Creator be a narrow-minded bureaucrat who hates and fears creativity? Would He despise Dante, Dostoevsky, Cervantes, Shakespeare, Kafka? Not to mention Michaelangelo, da Vinci, Raphael, Rembrandt. Or Brahms, Beethoven, Mozart. What an extraordinary Being this would be, indifferent to humour, paradox, speculation, drama, sculpture, art.

Should we worship such a Being as "better than ourselves". Should we consider such a travesty of a God worth worshipping, as He insists on praise, and deals out his avenging fire.

Murdo Ewen's God on the contrary is an inventive being, involved with humanity, delighting in humour, and in the infinite wonders of the world He has created, without forgetting the pain and suffering — necessities of freedom — to be found in the almost unimaginable inward and outward terrors of a prison camp.

I salute Murdo Ewen for his humanity, for his irreverent mimicry, for his bravery, and for showing that these are co-existent with compassion and profound religious understanding of a world which is at times beautiful and at times terrible.

Let me call him for want of a better term The Happy Warrior of whom Wordsworth wrote: exuberant, life-enhancing, hostile to injustice, a lover of the marvellous particulars of the world, yet aware of the darknesses and not a narrow Jesuitical theologian examining his navel by the comforting light of a demonic inferno.

By their fruits we shall know them. And because we respect Murdo Ewen, we respect his God also.

Iain Crichton Smith. (Iain Crichton Smith is a distinguished Scottish author, poet and broadcaster).

CHAPTER 1

I WAS LUCKY

IN 1953 when I was the Turnbull Trust preacher in Melbourne, Australia, I was asked to give a talk on my prisoner of war experiences. I described how along with my friend, Lieutenant James MacGavin, I nearly bought it in a German transport plane. Taken prisoner in North Africa, we were being ferried from Tunis across the Mediterranean to Naples. Shortly after leaving, the crew became highly agitated. Gesticulating wildly, they kept shouting "Spitfire", their tension increasing by the second. Then suddenly they began laughing and dancing and hugging one another. Grinning broadly at us, above the roar of the engines, they yelled, "Spitfire turn back!"

After the talk a man came up to me and said, "I have found your talk intensely interesting. My name is Dalrymple and I own a farm about one hundred miles up-country." To my surprise he asked me to be his guest for a couple of days. He added, "My wife and I are of Scottish descent. We would like to show you what a modern Australian farm looks like." I accepted the invitation.

The first night after dinner, sitting in front of a coal fire, Ian Dalrymple unfeignedly set out to cross-examine me. "Can you remember the exact date you flew from Tunis to Naples?" I found it rather surprising that he was so inquisitive. It took me two or three minutes to work out the timing. I knew I had been placed in hospital at Dulag Luft transit camp, Germany, on Christmas Eve, 1942. After a frightening experience in Naples, we arrived in Rome on the 21st. After two nights in jail, we were put on a train that took the best part of two days to arrive at Frankfurt-on-Main. "I've got it," I said triumphantly, "It was the 20th of December we left Tunis."

My host left the room. He came back with an RAAF log book which he opened and placed on my knees. Leaning over my shoulder and pointing peremptorily to one of the many entries, he barked, "Look at that." It read, "20th December, 1942, chased German transport JU 12 half way across the Mediterranean About to shoot it down. Glanced at the fuel gauge. Damn! Must turn back or end up in the drink."

Eefore dinner my charming hosts had offered me a whisky. I politely declined as I was a teetotaller at the time. After reading the entry in the log over a few times, I changed my mind and downed a generous Glenlivet. Picking up the log book, the ex-Spitfire pilot said, "Murdo, you don't know how lucky you are."

He was right. Luck has been my constant companion. It has pursued me down the nights and down the days of my whole life. I am unable to shake it off.

I was lucky to be born in Harris, one of the most beautiful of all islands under the sun. The west side of the Island is breathtaking. Mile after mile of silver-golden sand stretches as far as the eye can see. The combination of expansive beaches, turquoise-coloured sea and sharp silhouette of mountains in the background is unbelievably spectacular. It never ceases to excite.

A number of years ago, *The Sunday Observer* had a supplement listing the ten best beaches in Europe. It put two of them in Harris, Luskentyre and Hushinish. The two cemeteries on the west of the Island, Scarista and Luskentyre, have no equals anywhere for sheer scenic attraction. Both are situated by the edge of the Atlantic Ocean. On good days the murmur of the sea has an almost hypnotic effect. On stormy days the sight of huge Atlantic rollers thundering up the incomparable beaches is awesome.

The east coast of Harris, where I was brought up, is very, very different. Scattered along the deeply indented coast is a string of villages known as the "Bays." On the west the "machairs" by the sea are relatively rich and fertile. On the east the soil is woefully unproductive. Tourists, standing on the deck of the ferry The Hebrides as it approaches land, can't believe their eyes. What they see is a bleak, barren land of ice-scored rocks.

From the village of Tarbert in the north to Rodel in the south, winds the Golden Road. Planned and costed before the war, it was not built till the early fifties. In the interval inflation had rocketed, hence the name. The County Council did not have to pay a penny to the crofters for letting the road snarl its way through their precious holdings. They co-operated magnificently.

But why did people settle in such a bare uninviting place as the Bays of Harris? The answer is that they had no choice. They moved there under duress.

Faceless absentee landlords decided sheep paid better than people. Callously they evicted men, women and children off the good land capable of supporting them. The evicted were faced with a cruel choice, Canada or the Bays on the east of Harris. To begin with they refused. When the army was brought in, at the point of the bayonet, they opted for the Bays. It was such a miserable existence that later on many of them emigrated. In 1828 and again in 1850 more than six hundred sailed to Canada.

Those who remained had to learn a new way of life. On the west coast where the ground was so fertile there may not have been many luxuries, but there was no poverty. On the east there was hardly any soil worth speaking of. Driving along the Golden Road one can see the many "feannagan", wrongly translated lazy-beds. Sir Frank Fraser-Darling writes, "Nothing can be more moving to the sensitive observer of Hebridean life than these lazybeds of the Bays district of Harris. Some of them are no bigger than a dining table . . . carefully built with turves carried there in creels by the women and girls."

In order to survive, those evicted had to learn a new skill, how to fish in open boats in rough seas. With no capital the acquiring of boats and nets bordered on the impossible. Yet survive they did, despite the hardships.

In his excellent book, *Discovering Lewis and Harris*, James Shaw Grant writes, "Whenever I look at the miracle of man's endurance, four images float into my mind.

I see a battered merchant vessel steaming into Valetta at the height of the war in the Mediterranean with a Harris Captain — Angus Campbell — placid on the bridge. A Harris piper playing defiantly on the f'c'sle as his ancestors did throughout the centuries on many a bloody field.

I see Donald MacCuish, Scotland's leading authority on crofting law, sitting at the conference table, patiently drawing on a reservoir of knowledge both practical and academic, to illumine the darkness of civil servants to whom crofting was a mystery at best, and at worst an unmitigated nuisance.

I hear a preacher, Rev. Murdo Ewen Macdonald, in one of the wealthiest of Edinburgh churches, boldly tell his congregation of fur-coated wives, "We are waxing fat at the expense of hungry people . . . To glory in the affluent society . . . and preach Christianity to the hungry millions . . . is practical atheism at its very ugliest."

I hear thousands of listeners chuckling round their radios as they listen to a Harris crofter's son, Finlay J. Macdonald, embellish the simple incidents of his growing up with a story-teller's gift for the dramatic or absurd. How does such a barren countryside produce so rich a crop of seamanship, courage, intellectual ability, resolute crusading faith, light-hearted self-mocking?"

I don't know if James Shaw Grant knows that Captain Angus Campbell is my first cousin. I am named after his father. A swashbuckling war hero, Angus was awarded the O.B.E. for gallantry in action. He carried ammunition to beleaguered Malta. When German planes dive-bombed him, he got his piper to play "Cock o' the North." When he entered Valetta harbour, the piper played "The Campbells are coming." This had a terrific impact on morale. On one trip his ship received a direct hit and the bagpipes were damaged beyond repair. Angus wrote to Lord Inverclyde, President of the British Sailors' Society. He implored him to send a set of bagpipes as soon as possible. The citizens of Valetta were missing the skirl of "The Campbells are Coming." Lord Inverclyde contacted Admiral Cunningham and the bagpipes arrived in Malta on the next plane. After his widow's death, I inherited his O.B.E. medal and the celebrated bagpipes. My cousin, Willie Paterson, the civil engineer suggested we present the bagpipes to the British Sailors' Society. This we did and they are on show in their museum, with a neat brass plaque explaining their significance.

Finlay J. Macdonald was my second cousin. Author of a popular trilogy, he was one of the most brilliant communicators on radio and television in Britain. Alas, he is no longer with us. I was present at his funeral service. No one could help noticing the very wide spectrum of mourners. They included Members of Parliament, ex-Directors of the B.B.C., newscasters, media celebrities, university professors and lecturers, well-known authors, actors and actresses, and of course a good representation of crofters from the Hebrides. A tremendous tribute to a crofter's son who knew the meaning of poverty.

I am not related to Donald MacCuish, but his was a remarkable family that I knew well. The father died while the children were still young. The mother was an extraordinary woman. From her croft in the Bays of Harris she managed to send the entire family to University. Two became head teachers, two ministers and, as James Shaw Grant says, one, Donald John, a very able lawyer.

If I was lucky to be born in the Isle of Harris, I was particularly lucky to be brought up in Drinishadder, one of the most attractive villages in the Outer Hebrides. While place-name scholars are divided as to the meaning of Harris (Na-Hearradh), they are unanimous in their claim that Drinishadder means "Sheiling." An ancient custom, still practised in some parts of central Europe and Scandinavia, found its way to the Hebrides centuries ago. After the crops had been planted, the animals were rounded up and moved away to sheilings (Gaelic: araidhean; Norse: saeters).

The Vikings, who occupied the Hebrides for four centuries, established this tradition. After the islands were conquered in the 13th century, the inhabitants of Harris and Lewis continued the practice. Settled on the west of the island, as summer approached, they drove their cattle to sheilings, situated on the east, in what is now called The Bays. Drinishadder means the place of the sheiling.

The village with its twelve crofts kissing the sea, known as the Minch, is striking and picturesque. The view is gorgeous. From the top of Ben Drinishadder one can see The Clisham cluster of mountains in the north of the island, the much bigger mountains of Ross-shire in the east, the majestic range of The Cuillin of Skye in the south and St. Kilda some forty miles to the west in the wastes of the Atlantic. All this is enhanced by the numerous inlets and off shore islands. Drinishadder Bay was always busy. In summer, seals surfacing for breath, otters swimming gracefully, porpoises playing with spontaneous exuberance, northern divers plummeting from dizzy heights when they spotted mackerel or herring. In summer the seals never basked on the rocks from Mondays to Saturdays. But they always basked on Sundays. With absolute certainty they knew no-one would shoot them on the Sabbath.

To the west of the lovely village there was the common grazing. The moor (mointeach in Gaelic), I always found fascinating. There the sheep, ewes and lambs of all the crofts shared a pasture. The community organised three 'fanks' a year. In the month of June the sheep without lambs were sheared, in July the sheep with lambs, and later on in the autumn they were all dipped. At the third fank the policeman was always present to ensure that the dip was at the right strength. These were strenuous, sweaty exercises in which the black-and-white collie dogs played a prominent part. The day the lambs were separated from their mothers I always found sad. The plaintive bleating could be heard all night and in decreasing intensity for the next two or three days. As a wee boy I couldn't go to sleep, listening to their lamentations.

The moor stretched for at least two miles west of the village. Dotted here and there were numerous 'lochans'. Their colour changed as the light and clouds above them changed. Some were blue, some were silver, glistening with lilies. Others were jet black, exuding a threat. Within a mile of our home was a loch known locally as Loch Grannda (ugly loch). It was jet black summer and winter. The Norse and Celtic people were afraid of darkness. That may be the explanation.

These 'lochans' within easy walking distance of the village were something special. Not only were they lovely to look at and accessible, but more important, they were full of splendid trout (geal-dubh-breac). Many of them were owned by nameless absentee landlords living in the suburbs of southern cities. In a beautiful loch, within one hundred yards of our own house, the trout jump merrily in the evening. It is owned by a Harley Street surgeon, who along with a few yuppie friends visits it periodically.

The West Highlanders and Islanders have no conscience about poaching. This compulsive pastime they have never regarded as a sin. On the contrary they look upon it as a sacred duty. To the claim made by the Psalmist (probably a poacher), "The earth is the Lord's and the fullness thereof," the entire community would shout "Amen."

Shortly after I was appointed Professor of Practical Theology at Trinity College, Glasgow, I was invited to deliver a course of lectures in America on "Theology and Preaching." At that time I had no secretary and had to rely heavily on the University's typing pool. The title of the first lecture was "Preaching is a Divine Imperative." It came back typed, "Poaching is a Divine Imperative." Sound West Highland Theology.

In the mid-fifties our Church in Harris was up against it. The roof was in desperate need of repair. The Kirk Session decided to organise a mammoth sale of work to raise the money. The response was terrific. Crofters from all the villages along the Bays brought sheep, rams, ewes and calves for sale to support this special effort.

But by far the most original contribution was from Panny MacLeod, a godly man and a devout elder. He decided to go poaching on one of the best lochs on the moor. He poached from dusk to dawn and came back with forty-five speckled trout. These he auctioned at the Church sale of work. It caught the imagination of all present and the rush to buy the poached trout became a stampede. The sale of work raised well over £2,000, a substantial sum in the mid-fifties.

Farquhar Gillanders, a crofter's son and a native Gaelic speaker like myself, did well. One of my best friends, he ended up Registrar of Glasgow University. Greatly admired and loved by staff and students alike, he died in his early 'sixties. I miss him enormously. In the first edition of *Who's Who in Scotland*, under the heading "Recreation," Farquhar wrote "Illegal fishing."

I was born in a "white" house. When I was a wee boy there were as many as nine "black" houses (thatched) scattered through the four villages. I can recall one black house that shared the roof with the animals. From another in Drinishadder the smoke escaped through a hole in the roof — it had no chimney.

The black house was the traditional Hebridean dwelling. It is one of the most interesting relics of things past. It varied in size from twelve to twenty metres in length, five to eight metres in width. The walls were thick, more than three feet, as a rule. They were made of an outer and under layer between which earth and sand were packed. The walls were low, less than two metres. The couples, or opposite rafters, rested on the inner wall. The thatch was held down by heather ropes, anchored by heavy stones. Its low profile and rounded corners were the perfect answer to the fury of Atlantic gales.

My parents' house was a typical crofter's cottage. Two storeyed, the roof to begin with was covered with tarred felt. Such a roof proved vulnerable when the fierce winter south-west gales savagely hit us. More than once I have seen our roof holed and I remember the physical courage of my father, in the teeth of howling winds, pushing bags of hay into the holes.

The house was built against a hill and occupied an ideal position. To the left was the sea, less than a hundred yards away. To the right, more or less equidistant, was one of the most beautiful lochs in the Hebrides, Loch Plocrapool.

Every night I went to sleep listening to the murmur and the music of the sea. It was a simple house with no luxuries and no embellishments. At first it had no bath, no inside lavatory, no running water. Though I don't remember being hungry, there was little money. In the late 'twenties things were tough. Herring fishing had slumped, the Harris Tweed industry was in recession and unemployment was rampant.

By the late 'thirties things were very different. Tarred felt was replaced by rain-resisting slate. Tiny skylights had given way to storm windows. Crude stone fireplaces became sophisticated steel stoves and ranges. In the last fifty years there has been an astonishing improvement. In Harris at the moment most houses are comfortable, well furnished and fitted with the latest mod-cons. It goes without saying that the tourist trade has accelerated this significant development.

Two years ago at the end of a lecture tour in the U.S.A., two close friends, Bill and Mary Barnes, took my wife Betty and myself for a week's holiday to Bermuda. They adore the Island and have been frequent visitors since they were teenagers. One day we were walking along a road of scenic beauty. We stopped often to admire the rich profusion of flowers and gaze at the green-blue lagoons. Suddenly Betty, my wife, gave voice to an ex cathedra statement: "Bermuda is beautiful, but the Isle of Harris, where Murdo comes from, is more beautiful." The silence was shocking, but our American friends were too civilised to protest. Next year Betty and I had the pleasure of introducing Mary and Bill Barnes to Harris. One late afternoon we were walking on the Luskentyre sands, looking at the blue range of mountains just a few miles away, listening to the lazy surge of the sea. At one spot where the view was beyond words, Mary stopped dead and dogmatically declared, "Betty was right. Bermuda is beautiful but Harris is more beautiful."

Yes, I was lucky.

CHAPTER 2

AN ORAL CULTURE

THE Ceilidh, lamely translated in English as a "visit," was an important event. By some collective subconscious instinct a black house in the village was selected for the nightly come-together. What happened bears little resemblance to the kilted bonhomie extravaganza we occasionally see on television. No formal invitation was issued. The ceilidh addicts met in fair and foul weather all the year round. As a rule they arrived between eight and nine o'clock in the evening. And they settled themselves in front of a large, glowing peat fire. The gathering was a cross-section of the community. Old and young, male and female, married and unmarried, they mixed with effortless ease. The young boys and girls, always present, squatted on the floor. They looked and listened avidly.

There was no planned programme. The entertainment, for so it was in the best sense of the word, varied considerably from night to night. It could consist of the latest tittle-tattle, the most salacious village gossip. And then, without conscious effort, it would become deeply intellectual. It ranged from tales of ancient heroism like the exploits of Fionn and Cuchuillen, to profound and puzzling mysteries. Genealogy was a popular preoccupation. Long before the book and film Roots were thought up, the Celts were hooked on the subject. Politics had a prominent place. This interest stemmed from John Calvin, who was intensely interested in the relation between church and state. The crofters I listened to at the nightly Ceilidhs were much better informed than their so-called more educated, more sophisticated proletarian counterparts in the south. Sometimes a poem with a special appeal was recited, or a Gaelic hymn. The evening ended with appropriate thanks to the host or hostess. The Ceilidh at its best was highly entertaining and genuinely educative.

I remember attending a Ceilidh one night in a thatched house next to our own. The black house was full and fifty per cent of those present had to sit on the floor. That night the man who held the floor was a crofter fisherman by the name of Duncan Martin. In physique a giant, in temperament he was as gentle as a lamb. Well over eighty years old, I can still see him smoking his short stubby clay pipe. He puffed clouds of smoke from his black twist tobacco in the direction of the chimney. As he did, he unhurriedly unfolded the most dramatic of all his many adventures. I was a small boy, but the story I heard that night so impressed me that I can repeat it now almost verbatim.

At nineteen, Duncan Martin was a deck hand on a schooner that sailed to and fro between Scadabay (adjacent to Drinishadder) and Russia. It carried a cargo of salted herring and brought back a cargo of grain and Archangel tar. On one trip, the ship ran aground and the crew was arrested on a charge of spying. They were imprisoned. It would seem that in pre-Communist Tzarist days, the Russian rulers carried around a spy syndrome. Their secret service must have been exceedingly dim. A spying schooner, loaded with salted herring, manned by a Gaelic-speaking crew, is not remotely credible. Not even the British MI5, at its most inept, could concoct such a bizarre suspicion.

In those days, there were no electronic torture appliances. In their absence, the Russian secret service sent in a huge gorilla-like bruiser to extract information from the prisoners. He picked on the youngest and most fragile of the whole crew. A slender teenager by the name of Alasdair, a cousin of Duncan's. The gorilla knocked Alasdair about and kicked him viciously while he lay groaning on the floor. This went on for two days. It was then the rest of the crew appealed to Duncan Martin, the young giant. "You are the strongest man in Harris and Lewis, Duncan. You must intervene or your cousin Alasdair will be no more." Duncan answered, "I have never lifted my hand to man or beast and I am not beginning now." Next morning the Big Russian arrived exactly on time and got down to business as usual. After a savage battering, young Alasdair passed out and lay limp on the concrete floor of the cell, looking dead. Whereupon Duncan Martin stood up and walking over to the bruiser, gripped him by the wrists. "We swayed and strained against one another for a long time. Then I heard bones cracking (Gaelic — Chuala mi brac) and I knew I had broken the Russian's two wrists. He shambled from the prison with his arms hanging limply by his side. We never saw him again."

This was the authentic Ceilidh. It included high drama, clean entertainment, a warm camaraderie and a sense of community which belonged to the very essence of Gaelic culture.

Duncan Martin was one of the many splendid people this crofting community produced. It is not possible to do justice to them all. Invidious though it seems, I must restrict myself to selecting only a few.

There was Alasdair Campbell, the intellectual (a cousin of my mother) who lived in Scadabay, the village barely a mile away. As a young crofter, he was summoned before the Lord Napier's Commission of 1883. Lord Napier was charged with the task of conducting the first official inquiry into crofting conditions. And he was the first to get security of tenure for crofters. Alasdair was the only crofter in the district who did not need an interpreter. He was very fluent in English. At one session Lord Napier cross-examined him about the state of the cattle after a particularly bad crop failure. "You say the cattle were skin and bones, Mr Campbell. Could you be more specific?" asked Lord Napier. "Tell me, how emaciated were they?" Alasdair paused slightly and bowing politely answered, "My Lord, I'll tell you how thin they were. They were like Pharaoh's lean kine, you could only see them in a dream."

Alasdair Campbell was educated before the compulsory Education Act of 1872. The school was on his father's croft and was erected and financed by the Edinburgh and Glasgow Gaelic Societies. He knew Latin. After I went to the Junior Secondary School at Tarbert, every time I visited him he would monitor my progress in that language. A hard-working crofter, he was also what in those days was called the Compulsory Officer. This was the person appointed by the Education Authority to see to it that children attended school regularly. If a pupil was absent for a prolonged period, Alasdair Campbell would pay a visit to the family. His brief was to ascertain whether the protracted absence was due to illness, truancy or parental neglect. A conscientious servant and a born diplomat, he did his job for a pittance. In a voluntary capacity Alasdair was the community clerk. Whenever a letter had to be written to the Education Authority in Inverness, or to the Land Court, Alasdair composed it in copperplate writing and impeccable English.

And there was Angus Campbell (n'Aonghas Beag) who died at fifty-nine, to the sorrow of the whole Island. His mother died in childbirth and his four aunts (my mother being the youngest) brought him up. Beyond any doubt he was the greatest man Harris produced in my time.

A big handsome man with a first-class intellect, he had a delightful sense of humour. Regarded as the best mariner in the Minch, he was also a fine stone-mason, a boat-builder, a cabinet-maker, a useful plumber and an amateur marine engineer. A leading elder of the Church, he was at the same time a preacher of considerable skill.

The day I came home from prison camp in May 1945, he picked me up at Tarbert at 10 p.m. He took me home in a boat he had built himself, with an engine he had cobbled together from sundry bits, collected from various sources. The Greeks talked of the rounded personality and the Elizabethans of the versatile amateur. My cousin, Angus Campbell, powerfully embodied that classical ideal.

The technical skill which was his belonged to the whole family. His brother, Alick, was also a boat-builder, a superb stone-mason and carpenter. His sister, Morag, is the world's No. 1 Harris Tweed expert, weaving the cloth which was made of yarn, dyed with natural colours by hand. On a recent visit to Harris, Morag showed me her order book. One glance made it absolutely clear that she had business in Canada, Germany, Australia, most of all in the United States of America. Recently Morag was awarded the B.E.M.

In the wisdom of God, we are not permitted to choose our progenitors. If this were possible, not for a moment would I have hesitated. I would have chosen my father and mother.

Different in temperament, the two of them in a curious way were complementary. They were not stern, heavy-handed disciplinarians. As far as I remember, my father spanked me only once. It sprang from something which happened one Sunday evening while my mother and he were at church. We decided to teach our youngest brother, John, how to swim. Tying a rope round his neck we cajoled him to go out beyond his depth in the Loch. The idea was that if he got into difficulties we could easily pull him back to shore. The swimming lessons proceeded, but unknown to us, a neighbour reported the incident. And so, like the unjust steward in the Gospel according to Luke, we were called to account. After it was all over, my father solemnly declared he had spanked us not for swimming, not even for putting a rope round John's neck, but for breaking the Sabbath.

My father, Donald Alick, was an attractive man. About five feet ten inches in height, he had immense shoulders and was regarded as one of the strongest men in Harris. He died at the age of ninety-eight. His forebears, who came from North Uist in the late 18th century, were noted for their longevity. My great-great-grandfather, Lachlan Macdonald, made a hundred and ten. We have a copy of his death certificate procured from Register House, Edinburgh, and according to it, the cause of death was old age.

When I retired from Glasgow University, there was an unfortunate difficulty over my pension. Half my salary was paid by the University, the other half by the Church. As a result of an administrative misunderstanding, it took some time to arrive at an agreement. When at length the whole thing was amicably settled, I was sorely tempted to send a photostat copy of my great-great-grandfather's death certificate to the two venerable Institutions. If I had sent it, I would have scrawled at the top, "See what you're in for."

Blond, blue-eyed, with a fresh complexion, my father was a genius with children and animals. In some mysterious way he convinced them that he really cared and they responded to him as to no one else.

In the other house on the croft, a little boy of three got very badly burnt. Warming himself before going to bed, his night-dress caught fire. He was in a dreadful mess and we could hear his screams in our house fifty yards away. He would not let anyone come near him, doctor, nurse, parents, grandparents, uncles and aunts. Then my father was called. To everyone's astonishment, the wee boy stopped screaming and kicking and co-operated beautifully. For the next five weeks my father went over three times a day to bathe the child and smear ointment on the horrendous sores.

He was equally effective with animals. He talked to them as if they were human. Whenever they were sick he would stay up all night. Paradoxically, but perhaps perceptively, the community appointed him the cow executioner. I watched him in action more than once. Apparently there is a small hollow in a cow's forehead from which nerves lead directly to the centre of its brain. My father would delicately explore with his left hand till he found the hollow. Then with a short hammer in his right hand, he would strike with unerring aim from no more than half a foot away. The cow jerked and rolled over on its side unconscious. Long before the advent of tranquilliser pellets

17

and pain killing injections, this was quite a humane method.

I inherited my father's love of animals. I am sure environmental conditioning played an important part too. Which reminds me of how at the tender age of nine I rescued an otter.

I was looking for a sheep about to lamb, when I came across the beautiful creature caught in a trap. The trap was set by our cousin, Big Donald (Domhnall Mor). An elder of the church, he was also a hunter and one of the best shots in the Hebrides. An expert otter trapper, he made money from selling their hides. This supplemented the little he earned from a small croft.

My determination to free the otter was overpowering, but I was terrified. If I tried to prise open the jaws of the trap cutting into the otter's forelegs, it would snap at my hands with its ferocious teeth.

I sat by the edge of the loch and worked out a strategy. There was a byre half a mile away, the property of my two maiden aunts. In this byre there was a number of sacks used for carrying peats and potatoes. I ran all the way to it, appropriated six sacks and ran back to the spot where the otter was still struggling and snapping. I placed one sack over it and piled the five others on top. As I watched the small body writing and swirling under the sacks, I gingerly opened the teeth of the trap. Then I ran. I ran as I have never run before or since. Fear gave me wings. On top of a heather-covered hillock I waited for an hour. Then I returned to investigate. The otter was gone. There was blood on the rusty iron trap and on the grass.

I would not claim that my father was an intellectual, but he was an intelligent man. A born extrovert, he had a good sense of humour and had a fine baritone singing voice. A manager in the school for many years, in common with his fellow crofters he attached great importance to education. The education he lacked, he made sure his children got. He died full of years admired and loved by the whole community.

My mother was very different. Although my father was the prototype extrovert, she was what the psychologist Carl Jung calls an introvert or maybe an ambivert. Definitely an intellectual, she took pleasure in demolishing sanctified prejudices and time-honoured superstitions. Her education stopped at the elementary level. Nevertheless, she must have been a clever girl. Years later she was appointed the sewing teacher in Drinishadder school. A superb seamstress, she was good with her hands and adept at mending clocks. Once while on holiday in Harris, my wife, Betty, noticed that a clock, which was not working during a previous visit, was now keeping good time. "Who mended the clock?" asked Betty. "Myself did it" answered my mother.

Known as Catrìona Bheag (small Catherine), my mother was healthy and strong. She was nearly eighty-six years when she died. She had a prodigious memory, nearly total recall. At school, university and college, my teachers, to an embarrassing degree, used to compliment me on my memory. And I always found myself saying, "If I have a good memory, I got it from my mother." I should add that among my friends I have a reputation for a remarkable ability to forget things I am not really interested in.

Two days before he died, my brother Murdo was driving me from Edinburgh to Glasgow in a battered fourth-hand Rover car. As he slowed down approaching a roundabout, he suddenly said, "Murdo Ewen, would you agree that mother was the most intelligent uneducated person you have ever met?" I agreed that she was exceptionally intelligent, but would not accept that she was uneducated. I argued that in the formal sense she was relatively uneducated, but that in the nonformal sense she was very well educated. I referred Murdo to two famous Gaelic poets to illustrate what I meant. The first was Mary MacLeod (Mairi nighean Alasdair Ruaidh), the greatest of all Gaelic poets. She was exiled by the MacLeod of Dunvegan to a little island off Jura and died at the age of 104. She is buried in the transept of St. Clement's Church, Rodel, Harris. Mary MacLeod was the contemporary of John Milton and, according to discerning critics, was a greater poet than Milton. She could neither read nor write.

The second is the 18th century poet, Duncan Ban MacIntyre. He was a better satirist than Robert Burns. His vocabulary was astonishingly large and he used language with extraordinary flexibility and sensitivity. Like Mary MacLeod, he could neither read nor write. In sum in the non formal sense, MacLeod and MacIntyre were both brilliantly educated.

Both were products of a very rich oral culture. The cumulative wisdom of many centuries was passed down from one generation to the next, not through writing but through a spoken tradition. That is why crofters in the Hebrides, uneducated in the formal sense, are incapable of committing a grammatical mistake in their own language. When my brother and myself were in school in Kingussie and later at the Universities of Edinburgh and St. Andrews, our parents wrote to us in English. They could not write letters in their mother tongue. Fortunately the Cinderella status of Gaelic in our Island Schools is no longer countenanced. Comhairle nan Eilean (W.I.I.C.) encourages Bilingualism from the day boys and girls who go to school. I applaud this policy.

The sense of cohesion which is a feature of this unique community is not the result of an edict or of a directive from on high. It is the by-product of a coalescence of pressures converging from various directions. The Church standing at the centre was one. When I was growing up, the majority of people worshipped twice a Sunday. The mid-week prayer meeting was packed and family worship was conducted in most houses. The school serving three adjoining villages was another. Irrespective of sectarian divisions, boys and girls were educated together. I am sure this had a unifying influence. There were other sundry activities which helped to bind us together — peat cutting, sheep shearing, fishing. These were team efforts. We cooperated because we needed one another.

In the mid-twenties, when I was still at the primary school, there were no luxuries but what we ate day by day was of a high quality. When I came out of prison camp in 1945, I had to spend some time in Bangour Hospital to get my wounds sorted out. I was treated by A. B. Wallace, at the time the leading plastic surgeon in Scotland. We became good friends. Between operations, he would take me home for weekends to his home in Edinburgh.

One day, he was giving a tutorial to medical students on how to do a muscle graft and he chose me to demonstrate the difficulties involved. When the tutorial was finished, he suddenly said, "Murdo Ewen, you have excellent teeth. Tell the students what your diet was when you were growing up in the Island of Harris." I thought for a moment and answered — "Fish on Monday, fish on Tuesday, fish on Wednesday, fish on Thursday, fish on Friday, fish on Saturday, meat and broth on Sunday." "That explains it," concluded A. B. It was a good diet, as nutritious as it was monotonous.

In a predominantly Presbyterian climate, there is one apparent contradiction I have found fascinating, the co-existence of a narrow fundamentalist theology with a robust salty earthiness. Periodic outbursts of revivalistic fervour have not succeeded in suppressing a healthy ironic irreverence. Let me give one example.

John MacKinnon was an elder of the Free Presbyterian Church in Tarbert, Harris, the denomination which excommunicated that godly and brilliant man, Lord Mackay of Clashfern. John's minister, the Rev. Donald Macdonald, despite his narrow naive theology, was a very nice man, highly regarded throughout the island. The last Sunday of the month, he conducted a service in the village of Stockinish in the south of Harris. As the Rev. Donald didn't drive, he had a regular driver called Donald Archie, whose nickname was Jehu, that impetuous character in the Old Testament who "driveth furiously." On the way back from Obbe one Sunday, Donald Archie failed to take the sharp bend on the edge of Loch Direcleit, just outside Tarbert. The car landed in the Loch. The Lord only knows how the minister and his driver survived, but survive they did.

So impressed was the Rev. Donald by his miraculous escape that whenever he preached on salvation, he reminded his congregation of how the Lord saved him when he was submerged in Loch Direcleit. This continued month after month, year after year without let up. The eccentric elder, John MacKinnon, had enough. He decided to put paid to the escape from Loch Direcleit once and for all. A born opportunist, he took his chance when he was asked to lead in prayer one Friday Communion Question Day. His prayer sounded as if he was conducting a seminar for the enlightenment of the Almighty. It proceeded like this. "Better than any of us, you know Lord that circumstances in the world to come are quite different from the one in which we live. For example, take the parable of Dives and Lazarus in the Gospels. Lazarus was a poor wretch in the present world, sitting outside the gate of the Temple with his beggar's bowl, accosting the passers-by with his ingratiating whine. But in the world to come! No beggar him! He went straight to Paradise where he possessed riches beyond compare. Bliss was his for all eternity. But Dives, what happened to him? I'll tell you Lord. In this world he was what they call in the other language (English) a millionaire, with many servants and flunkies at his beck and call. But in the next world he was poorer than Lazarus the beggar ever was. He did not go to Heaven, he went to Hell to the very bottom of Hell which is the hottest." At which point there was a dramatic pause which John ended thus. "Dives would not be the one to complain if he had been dipped in Loch Direcleit." That did it. The miraculous escape was never again mentioned.

Ever since I came to think for myself, I have rebelled against the negative aspects of Hebridean religion. But at the end of the day, I would agree with John MacLeod, one of the brightest, most literate, most provocative of recent Scottish journalists who shocked many Hebrideans with his scathing analysis of what he calls the "Malaise of the Gaels." At the end of many savage strictures he concludes on this positive note: "There are no people on the face of the earth as warm-hearted, as humorous, as hospitable as the folk of the Outer Hebrides." I agree.

CHAPTER 3

ANATOMY OF A COMMUNITY

THE little school by the sea was the axis round which the crofting community revolved. It was in this two-teacher school that children from the three villages, Scadabay, Drinishadder and Meavag, began their education. The vast majority left at the age of fourteen. The minority, fortunate enough to win bursaries in a fiercely competitive contest, moved on to a Junior Secondary school some five or six miles away. It was called Sir Edward Scott's Public School.

My first day at the village school was a traumatic experience. Introduction to the process of learning in a foreign language at the age of six is somewhat confusing. My entire English vocabulary amounted to two words, "yes" and "no". The teacher, though a native Gaelic speaker, taught all lessons in English. There were over sixty pupils attending Drinishadder school the day I enrolled. When the number dwindled to three or four a few years ago, the school was closed. Another grim reminder of the relentless depopulation which has ravaged the Hebrides over decades. Successive governments, whatever their political hue, have loftily ignored the problem.

The Headmaster was a unique character. His nickname was "Calum a Chadail", translated "Sleepy Malcolm". It was an accurate description. Every morning we arrived punctually at 9 a.m., but there was no sign of the sleepy one. The boys played shinty. The girls pre-occupied themselves with pursuits less vigorous. About half past ten, sometimes eleven, an unkempt, unshaven Calum would suddenly appear and blow his whistle imperiously. We may not have been the best scholars in the Island of Harris, but when it came to shinty, we had no equals.

I am not suggesting that Sleepy Malcolm was a disaster. Far from it; he was a good teacher. I can still see him striding up and down the long classroom gesticulating, an inspired communicator. His favourite subject was history. On Napoleon and Wellington few could stimulate like him.

His was a short fuse. At times his temper would erupt like an overheated Vesuvius. These occasional outbursts may have been connected with Sleepy Malcolm being wounded, gassed and imprisoned in the First War.

This I learned to my cost one afternoon. In the middle of a geography lesson, the Sleepy one pounced on a boy called Angus, who shared a desk with me. Angus was a superb athlete but could not be remotely described as an intellectual. The Headmaster thundered, "Angus Macdonald, what are the MacGillicuddy's Reeks?" Before Angus could confess his total ignorance, there was a knock at the door. Sleepy Malcolm rose from his desk and went out to investigate. While he was away, Angus asked me frantically, "What are the MacGillicuddy's Reeks?" To my eternal shame I told him, "They are a Tribe who came to Ireland under Julius Caesar and they have remained there ever since."

When at length Sleepy Malcolm returned and asked the question once again, Angus repeated what I told him like a performing parrot. He was summoned to the floor, the gladiatorial arena where retributive punishment always took place. The cross-examination began. Angus, no budding scholar, was a genuinely nice boy. Loath to betray me, he proceeded to prevaricate. When the Headmaster shouted, "It was Murdo Ewen who put that into your head?" Angus, terrified out of his wits, nodded. It was my turn to enter the arena. Sleepy Malcolm, with studied unhaste, opened his desk. From its depths he removed the dreaded Lochgelly tawse. Commanding me to cross my hands, he gave me six of his ferocious best.

The rest of the class, who looked on, were furious. They felt deeply that the punishment did not fit the crime. So next day, at the lunch time break, they dug up a number of eels from the shore on which the school literally stood. They deposited the slimy wriggling creatures in the Headmaster's desk among all sorts of important papers including the Register. At the inevitable Court Martial that followed, the ranks stood firm.

I said Sleepy Malcolm's favourite subject was History. Next to it was Navigation. The moment the month of June came in, he would send the girls home at 3 p.m. The boys he dragooned into boats which he had borrowed from neighbouring crofters. For the next two hours, he would teach us how to set sail, lower it, tack against the wind and steer by compass. No wonder the three villages produced so many first officers and sea captains.

The pupils in Drinishadder School were the children of crofters who had little or no money in the late 'twenties and early 'thirties. Unemployment was high. Herring fishing was in the doldrums and the ancillary Harris Tweed industry was going through a bad patch. Despite this, the village of Drinishadder managed to send a surprisingly high proportion of boys and girls into the various professions.

My older brother, Murdo, did not distinguish himself at the village school. Like so many others, he left at fourteen years of age. Two years later, motivated by the ambition to become a minister, he gained entrance to the Junior Secondary school at Tarbert and later to Kingussie Secondary School. There he got the requisite number of passes to qualify for entrance to Edinburgh University. After completing an M.A. degree, he took his theological training in Christ College, Aberdeen.

Murdo served three congregations in Islay, Glasgow and Edinburgh. There, at the peak of a very fine ministry, he died of a heart attack at the age of fifty-four. Intelligent though he was, he would not claim to be a scholar. Nor was he an outstanding preacher. As a pastor, though, I have not met his superior in the whole of the Church of Scotland. Incredibly generous, he really cared for people. The night before he died, he procured a television set for a woman who was bed-ridden for ten years. He carried it up three flights of stairs, plugged it in and got it working. He opened up for her a new universe. A pastor to the end.

John, the youngest in our family, was quite different. He too left school at fourteen. While still a teenager, he joined the Merchant Navy. At the outbreak of war in 1939 he transferred to the Royal Navy where he had a distinguished career.

The first Victoria Cross of the Second World War was awarded to the Captain of the *Rawalpindi*, an armoured liner death trap escorting a convoy to the U.S.A. He was the father of Ludovic Kennedy, the well-known writer and T.V. personality. Captain Kennedy, in order to let the convoy get through, engaged a German Battleship, the most powerful afloat at the time. With brilliant seamanship and unbelievable courage, he fought for two hours, letting the convoy escape. At the end, the inadequately armoured liner was blown out of the sea. Captain Kennedy was killed. He was awarded the Victoria Cross. No-one deserved it more.

A few hours afterwards, at dusk, John, an able seaman, was at the wheel. With his excellent eyesight he spotted objects bobbing in the sea. When he reported to the Commander in charge of the watch, he was told he was hallucinating. At the end of an acrimonious argument, the Captain was called. He ordered the ship to turn round and within half an hour the survivors of the *Rawalpindi* were rescued. For his alert seamanship John was Mentioned in Dispatches.

On D-day, John was Chief Petty Officer of a minesweeper lifting mines along the coast of Normandy, hours before the main assault took place. One mine exploded, wounding him badly. He carried on as if nothing had happened. For courage and tenacity in face of the enemy, he was awarded the Military Medal.

John had an outrageous sense of humour. He was the best mimic I have ever known. Any preacher he heard he could impersonate to perfection. His portrayal of one Elder leading the evening congregation in prayer was so comically and cruelly accurate that the entire family was reduced to helpless laughter. Sunday night was Theatre in our home.

After the war, he went to college, studied hard and got his Master's Ticket. He married a very charming girl called Helen Stephen. They had two children. Alison qualified as a teacher. Ewen (named after me) is both a lawyer and a Commander in the Royal Navy. The two of them have inherited their father's sense of humour.

Angus, the eldest, owns the ancestral croft. Like the majority of the boys and girls in the community, he left school at fourteen. He could easily have moved on to a higher education level had my parents been able to afford it. We still have a letter in the house from that great man, Murdo Morrison, Director of Education for Inverness-shire. In it he claimed Angus was one of the most intelligent pupils he had come across in the whole county. He guaranteed him a bursary if he wanted to go to a secondary school. Such was the high rate of unemployment in the Western Isles at the time that my parents could not implement the generous offer. So Angus, while still in his teens, like most Hebridean lads, joined the Merchant Navy. When I was going through secondary school and university, desperately hard up, registered letters used to arrive from sundry seaports all over the British Isles. The money enclosed ranged from two pounds to a single ten shilling note.

My first Headmaster, the legendary Sleepy Malcolm, at length retired to Edinburgh. Shortly after I had been appointed to the Chair of Practical Theology in Trinity College, Glasgow, I happened to call on him. By this time he was in his middle eighties and blind. I rang the bell and waited. I could hear him shuffling slowly along the hall. "Who is there?" rasped the well known voice. "One of your former pupils, Sir," I shouted. "I have had many former pupils. Which one?" he bellowed. "Murdo Ewen from Drinishadder, Harris", I answered. The door opened. The blue sightless eyes looked straight through me and he said, "Murdo Ewen, you may be a Professor, but your brother, Angus, was cleverer than you."

Angus, through no fault of his own, missed a higher education, but his family did not. He and his wife, Mary, worked hard to enable Catherine and Chrissie to become teachers, Donald Alick an engineer, Annie a nursing sister and Dolina (twice a beauty queen) a secretary. This is in the Highland tradition. Parents who did not make it themselves are doubly determined their children will.

The next croft, Number 9, supported four families. They produced four teachers, an engineer, a police inspector, a banker and an officer in the Merchant Navy. Number 8 produced a teacher and a mercantile marine officer. Number 7 produced a minister and a wireless operator. Number 6, two teachers, an engineer and a banker. The MacLeods of Croft 5, our cousins, were a particularly able family. Katie and Rhoda graduated in Jordanhill College of Education in Glasgow, and became headmistresses. Their brother, Donald Alick, did not go to college; he joined a bank. In time he became general manager of the British West African Bank. He made the front page of *Time Magazine* and, in recognition of his outstanding abilities, was awarded the C.B.E. The other two members of the family, John Angus and Rachel, denied the privilege of a higher education, were, I am sure, equally intelligent. John Angus with his engaging stammer was one of my favourite relatives.

The MacLeods and ourselves were very close, perhaps because our grandparents were evicted from their crofts five times. When in the late 'twenties they emigrated to North Uist, my father helped Alick MacLeod to build the new house.

How did a village of twelve crofts manage to send so many into the professions? One of the various explanations is that the community was motivated by the ambition to opt out of a bleak economic future. Another is the prestige accorded to teachers and the inordinate importance attached to learning. Again, the village was innocent of distractions: no radio, no television, no discos, only an occasional newspaper. Speculations beyond objective analysis, one irreducible fact remains. The remarkable educational achievement of this village, pointing to a reservoir of a basic genetic ability.

Even more than education, religion was at the centre of the stage. I doubt if any part of Europe is more Church orientated than the Hebrides. Since the end of the 18th century, the Sabbath has been observed with oppressive rigour. I am prepared to admit that this stern discipline has some by-product benefits. But I am also bound to say that solemn sabbatarianism in no way demonstrates the joy of the Lord.

From my earliest memory Duncan MacLeod was my minister. He did not baptize me. His immediate predecessor, the Rev. Mr Campbell, did. If I have any schizophrenic tendencies, this surely is the explanation.

Tall, straight as a lance, with high cheek-bones, deep blue eyes, a cleft chin and dark hair, he looked like Abraham Lincoln without the beard. A saintly benevolent dictator, he bestrode the Island of Harris like a colossus. Dr. Roderick Smith, one of my oldest and closest friends, assisted him in the very late 'twenties. He agrees with me that Donnachadh Mor (Big Duncan) was the greatest minister he ever met.

A good scholar, the Rev. Duncan could teach English, Gaelic, Maths, Latin, Greek and Hebrew up to university standards. Only a few bursaries were awarded in the fierce competitive educational arena so the parish minister came to the rescue. In his study in the lovely manse by the sea, he tutored many lads, drilling them mercilessly till they passed the "Prelims." This gained them entrance to university.

His Alma Mater, Aberdeen University, on learning of his unique contribution to Hebridean Education, conferred on him the honorary degree of Doctor of Divinity. I like the citation which described him as "The University of the Outer Hebrides." The whole community, including the Free Presbyterians, rejoiced when they heard of this well deserved honour. Towards the purchasing of a gown and hood, these crofters in their straitened circumstances contributed magnificently.

The Sunday after his graduation, the spectacle of boats from every village converging on Tarbert for the morning service, was very moving. The Church was packed. Silently they waited till the door at the back of the pulpit opened. Then the tall figure resplendant in full academic regalia made his appearance. After he pronounced the Benediction, he warmly thanked them for their generosity. Then he said, "I'll tell you what I am going to do. I am going to birl three times, so that you can see this gorgeous gown and hood from every possible angle. Take a good look for this is the last time you'll ever see them." There was a spontaneous burst of laughter. Sitting beside my father in the family pew, I sensed the pride mingled with affection that pulsated through the congregation.

I would not describe Duncan MacLeod as a popular preacher, but he was without compare the most intellectual preacher in the Hebrides. Transparently honest, he was absolutely fearless. His Rambo robustness, his engaging eccentricity, his generosity and erudition, all marvellously mixed, made him the unique person he was. Under him, a congregation of just over 200 members produced nearly thirty ministers. I doubt if such a statistic can be surpassed anywhere in the Church of Scotland.

The Hebrides have produced spiritual giants like Duncan MacLeod and Angus Campbell. They have also produced pillars of neurotic scrupulosity. At an early age I became aware of the split down the middle, the fissure at the centre, what Bonhoeffer, theologian and martyr, calls "the bifurcation of Realilty." Nowadays we tend to speak of it as the "sacred secular dichotomy." While this split exists everywhere in Christendom, it stands out perhaps more sharply in the northern Outer Hebrides than anywhere else. The moment men and women join the Church they are under pressure to renounce what could be reasonably regarded as legitimate pleasures and interests. This includes recreations like secular music, athletic activities and dancing. At the same time, there exists a surprising tolerance towards tobacco and alcohol.

This life denying puritanism has no Biblical foundation whatsoever. It is the very antithesis of what Jesus meant by "the life more abundant." This brand of religion does not increase zest for living.

Instead it has a devitalising effect. Its sponsors fail to see that whatever nourishes personality and broadens its horizons is good. By the same token, whatever inhibits the human spirit, robbing it of spontaneity, is bad.

This moribund Theology we must castigate as the God-distorting heresy it undoubtedly is. Who created the secular world anyhow? Was it Satan standing over the world of the Spirit? No! It was God the Father Almighty! He is Creator of all things in heaven and on earth. He holds the whole world in His hand. He is responsible for our spiritual longings and aspirations, our scientific discoveries, our classical music, our Beethovens, Bachs and Mozarts. Yes! God our Creator and Redeemer is responsible for everything.

A God who exalts the Spirit and despises the Body is not the God and Father of our Lord Jesus Christ. The God who becomes incarnate in Jesus is unambiguously life-affirming. He is infinitely less squeamish than many who profess His Name. That is why I am so critical of the fervent pietistic sects which periodically descend on the Hebrides. Mindlessly they do much damage. They prefer Emotionalism to Intellectualism — an emphasis alien to the Highland and Hebridean culture. Why do they not expend their evangelical zeal on people who are in desperate need of conversion, drug addicts in our cities, the disadvantaged in the deprived sectors of our society? Why do they insist in mounting evangelical campaigns in the most religious community in Europe.

In the Highlands and Islands we desperately need the kind of preaching which communicates the great theologians without fear or favour. In short, courage and intellectual integrity. To be a good minister, one has to be tougher than a commando or a paratrooper. I have been all three and I ought to know. One of my favourite definitions of theology is "Critical reflection on the Christian message." This kind of theology prefers flexibility of attitudes to fossilised virtues. It prefers the promotion of life fulfilment to the preservation of stale and smelly religious orthodoxies. A revolution, spiritual, social, economic is an urgent imperative. I firmly believe it lies in the hands, not of our so-called elders and betters, but in those of the young.

CHAPTER 4

DRUDGERY AND ROMANCE

WHEN I was approaching thirteen, I won a bursary which enabled me to move to Sir Edward Scott's junior public school in Tarbert some six miles away. It was the only town Harris could boast of and was regarded as the capital. From Sunday evening to Friday morning we stayed in digs. After school on Friday we walked all the way home. On Sunday evening, whatever the weather, we made the return journey. It was not till the early 'fifties that the Golden Road was built. It enabled the population of the Bays of Harris to replace sailing boats and foot-slogging with bicycles and cars.

I was fortunate in my lodgings. With my brother, Murdo, my cousins, Rachel and Donald Alick, we stayed with Seonaid (Janet), married to John MacLeod, a first cousin of my father. Seonaid could be described as a larger than life character. She was a staunch sabbath-observing Free Presbyterian who took a dim view of the Church of Scotland. Genuinely kind, she fed us well. Her motto was, "Growing boys must be fed." Each Sunday evening, after we returned from our homes, we were imperiously summoned to family worship at precisely 9 o'clock.

I remember vividly what happened on one of those solemn Sunday evenings. The lodgers had gathered in a large upstairs bedroom, directly above the living-room. We began fooling around. John Angus, Seonaid's first-born, butted me in the stomach. Staggering back, I fell heavily across a double bed. It collapsed with an almighty crash. The noise reverberated throughout the whole house. My brother and fellow lodgers suggested I descend the stairs and appraise Seonaid of the calamity. My courageous descent felt like the long walk to the gallows. Seonaid had heard the deafening crash. As I entered the living-room, I saw her seated in an easy chair beside a blazing peat fire. Paralysed with fright, I stammered out my abject confession. My landlady transfixed me with a merciless steely gaze. After a long silence, she pronounced sentence, "Murdo Ewen, I can forgive you for breaking the bed. What I cannot forgive is that you broke it on the Sabbath day."

During family worship, I was in a chastened mood. After it was over, John, Seonaid's husband, beckoned me aside. With an amused glint in his eyes, he said, "Murdo Ewen, I would not lose any sleep over breaking the bed. It's ancient, it should have been thrown out ages ago."

It may interest you to know that John Angus, the instigator of what seemed to me at the time a major disaster, has turned out to be a model citizen. An industrial chemist by profession, he has a number of inventions to his credit. A devout elder of the Church, he writes well in Gaelic and English and is also a poet. Whenever we meet, and that I am sorry to say is infrequently, we both recall that fateful happening, one Sunday evening, just before family worship.

My going to Sir Edward Scott's public school, (a comprehensive), was probably the best thing that ever happened to me. In the fierce competitive arena in which scholarships were won, how I got one will ever remain a mystery. The truth is that in the little village school I was not all that highly motivated. If the county bursary had not been awarded, I know what would have happened. Along with my brothers, Angus and John and the majority of young men from the Outer Isles, I would have joined the Merchant Navy. In time, if I had mustered enough ambition and worked hard, I would probably have got my "Ticket." It was not to be. The winning of that much coveted bursary shaped my future. Things could never be the same again.

My first day at Sir Edward Scott's, I sensed I had entered a larger and more exciting world. Wider horizons had opened up. Possibilities, hitherto undreamt of, began to beckon. But, with the sense of exhilaration, I was also conscious of a distinct feeling of unease.

Those of us who came from the crofts looked upon Tarbert as a kind of metropolis. It had a main street, a cluster of shops, a post-office, a bank and a pier at which the MacBrayne steamer called three times a week. MacBrayne's seemed to have a monopoly of Hebridean and Highland piers. So much so that an unknown versifier parodied the well-known metrical psalm to read:

The earth belongs unto the Lord
And all that it contains
Except the West Highland piers,
They belong to MacBrayne's.

Tarbert, the capital of the Island, had a collection of important personages. They were the Minister, the Banker, the Surveyor, the Factor, the Policeman and the Clerk of Works. In the presence of these Olympian characters we felt rustic and inferior. We assumed their children had a distinct advantage and that, come the exams, they would slaughter us. How wrong we were! The crofter boys and girls turned out to be good scholars.

The small Junior Secondary school in Harris was one of the best in Inverness-shire. I am not boasting when I claim that a high proportion of the county's competitive bursaries were won by the pupils of Sir Edward Scott's.

There was Willie MacPherson, who taught maths. A stockily built shinty player, he was the best-natured teacher I have ever known. His patience knew no weariness, especially with those who had convinced him they had a "maths block." Never once did he commit the heinous sin of being clever at a pupil's expense. He did not use the strap, but I don't remember anyone ever taking advantage of him. At Junior and Secondary school, maths was my best subject. The credit goes, not to innate ability, but to this splended teacher.

Peter MacLeod, who taught English and Latin, was a very different man. Willie was short, compactly built, with dark curly hair. Peter was a blond blue-eyed Lewisman, tall and massive and handsome. He was not as even tempered as MacPherson, not by a long chalk. In the middle of a lesson, he would suddenly lose his cool. When he did, we lesser mortals trembled the way the Children of Israel did when Jahweh thundered from the summit of Mount Sinai. Despite this, I regard him as the most brilliant of all my teachers, with the possible exception of Professor D. M. Baillie of St. Andrews University.

In the two languages he taught, his main thrust was to build up an extensive vocabulary and a sensitive use of language. Though he by no means ignored grammar, he was determined not to get pupils embogged in the quagmire of nit-picking syntax.

Striding up and down the classroom, he would suddenly turn his back on us, go over to the blackboard and chalk words like phenomenon, invidious, travesty and dichotomy. Then, wheeling round, he would stab a forefinger in my direction and bark, "Murdo Ewen, stand up and use these words in sentences of your own making." A gruelling discipline, but in the end hugely rewarding.

In my time, I have been through commando and paratrooper battle schools. To say they were tough, is a misuse of language: they nearly killed me. I doubt if they were as cruelly rigorous as Peter MacLeod's language laboratory in Sir Edward Scott's Junior Secondary School in Harris.

A brilliant communicator, Peter MacLeod was a hard-working teacher, who conscienciously did his home-work. His real ability was his capacity to motivate. He loved the two subjects he taught and this love was contagious. Under him, home-work was not a dreary chore. It became an exhilarating adventure. How very fortunate we were in that modest school. We collided with a brilliant communicator and he excited us by opening up for us the worlds of Robert Louis Stevenson, Walter Scott, Charles Dickens, Shakespeare, Shelley, Keats and Wordsworth.

The Headmaster, Angus Macdonald, was "sui generis" — absolutely unique. The subjects he was supposed to teach were Gaelic and Art. In these fields he was highly competent. But, exercising his privilege as Head, he dabbled in a number of other subjects, English, Latin, Algebra. Geometry he never tackled, we noted with cynical interest.

My only claim to fame is that I was the one who bestowed on him his nickname, "The Blus." In his strenuous efforts to teach us Algebra, he would say A blus B instead of A plus B. To this day, among his former pupils, some of whom hold positions of national importance, he is affectionately known as "The Blus."

The Blus did not pass any Highers. Neither did he go to any College or University. He must have been intelligent, for at a fairly early age he was appointed a "Pupil Teacher." So impressed were His Majesty's School Inspectors by his ability to motivate pupils, that he was appointed Headmaster in the village of Stockinish, South Harris. It must have been a tough furrow to plough. Whenever we fell from grace, we were summoned into his presence. Glaring at me with righteous anger, he would say, "Macdonald, I have a good mind to send you back to Stockinish." And when I replied with equal righteous indignation, "But, Sir, I don't happen to come from Stockinish," he would shout, "It doesn't matter." To the Blus, the village of Stockinish must have represented an educational Siberia to which all miscreants were exiled, never to return.

The Blus was not good at Albegra, but insisted on teaching it. When he got stuck in the murky depths of a quadratic equation, he would say, "Murdo Ewen, come out here and show these donkeys how to do it." At which point I experienced what some American psychologists call an Ego inflation. After arriving at the correct conclusion, I went back to my seat, thinking of myself more highly than I ought. This was too much for my classmates. They ganged up on me and delivered a mafia ultimatum, "Murdo Ewen, if you don't get stuck in the middle of a quadratic equation, you will come to a sticky end." The next time I was called out, Laurence Olivier himself would have been proud of me. I put on a great act, frowning furiously, rubbing out every false conclusion I had come to and trying all over again. At last I said, "Sorry Sir, I'm stuck," to which the Blus replied, "Back to your seat, you're just as stupid as the rest of them."

Recently a much larger more modern school has been built in Tarbert. At the time the catchment area included the islands of North Uist, Benbecula, South Uist and Barra. It now takes pupils up to the 6th year. Previously they had transferred to the well-known Nicolson Institute in Stornoway after their 4th year. The Regional Council (Comhairle nan Eilean) wanted a former pupil of Sir Edward Scott's to open the new school. I felt highly honoured that I was chosen.

Betty, my wife, was included in the package and we both got the red carpet treatment. We flew to Stornoway and were lavishly dined and wined at the Council's Headquarters. Then we were driven down to Tarbert, where the welcome was equally impressive. The evening the new school was opened, the assembly hall was absolutely packed. There were former and present pupils, parents, grandparents, well-wishers from all over the Long Island. The Headmaster at the time was an Englishman. A former Regimental Sergeant Major, he had a reputation for bluntness. He had unearthed the Blus report on myself at the end of my final year. It was very laconic. It read, "Bright, mischievous, will either go far or come to grief." I suppose it could have been worse.

After winning two bursaries, the County and the Highland Trust, I moved to Kingussie Secondary, which had a good reputation. I could not go to the splendid Nicolson Institute, only thirty miles away. Stornoway was in the county of Ross and Cromarty, Tarbert was in the county of Inverness-shire. In those days the boundaries were so rigid that there was no exchange of bursaries, so I could not qualify for a bursary there. Since Comhairle nan Eilean has come into existence this is no longer the case. On my 5th year, I managed to acquire five Highers — English, Latin, Gaelic, Maths and Science — and, at the age of eighteen, made my way to St. Andrews University.

Kingussie, in company with Portree Secondary and Royal Academy, Inverness, was small, but it had a name. There were four first-class honours on the staff and the classes were very modest in size.

I lodged in a house called "Hillside" on the edge of the little town. The landladies were two unmarried sisters, who were really good to us. There were five lodgers. Alec Hugh Macaulay, the best soccer player in the school, now a retired minister. Hugh Morrison from Barra, who succeeded his father as Post-Master in the Island. Ewen MacKay from Harris, who became a teacher. He was humorous and very good natured. Murdo, my brother, joined us a year later and like myself ended up a minister.

The boarding style was most unusual. I have not come across anything like it. The students from the Islands paid the landlady a modest sum for their rooms. They then opened accounts with the butcher, the baker and the grocer. They were paid at the end of each term when we received our bursary instalments. This rather unique arrangement was supervised by a high-powered committee. It was composed of the Parish Minister, the Doctor, the Headmaster, the local Journalist and the Grocer in the main street. They took their duties with the utmost seriousness. From time to time, we were summoned by this august body. If, after careful examination of our bills, they found we were over-indulging in chocolate biscuits at the expense of meat and fish, we were given a severe dressing down.

I look back on Kingussie School with affection. It was, in fact, a mini-university. I cannot possibly exaggerate how much I owe to it. Over the generations, this modest school has turned out a number of notable scholars. Diarmad MacLennan, Professor of Philosophy in McGill University and a Gifford Lecturer, was perhaps the most outstanding. The number of teachers, doctors, lawyers and ministers it sent to university is impressive. The staff were outstanding.

There was Betty Campbell, the principal teacher of English. Good-looking and good-natured, she was a first-class honours of Edinburgh

University. I don't know why she took a liking to me, but she did. Though I was painfully shy, she coaxed me to participate in the town-school debates. In other words, she was responsible for launching my public speaking career. Many years later, when I was appointed to the Chair of Practical Theology in Glasgow, she sent me a sweet and affectionate letter.

James Giles was the Classics master. Dapper, red-headed, hardworking, we thought over-zealous on homework. A good scholar, he produced a Latin grammar which was in considerable demand. The only teacher to possess a car, he was exceptionally kind to myself and my close friend, Archie MacRury. The odd Saturday, he would drive us to Inverness forty miles away. In Burnett's restaurant, he would treat us to a slap-up meal. Then he would take us to the Pictures at his own expense. Just before midnight, he would deposit us at our respective lodgings in Kingussie.

John Steele, the youngest member on the staff, was immensely popular with students and colleagues. Mild in manner, he was also charmingly absentminded. Along with his unfailing courtesy, he had a wicked sense of humour. This he sometimes used to great effect at our expense. There was no resentment, because we liked him. We knew he was basically a kind person. His principal subject was Gaelic. He also taught pupils up to 'O' Grade in Latin.

Donald Morrison, the Science master, was a lovable eccentric. A double first of St Andrews University, he was appointed a Lecturer in Chemistry there. He did not get on well with his irascible Professor, so he chucked it and opted for Secondary School teaching. We gave him the nickname of Professor Corki. In the children's comic, this was the Professor who in his laboratory always blew himself up. Formidably erudite, he was as much at home in English, Latin and Greek as he was in Physics and Chemistry. Betty Campbell assured me that he knew far more about Shakespeare than she did. I was very fond of him and he was responsible for my going to St. Andrews.

The Headmaster, Mr Brewis, was an Englishman and his subject was Mathematics. As Maths was my best subject, we got on famously. A warm-hearted man, he would occasionally lose his temper. This happened when we failed to grasp what he called the straightforward simplicities of solid geometry. He loved the Highlands of Scotland and he had a special regard for his Gaelic-speaking Hebridean students.

His humanity is revealed by one incident in which I was comically involved. I had the temerity to enter for the Highland Trust Bursary competition. It included papers on English, Latin, Maths and Scripture. My teacher on Scripture was a certain Miss MacKay and I have not met anyone I was more frightened of. The Germans I fought behind the enemy lines in Tunisia were benign in comparison. A rigorous sabbatarian, she was biblically a fundamentalist to her backbone and back-teeth.

In the last period in the afternoon she endeavoured to expound for our enlightenment the parable of the sower. Glaring at us malevolently, she barked, "How many soils are in the parable?" A retarded volunteer from the back of the class suggested one. "You are an imbecile," snapped Miss MacKay. Another, slightly less retarded, said two, while someone else argued for three. It was then Miss MacKay made a fatal error. "Any advance on three," she sneered. Sitting at the centre of the class I shouted, "Three a half." Her volcanic reaction would put Vesuvius to shame. She splutterred with incoherent rage. She screamed, "Macdonald you are a blasphemous rude wretch. Leave the room immediately. Report to the Headmaster, who will mete out the appropriate treatment." This meant the belt.

I wended my way to the Headmaster's room. It was like the long walk to the gallows. When I told him I was sent by Miss MacKay, I could discern a look of great pity spreading over his face. "Sit down, Murdo Ewen, tell me the worst," he said in a kindly manner. I told him about the Scripture lesson and my unhappy estimate of the number of soils. Looking at me quizzically he asked, "Murdo Ewen, were you really guilty of blasphemy?" "Not intentionally, Sir," I answered. "And why did you say 'three and a half' in what was a serious religious lesson?" I answered, "Well, Sir, I picked it up as I listened to auctioneers selling herring on the pier at Tarbert, Harris." His reaction took me by surprise. He placed his feet on the desk, leaned back as far as he could in his chair and laughed uproariously.

When he recovered, Mr Brewis leant forward over his desk. Summoning up a conspiratorial look he said, "Murdo Ewen, I am not going to belt you, but you have to be a good actor. Go back to Miss MacKay's room and conjure up a look of utter misery. Sit sullen and silent at your desk. From time to time throw an angry glance in her direction. Goaded by your dumb insolence she will explode and shout at you, 'Macdonald you are a blasphemer. You asked for it and you got it.'" This is precisely what happened. It worked like a charm. After school Mr Brewis stopped me outside the gate and raised an eyebrow. I looked him in the eye and said, "Sir, I am seriously thinking of making the stage my career." He punched me playfully in the stomach.

This small school was terrific. It helped to make me. In St. Andrews University my lecturers in English, Latin and Chemistry cross-examined me about my teachers at school. They assured me I could have skipped the first year and would have felt comfortable in the second.

A word about the title of the chapter. I have borrowed it from Professor Alfred Whitehead's stimulating book, *The Aims of Education*. A mathematician and a philosopher of the first rank, he was one of the last of the polymaths. In this book, he argued that Education, properly understood, had two dimensions, drudgery and romance. To become a good novelist, a good poet, a good philosopher, a good theologian, a good preacher, even a good footballer, we have to serve a gruelling apprenticeship. This discipline builds a solid foundation which will support higher achievements. But drudgery without romance will only get us to a pedestrian level. The really good teacher is someone who has the ability to fire the imagination. They open our eyes to exciting beckoning vistas. The good teacher at every rung of the educational ladder, elementary, junior secondary, secondary, college or university, will do for us what Chapman's Homer did for Keats:

Then felt I like some watcher of the skies
When a new planet swims into his ken;
Or like stout Cortez, when with eagle eyes
He gazed at the Pacific

CHAPTER 5

ALMA MATER

ST. Andrews has a haunting beauty. It communicates itself immediately to those who see it for the first time. There is an atmosphere, mysterious and indefinable, which clings to its very stones. The beauty cannot be explained by three broad parallel streets converging upon an ancient cathedral; nor by the ageless tower of St. Rule, brooding over the tomb stones at its foot; nor by the 16th and 17th centuries stately houses in South Street; nor by the wide golden expanse of the west sands. No! The beauty of St. Andrews, that grey city by the sea, is something else. It is like the beauty of a woman, a great painting, a moving symphony, or Loch Duich in Wester Ross. It defies analysis.

The game of golf, now a lucrative obsession the world over, was invented in St. Andrews. We have no precise date, but scholars claim it happened shortly after the founding of the University in 1412. We know that John Napier, a St. Andrews student, invented logarithms. But we don't know the name of an earlier intellectual who invented this intriguing and maddening pastime. He remained anonymous for one simple reason. This new time consuming activity came to be officially discountenanced. Because it had become more popular than archery which was compulsory, it was punishable by an Act of Parliament.

In the Age of Faith, pilgrims in large numbers made their way to the shrine of St. Andrews. Today pilgrims in even larger numbers from every corner of the globe make their way to a very different shrine, the Old Course. To those who take this ancient game seriously, the Old Course has become the Holy of Holies.

It is a happy coincidence, or is it providential, that the old grey city is more dominated by golf than any other. At the same time there is no city in Europe more dominated by its university than St Andrews.

The craggy sage, Thomas Carlyle, never extravagant with his compliments, paid this tribute to St. Andrews: "You have there the essence of all the antiquity of Scotland in good and clean condition." Dr. Samuel Johnson, not notorious as a Scotophile, put it thus: "St.

Andrews seems to be a place eminently adapted to study and education." As for myself, I would be content to repeat the words of the psalmist, "Yea I have a goodly heritage."

In October 1933, at the age of eighteen plus, I matriculated. The total number of students was slightly less than five hundred. Despite its smallness, the University of St Andrews was not provincial. Most of the students were Scottish, but a surprisingly high proportion came from English public schools, the U.S.A., the continent of Europe and the Third World. The women's student union and the men's, at the time not mixed, were very active. There were many lectures on social and political issues, on religion and literature. And there was the Debating Society. As a member I acquired a certain amount of confidence in public speaking. In the various societies friendships were formed across faculty and departmental lines.

Sir James Irvine was the Principal and had been since 1921. A brilliant promoter, he was also an able administrator. One of his ambitions was the development of students' residences. In this he was very successful. He managed to secure the handsome benefaction of £700,000 from an American Scot millionaire. This enabled him to build St. Salvator's Hall, facing the old ruined Castle. There were others like Women's Hall, Chattan and Dean's Court. Proportionately this small University was the most residential in Britain. Before he became Principal, Sir James was Professor of Chemistry and had an international reputation in the chemistry of sugars. He also played an important part in developing the gas-mask, used against poison gas in the First War. He was a man of great charm who proverbially could wile the birds off the trees. In an interview he gave you the impression that you were the most important person in the universe.

This most ancient and by far the smallest of Scottish universities simply bristled with world-class scholars. Sir D'Arcy Thomson, whose intellect was as massive as his physique. His was the eccentricity of true individuality. With his blue eyes and red beard, he was indeed an arresting figure. I often watched him striding up and down South Street, a parrot perched on his shoulder. Sir D'Arcy belonged to the ranks of the almost extinct breed we call "Polymaths." Professor of Natural Science, he was a scholar of international renown. When the Chair of Greek fell vacant, he applied for it and was bitterly disappointed when he did not get it. His magnum opus was "Growth and

Form." According to some scholars, it is the most gracefully written textbook of all the sciences in any language. It has gone through many editions and is still quoted.

The Oxford Group, an American import which indulged in the public confession of trivial sins, somehow or other succeeded in getting Sir D'Arcy to one of their meetings. The next day a friend asked him what he made of it. Snorting loudly into his red beard, Sir D'Arcy replied, "There wasn't a decent sin among them."

The twin departments of Latin and Greek were very strong. W. M. Lindsay, Professor of Humanity, was one of the foremost Latin scholars in Europe. He was an Olympian who dwelt apart. During my entire stay in St. Andrews, I never once clapped eyes on him. He was only accessible to honours and research students. He met them not in a classroom but in his study looking out on the west sands.

This story is told of him and I am sure it is authentic. Balliol College, Oxford, offered to make him a Fellow. He declined unambiguously. He then added that he had only one ambition left, to become Provost of Pittenweem, the little fishing village in which he was born and brought up. This sentiment was discreetly leaked by his colleagues. Within a couple of years, he was elected Provost of Pittenweem. Professor Lindsay personifies the high excellence of traditional non-expensive Scottish Education.

Herbert Rose, Professor of Greek was built on Falstaffian proportions. He was the most eloquent and persuasive advocate of a classical education I have ever heard. Exposure to the classics could equip any person for any post in the Army, Navy, Civil Service, Politics and the Church. This sanctified myth he accepted uncritically. I have no wish to denigrate a classical education. In a modest measure I have benefited from it myself. But I do not endorse Professor Rose's deification of it. I have met many of its polished products in war and peace. They did not impress me as all that liberated. The very opposite. In some cases this kind of education succeeded only in strengthening their cast-iron prejudices.

During the First War, Professor Rose served, not as an officer, but as a private. At the end of June 1918, he was elevated to the rank of Lance Corporal unpaid for showing intelligence above the average. Every day in fair or foul weather, summer and winter, he swam in St. Andrews bay. A spectacle marvellous to behold. You could hear him blowing like an oversize porpoise.

In the thirties, perhaps the strongest departments in the university were those of Philosophy under Professor George Frederick Stout and Moral Philosophy under Professor A. E. Taylor. Stout made his mark in two disciplines, Metaphysics and Psychology, no mean achievement. Stout had pioneered the study of the Association of Ideas. This breakthrough Sigmund Freud implemented in his celebrated clinic in Vienna.

I took general and special Philosophy under him and I have never regretted it. We soon discovered that Freddie loathed Bertrand Russell. Neither was he greatly enamoured of Thouless, the psychologist. The class pooled its considerable ingenuity in asking tricky questions. We would get Hamish Fraser, a model of impeccable behaviour to pose them. Freddie always lectured with his eyes shut. I suppose it helped his concentration. Hamish, with excellent timing, would interrupt Freddie in full flow: "Excuse me, Sir, but didn't Bertrand Russell say?" Stout's small frame shivered with uncontrollable indignation. "Did I hear someone mention the name of that fool Bertrand Russell?" "Yes Sir," answered Hamish in his mildest manner, "I did." Whereupon Freddie would open his eyes and shout in a shrill voice, "Fraser, I taught Bertrand Russell all the Philosophy he knows and God knows that isn't much." It worked beautifully. Walking across the quadrangle after the lecture we laughed our heads off. Thouless, the well-known Psychologist, was another of Professor Stout's pet aversions. Again Hamish would interject, "Did not Thouless say somewhere?" Freddie would indulge in his characteristic cackle and remark, "Thouless. His name should be 'Soulless.' In one of his books he has misquoted me three times."

I believe Freddie Stout was the most absent-minded academic in the whole of the English-speaking world. All the lies told about him are true. He personified goofieness. There was no-one in his class.

The story I am about to tell is told of others. I am convinced Freddie Stout was its 'fons et origo.' He was asked to lecture to that august body, the British Association, in Edinburgh. He didn't drive, so he had to go by rail. At Leuchars junction, where one always changed, he walked up and down the platform waiting for the next train. Suddenly he realised he had forgotten where he was going. From a public phone-box he rang up his long-suffering wife. "My dear, I am at Leuchars station waiting for the next train. My mind is blank. Where am I supposed to go? I have no idea." Impatiently she answered, "Freddie, you fool, look at your ticket." He had bought a return ticket and had put the two halves in separate pockets. He extracted the wrong half and returned to St. Andrews.

I cannot vouch for the above story, but I can for the following one. One day in the special Philosophy class, Freddie took us into his confidence. "I have an appointment with the Principal at 12 noon. Will you stop me at 11.50? Be sure to do so for I have forgotten the appointment five times already." I made it my mission in life to get Professor Stout to the Principal in time. Taking my watch off my wrist, I placed it on the desk in front of me. I worked out the time it would take Freddie to shuffle down the stairs, walk across the quadrangle and climb the two flights of stairs leading to the Hepdometers room where the Principal received people. I decided to give him the signal at quarter to. On the second I said, "Excuse me Sir." He was lecturing with his eyes shut and paid no attention. After a discreet pause, I said again, "Excuse me, Sir." Still no response. At this point I panicked. I shouted at him, "Sir you have an appointment with the Principal." He opened his eyes and snapped, "Macdonald, shut up, you are determined to prevent me finishing this lecture." Freddie did not keep his appointment.

Professor Stout lorded it over the twin disciplines of Philosophy and Psychology. I think he was the last to do this in Scotland. By the time he retired Psychology as an academic discipline had won worldwide recognition. All universities of standing in the western world have now a Chair in the subject. How fortunate I was to study under Freddie, the eccentric genius. It is largely to him that I owe my abiding interest in Philosophy and Psychology

In those days the relationship between staff and students at our universities could be described as formal and correct. Since the war, this has undergone a radical change — for the better in my opinion. Gaelic-speaking students were conditioned to place their teachers on a pedestal. We were taught to look up to them and never argue. This respect was so much part of our psyche that it was almost impossible to overcome it. It was at St Andrews that to my own utter astonishment I made the break through. I did not take the initiative. It would never have occurred to me. Several of my teachers were responsible for it. This I suppose is what the theologians mean by Grace.

It all began with Blyth Webster, Professor of English Language and Literature. When I arrived at St Andrews, he was the Director of Studies in the Faculty of Arts. I was summoned to an interview in his retiring room. After two minutes or so he said, "You are a Gaelic speaker. I know it from your voice." "Yes, Sir, Gaelic was my first language." I answered. "And you have an inferiority complex about your English, haven't you?" "Yes, Sir, I suppose I have," I grudgingly conceded. Dramatically, he opened a drawer of his desk, took out a key, walked across the floor and locked the door. Dangling the key in front of my face he said, "Macdonald, I will not let you out till you say goodbye to your inferiority complex in this very room." Then, sitting down, he went on in a more reasonable tone. "Gaelic, far from being a handicap, is a distinct advantage. The last first-class honours I awarded was to a Gaelic speaker." He unlocked the door and let me out.

The talk must have done me good. At the end of session I got a first-class certificate and was runner-up in the class. I found it encouraging that I could more than hold my own with the confident and articulate products of the English public schools.

Blyth Webster was a very handsome man with grey wavy hair. He wore a bow tie and was always expensively suited. All the girls adored him.

Flamboyant in style, he may not have been the best scholar in the university, but he was by far the most popular lecturer. From the moment he opened his mouth, he arrested attention and retained it to the end. His lectures on Hamlet and King Lear were unforgettable.

To my amazement, we became friends. I had many afternoon teas with him in his book-lined study at Number 52 South Street. There, as I sat in a well worn leather-covered chair, he would ask me endless questions about my background, my family and my schooling. The friendship continued. When, years later, I was called to the parish of Portree, Isle of Skye, his congratulatory letter was one of the nicest I received.

The next who helped me in the exciting break through was Terence Bruce Mitford. Lecturer in Latin, after the war he was elevated to the prestigious level of Reader. By that time, he had acquired an international reputation as an outstanding amateur archaeologist.

During the war, he was a commando. Broad-shouldered, athletic, a polished, erudite product of Oxford, he was one of our favourite lecturers.

Quintessentially English in manner and speech, more than anyone I have ever known, he loved the Outer Hebrides. This curious interest and unflagging affection stemmed from a rather extraordinary happening.

One summer, walking in North Harris, T. B., as he was affectionately called, lost his way in a thick mist. Literally he bumped into a man approaching from the opposite direction. This indistinct figure turned out to be the Postman who lived in the village of Croleadha, arguably the most isolated in the British Isles. When T. B. asked him to direct him on the way to Stornoway, the shadowy stranger in a heavily accented Gaelic accent answered, "You will never make it in this mist. Come home with me, stay the night, and tomorrow morning I'll act as your guide on the road to Stornoway." This was the beginning of the most remarkable friendship I have ever known.

That night, before going to bed, T. B., the Oxford scholar, learned to his astonishment that Murdo Macdonald, who had rescued him in the mist, had never been to school. His astonishment rocketed to an astronomic level when he discovered Murdo had acquired a mastery of English, Latin and Greek. In Latin "Caesar in Britain and Belgium" he could translate better than his honours students. In New Testament Greek he was as much at home as he was in Gaelic. More shocking still was the realization that this so-called uneducated crofter knew more about Shakespeare's First Folios than he did.

The friendship which had its origin in the mist, developed into a beautiful one. It was a David-Jonathan relationship against all the odds. The Oxford Scholar and the Crofter Postman wrote to each other once a week and exchanged books. One icy winter Murdo succumbed to pneumonia. T. B. sank into deep grief. I was still a student, but I believe my pastoral help at this time defined and deepened our relationship.

T. B. and I came from very different backgrounds but we became close friends. I was good at Latin, but that in no way explains it. My name was Murdo and I came from Harris. What better foundation for an authentic friendship? Years later when my Alma Mater conferred on me the honorary Doctor of Divinity, T.B. was over the moon. The evening before the Graduation, he arranged a terrific dinner in his lovely house in the Laid Braes. Present were all the surviving Professors and Lecturers who had taught me. I had to pay for my supper. In other words, I had to mimic them all. It was a splendid evening.

My friendship with Donald Morrison, Professor of Moral Philosophy, is rooted in comedy. By my second year at St Andrews I had acquired a reputation as a good mimic. Given half a chance, I was more than willing to demonstrate this meretricious talent.

One day the learned Professor had to go to a funeral and was late for his class which included that most charming of all Roman Catholics, Cardinal Gordon Gray, who insisted that I give them a lecture during Professor Morrison's puzzling absence. My ego hugely inflated, I proceeded to do so. Stepping on the the platform behind the lectern which the Professor always used, I began to expound Plato's "Republic." In particular, his famous parable of "The Shadows in the Cave" which explained the difference between "Appearance and Reality." I am not exaggerating when I claim I could impersonate him well. He spoke out of the left side of his mouth. The effect sounded conspiratorial as if he had served a long sentence in Sing Sing prison in America or Barlinnie in Scotland. I was enjoying myself when suddenly the laughter subsided and I could see the frozen look on the collective face of the class. I knew something had gone disastrously wrong. Then I heard Professor Morrison's lugubrious tones, "Macdonald do you mind if I take over?" Retreating to my seat, I sat there in abject misery. Recently an increasing number of unruly students had been sent down. I was convinced I was going to be the next in the queue. What would my parents say? They had sacrificed so much to send me to secondary school and university. They even had to sell a cow to pay my travelling expenses. What would they say?

Next morning apprehension increased when I received a letter from Professor Morrison. It was an invitation to lunch with him in Macarthur's Cafe in South Street at 1 p.m. I arrived in very good time, my knees playing the "Road to the Isles" against one another.

Inside, the Professor ordered a three-course lunch — soup, meat with vegetables and a pudding. Half way through the pudding, he fixed me with an Ancient Mariner look. He asked me, "How many of my colleagues can you do?" With what I hope was appropriate modesty I answered, "I can do a few of them Sir." The glittering eye transfixed me. "Macdonald I asked you how many?" I decided to be honest. "Well Sir, I can do Professor Stout, Professor Rose, Professor Blyth Webster, Dr Reginald Jackson, Dr John Wright, T. B. Mitford. Over the way at St Mary's College I can do Professor Duncan, Professor Dickie, Professor Baxter, Professor Forrester and the Janitor Mitchell." "And myself," my host added. "Well, after a fashion, Sir." "No! Not after a fashion," Professor Morrison expostulated. "Macdonald, I listened to you for five minutes expounding Plato's parable of 'The Shadows in the Cave' and you can do me better than I can do myself."

He asked me to do George S. Duncan, Professor of New Testament Language and Literature, who spoke in a curious bleating voice. He sounded like a sheep permanently gone astray. So I impersonated him preaching on the text "How much better is a man than a sheep." I did Professor Stout disembowelling Bertrand Russell. I did Professor Rose, snorting loudly as he handed back our Greek proses with blasphemous comments. I did Reginald Jackson, the epitome of mind-stunning incomprehensibility. I did Professor William Forrester praying, "For those who are in prison and those who ought to be."

Donald Morrison laughed uproariously. The tears streamed down his face. I have never had a more appreciative audience. After each performance he would beckon the waitress and order, "Give the young man another chocolate pudding." I left Macarthur's Cafe with eight chocolate puddings inside my very extended stomach. I have not eaten a chocolate pudding since.

At the end of the academic year I was awarded the medal in Higher Moral Philosophy. My cynical friends accused me of getting it, not because I was a good philosopher, but because I was a good mimic. Perhaps they were right, but I would like to think Professor Morrison was slightly more objective.

My energies were not exclusively confined to the purely academic. I became heavily involved in extra-curricular activities. I feel convinced that this kind of involvement enhanced and enriched my education. My first year I joined the Inter-varsity Fellowship (I.V.F.). Recoiling against their theological conservatism and insipid social concern, I found myself gravitating towards the Student Christian Movement (S.C.M.).

It was in this religious group I struck up a friendship with Robin Ross, President of the Debating Society. He persuaded me to join. Incredibly I was an instant success. Within a year I was picked to debate against Oxford University. To this day I remember the subject, "That the masses are the Barbarians threatening the future of civilization." I was more nervous than I was when I was dropped behind the enemy lines in North Africa. Leading the counter motion, I accused the Public School system of Education of the wrong kind of elitism. I accused it of not being in the slightest interested in stimulating the considerable intellectual ability of Britain. Greatly enjoying myself, I was rudely interrupted. The leader of the motion leapt up and in a well-bred Oxford accent intoned, "Mr Chairman, I demand an interpreter." It was not easy to go on after that, but against all the odds, St. Andrews won the debate.

In Athletics, my achievements were modest but gratifying. In soccer I was a useful right back. According to my opponents, I was a dirty one. I deny it. Not once did I ever set out to hurt anyone. Honestly I was not all that skillful. There were only two things in which I excelled. I could belt the ball a considerable distance up the park. And when the outside left got past me, as he invariably did, having a fair turn of speed I always overtook him. Then I shoulder heaved him over the touch line. To put it bluntly, I was not a good footballer, but I had a low centre of gravity and a high co-efficient of aggressiveness.

In boxing I fared much better. By the end of my second year I was welterweight champion of the University. Even more surprising, though comparatively short of stature, I was the hammer champion of St Andrews.

The friendships formed with fellow students were a very important part of my education. As the University was small, these leapt across faculty and departmental boundaries. Two of my best friends were medical students, Tommy Porter and Duncan MacRae, the brilliant Scottish Rugby Internationalist.

Naturally most of my friends were in the Faculty of Divinity. These were the Gaelic-speaking students. Norman Macdonald, the best all-round athlete in the University. John Ross, Angus MacKay, Angus MacCuish, John Alick Macdonald, Calum MacCorquodale and Colin MacKenzie. They all became parish ministers and fulfilled the promise which was so apparent to their teachers at St Andrews.

There were four friends with whom, despite the long war separation, I remained particularly close. One was George Johnston, an excellent golfer and now retired. Another was Jim Porteous, a superb minister and a most attractive human being. Jock Skinner lodged with me for five years in the famous "Bunk", 25 Abbey Street. In classes, in college prayers, in his parents' home many weekends, we were inseparable. Jock had a good mind and a crisp, delicate command of the English language. He was an outstanding athlete. This, combined with his warm spontaneous friendliness, made him the most popular student at St Andrews. The fourth of my closest friends was John Brown, with whom I am in touch to this day. A good scholar, he has had successful ministries in all the parishes he served. The Doctor of Divinity his Alma Mater conferred on him gave me greater pleasure than my own.

As I said before, the relationship between professors, lecturers and students, though more formal than it is now, was on the whole healthy. That is illustrated by the celebrations staged at the graduation of William Wallace Philp, one of the most colourful characters in the University. He had taken eleven years to complete an ordinary M.A. degree. The normal time was three. When the great day arrived, his fellow students put on a magnificent show. With the blessing of the Principal, Sir James, they borrowed a cannon from Leuchars aerodrome only a few miles away. Mounted on a platform with wheels they pushed it down North Street, stopping at the Younger Hall where all graduations took place. The timing was military in its precision. When William, grossly overweight, walked across the platform and knelt before the Principal who patted him on the head and intoned, "et super te", a signal was given. The cannon roared shattering the silence. After the noise subsided, a group of students in the corner of the gallery, playing tin flutes, sang softly, "Abide with me, fast falls the eventide." It was great fun.

The decision to study for the ministry was an agonising one. Like Jacob at the Brook Jabbok, I wrestled with it for a long time. I have never laid claim to a cataclysmic dramatic instantaneous Damascus Road experience; nevertheless, when at last I made up my mind, I believe the decision was authentic.

Three people helped me to arrive at a very difficult decision. The first was my own minister, Dr. Duncan MacLeod, the greatest minister I have ever known: the second was my cousin, Angus Campbell, the best rounded personality I have known: the third was Jock Skinner, a fellow student and fellow lodger, who became a close friend. Remarkably attractive, he was an unorthodox and eccentric saint. I suspect that all saints, whatsoever denomination they belong to, are unorthodox and eccentric.

CHAPTER 6

ST. MARY'S

THE quadrangle of St. Mary's College, dominated by the great Holm oak, under whose shadow pigeons strut confidently, has a curious tranquility. It stands in marked contrast to the turbulence which engulfed St. Andrews in 1538. That is the year in which the Papal Bull, responsible for its existence, was promulgated.

Prior to the Reformation the teaching at St. Mary's was rigidly scholastic. After the Reformers triumphed, especially under the leadership of Andrew Melville, the College was directed exclusively to the training of ministers. To this day it remains the University's School of Theology.

Before the Union in 1929 of the Established Church of Scotland and the United Free Church there were four Regius Chairs in St. Mary's. These were Divinity, Old Testament Language and Literature, New Testament Language and Literature and Ecclesiastical History. After the Union, two more Chairs were added, Systematic Theology and Practical Theology which included Christian Ethics. The new Chairs were founded by the Church of Scotland.

St. Salvator's College, separated from St. Mary's by South Street and Market Street, was barely two hundred yards away. But the first thing I noticed was that the atmosphere in the new quadrangle was warmer, less formal, more intimate. I sensed it my first day there. The Professors who taught us were all ordained ministers. Most of them had served in parishes in various parts of Scotland. All of them were distinguished academics and some had a world-wide reputation. At the same time they were dedicated to the task of vocational training. Their job was to turn out good ministers.

The Professor of Old Testament, Sandy Honeyman, was the youngest Professor in the four Scottish Theological Colleges. A brilliant linguist, I remember him saying once, "There isn't such a thing as Old Testament Theology." He was a good teacher who never put a student down in class. Unassuming and non-aggressive he always was, except when seated behind the wheel of a car. There at least seven demons took him over. He was once caught by the police for speeding and in due course had to appear at the Sheriff Court in the town of Cupar only ten miles away. The afternoon he had to present himself before the magistrate, a number of us went into his lecture room. There on the blackboard we laboriously copied out in Hebrew these words from the Second Book of Kings, chapter 9, verse 20: "And the driving is like the driving of Jehu, son of Nimshi, for he driveth furiously." Next morning at 11 a.m. there was a full attendance at class waiting for his reaction. Sandy, as we called him behind his back, looked at the blackboard, smiled gently and said, "Yes, but the difference is this, he wasn't fined and I was." We cheered him to the echo. Far from being annoyed, he looked actually pleased.

The Professor of Ecclesiastical History, James Houston Baxter, was quite a character. He came from Glasgow and had the typical Glaswegian irreverent sense of humour. He was somewhat peeved that George S. Duncan was elected Principal, a position he dearly wanted. So we became accustomed to the occasional snide joke at Principal Duncan's expense. At the end of one lecture at the discussion stage, a student asked, "Professor Baxter, can you tell me where I can find Professor Duncan's book on *The Ephesian Ministry* in the Library?" To which Binky (his nickname) replied, "Try the fiction section, Mr Fraser."

Binky had an encyclopedic mind. A good classical scholar as well as a good Historian, he was working at a Dictionary of Medieval Latin during my time at St. Andrews. Now and again he would ask us over to his house in South Street to help him arrange the Dictionary in alphabetical order.

In the class, his off-the-cuff digressions were far more interesting than his formal lectures. Often the stimulating asides would take up to fifty minutes, and what he had to say on Augustine, Luther or Calvin was crowded into ten.

Next to Compton Mackenzie, Binky was the most fluent and polished conversationalist I have ever listened to. In College Chapel his prayers, which I am sure he never prepared, were models of perfection. I learned a great deal from James Houston Baxter.

The Professor of Divinity, Edgar Primrose Dickie, was still a young man when he left St. Anne's church in Edinburgh to occupy the oldest Theological Chair in Scotland. In the First War as a very young officer, he won the Military Cross. Taking firsts in Classics and

Philosophy, he continued to demonstrate this versatility for the rest of his academic career. In addition to weighty publications such as *God is Light* and his translation of Karl Heim under the title of *God Transcendant*, he wrote a delightful book of children's addresses to which many ministers are indebted. And over the years, his contributions to *Punch* were highly amusing. Of all members of staff, Edgar was the friendliest. If he met a couple of us in a spare period, he would say, "What about a coffee and blether at Macarthur's?" In St. Andrews, Edgar was the first to make the very important breakthrough in a more relaxed staff-student relationship. He treated us as equals and we felt absolutely at home in his company.

Edgar was genuinely irenic. Always good-natured whatever the provocation, he never once pulled rank. There were some students who were puzzled by the fact that a man who was a war hero could be so gentle, so patient and so understanding. It is a puzzling phenomenon that merits research. In the last war, I got to know tough swashbuckling heroes, yet, in the realm of personal relationship, they were devoid of any aggro. In my year, there was a student who was not the brightest in our midst. He combined a super-abundance of brass neck with a capacity for asking meaningless questions. The rest of us were annoyed, muttering angrily under our breath. I don't remember Edgar ever losing his cool. He would listen courteously to Mr X's vacuous imbecilities. Then, blinking benevolently, he would answer, "Mr X, that is an interesting train of thought. I must confess I haven't thought along these lines myself."

Edgar Dickie was very good to me. The three years I studied under him, his warm friendship meant much to me. The friendship stretched and developed over many years. When I was awarded the honorary degree of Doctor of Divinity, Edgar and his hospitable wife, Ishbel, invited Betty and myself to stay with them at their lovely home, "Surma," the night before the graduation. Years later, we were their special guests at their golden wedding celebration. Edgar was a superb teacher and a great friend.

The first Professor of Practical theology and Christian Ethics in St. Andrews University was William Roxburgh Forrester. He had a long and distinguished ecclesiastical pedigree. His father was a minister as was his grandfather before him. The Roxburgh prize, awarded to the best examinee in scripture in the four colleges, was established by his maternal grandfather. I won it in my time and that endeared me to him.

Willie, as we called him, took a first in Mental Philosophy at Glasgow University. He came to St. Mary's, not from a posh church in the suburbs, but from one in the toughest slums of Edinburgh. With his excellent academic record, his involvement in church and community, he was eminently qualified for the post to which he was appointed.

No. 54 South Street, where they lived, was a remarkable home. Willie and his wife, Isobel — a cousin of the two brilliant Baillie brother theologians — had an ever open door. All students, whatever their country, creed or colour, were welcome. This meant a great deal to me personally. At the Christmas holidays, I could not afford the return fare to the Outer Hebrides. It was cheaper to stay behind in St. Andrews. During the festive season, the Forresters, with characteristic generosity, made me one of the family.

For some reason or other, Willie Forrester credited me with a prodigious memory. In his seminars on Preaching, he would urge us not to enter the pulpit without either a full manuscript or notes, copious or otherwise. Then he would add, "With the exception of Murdo Ewen Macdonald." In time this compliment became embarrassing to me and irritating to the rest of the class. A few months afterwards, my fellow students got their own back with a vengeance.

Professor Willie refused to wear a clerical collar and was a sworn total abstainer. In this particular lecture, he was warning us of the danger of resorting to alcohol when a minister is nervously exhausted on a Sunday evening. This he would point out is how the brilliant popular preacher, Slater, came to grief. He began drinking a glass of sherry after the evening service and this was his undoing. Then, looking at us earnestly, he would plead, "Gentlemen never drink, however tired you are on a Sunday evening." With something amounting to psychic rapport, the rest of the class shouted in unison, "With the exception of Murdo Ewen Macdonald."

Willie was the Pastor to whom all turned in time of trouble. He died at an advanced age. I attended his funeral in Edinburgh and was very impressed by the number of his former students who were present. They came to salute the memory of a good teacher, a good pastor and one of the most lovable of men.

George S. Duncan, Professor of New Testament Language and Literature, and Principal of St. Mary's College, was not a parish minister, but during the First War, he was Chaplain to Field Marshal Douglas Haig. Their relationship was marked by mutual admiration and considerable affection. After the war, Earl Haig, as he was by then, became Chancellor of St. Andrews University. I am sure the noble Earl played a prominent part in the appointing of his beloved Chaplain to the Chair of New Testament. I am not hinting at any unseemly nepotism. George S. had a distinguished academic record, a first in Classics at Edinburgh and Cambridge.

His books, *The Ephesian Ministry, The Epistle to the Galatians* and *Jesus Son of Man* earned for him an international reputation as a good scholar. But he was more than an able academic. He was very human, a devout Christian and deeply interested in the selection and education of ministers. Those of us who studied under him were not one bit surprised when he became Moderator of the General Assembly of the Church of Scotland, an honour he served with distinction.

Of all the academics and ministers I have known, George S. Duncan was the most transparently honest. Deviousness was a word he did not even begin to underestand. Skulduggery in any form, however sophisticated, he despised and condemned in blistering terms.

It was well known that Sir James Irvine, Principal of the whole University and George S., Principal of St. Mary's did not see eye to eye. Sir James was a very successful promoter of the university's interests. What he aimed at, he invariably achieved. He succeeded in putting a small university in an isolated corner of Scotland on the map. No mean accomplishment. In pursuit of this laudable ambition, he did not allow himself to become embogged in neurotic moral scrupulosities. In other words he was the very antithesis of George S.

When at length Sir James was gathered to his fathers, George S. experienced feelings of guilt. I am flattered that he made me, a former student, his father confessor. "Murdo Ewen, you may know that Sir James and I were not exactly bosom pals." "Yes, Sir, I do. It is universally accepted that you were not exactly a David and a Jonathan." Then, intoning the Latin tag, "De mortuis nihil nisi bonum," (about the dead speak nothing but good), he glared at me and added, "But Murdo Ewen, if I were writing his epitaph it would read, "He being

56

dead yet sneaketh."

George S. Duncan was far more than a renowned scholar. More important, he was a warm-hearted, caring human being. He always remembered his former students. Wherever they were, he kept in touch with them. He followed their careers with unflagging interest. When my wife Betty, who is American, arrived in Scotland in 1946, I had an affectionately rude letter from my former Professor. He invited us to come over to St. Andrews and spend a few days with his wife, Muriel, and himself. He ended his letter with these words, "I want personally to tell the dear girl what an outrageous rascal she has married." Betty was overwhelmed by the beauty of the ancient town and her warm reception. There is no one who loves St. Andrews more.

Has God a sense of humour? The answer very definitely is in the positive. Psalm 2, verse 4. "He that sitteth in the heavens shall laugh."

I feel convinced that the Maker of Heaven and Earth arranged that George S. Duncan was Moderator of the General Assembly the year the Women's Temperance Association was celebrating its centenary. The Moderator was saddled with many duties and one was to address this august and formidable body in the Usher Hall. From the platform, he found himself looking at approximately two thousand dedicated teetotallers. Scowling at them benevolently as was his wont, he went on, "My congratulations! You are one hundred years old today. Considering your advanced age, you look so young and fresh and vigorous. Indeed you remind me of that celebrated gentleman, Johnny Walker still going strong." The Psalmist is right, "He that sitteth in the heavens shall laugh."

George S. was incredibly good to me. He treated me as if I was a member of his own family. When I was called to the parish of Portree, he insisted on introducing me to the congregation. He told them of my academic attainments in embarrassingly generous terms. Then he switched course, "Your new minister is a superb mimic. He can impersonate at a conservative estimate a dozen Professors and Lecturers in St. Andrews. If you do not want to be caricatured comically but not too cruelly, be nice to him."

His reference on my behalf when I was appointed Professor of Practical Theology in Trinity College, Glasgow, reads: "Dr. Macdonald has always been a virile and independent thinker. He gave proof of his intellectual ability when, at St. Andrews, he was medallist in all departments of the Divinity curriculum apart from Hebrew. I may add that my honoured colleague, Professor D. M. Baillie, had a high opinion of Dr. Macdonald's intellectual powers."

It was sensitive and shrewd of George S. to include D. M. in his testimonial. If D. M. had been alive, he would have been my No. 1 referee. By this time, D. M. Baillie was recognised as a world-class theologian. In Scotland he was revered. Including his estimate of me did me no harm.

Donald MacPherson Baillie, Professor of Systematic Theology, was a giant who towered over his colleagues not just in St. Mary's College, but also in the whole University. He combined a native shyness with a unique capacity for making friends. Underneath the diffident exterior there bubbled a boyish irrepressible sense of humour.

His two major published works were, *Faith in God and its Christian Consummation*, and the Christological classic, *God was in Christ*. The timeliness and the lucid brilliance of the latter pushed Donald Baillie into the forefront of world theologians. Impression followed impression in quick succession. From the ends of the earth, students came to sit at his feet. Posthumously three other books were published, *The Theology of the Sacraments* and two volumes of sermons.

If it is asked why this original thinker did not publish more, the answer is simple. Considering his physical frailty and his asthma, the miracle is that he accomplished so much. After his death, among his papers there was found some six hundred and fifty carefully written sermons and as many even more carefully composed prayers.

I do not regard myself as one of the great preachers, but I do possess a certain amount of pulpit skill. This in large measure I owe to Donald Baillie. He heard me preach in Martyrs' Church one Sunday. On Monday, he invited me for afternoon tea to "Crask," his lovely house overlooking the west sands. I had hardly sat down when he said, "Murdo Ewen, I have bad news for you. You have the making of a popular preacher." I began to laugh, but he cut me short. "It is no laughing matter, it's a very serious business. Your strength in the pulpit is your ability to arrest attention and retain it to the end. Your weakness is your use of language and illustration. And your conclusions in the two sermons I heard were prolix and predictable. If you are willing, I'll be your preaching mentor from now on. You will deliver me a sermon fully written not later than Wednesday morning. I'll return it corrected on Thursday, so that you will have time to re-write it before Sunday. Do you agree?" "Yes Sir," I croaked.

What D. M. did to the first sermon I submitted, still hurts me. He changed it out of all possible recognition. The red ink he used was indecently spattered over every page. It looked like the field of Waterloo after the battle. Discarded adjectives and adverbs were lying all over the place waiting for burial. He summoned me to his study and the seminar that followed was tougher than any commando course I have been through.

Roaming round the study, he would suddenly stop, jab a forefinger at me and shout, "Listen to this sentence. It is long, rambling and convoluted. How can you expect anyone to take it in?" Then he would come over to where I sat. His grey-blue eyes would look into mine without any mercy. "Murdo Ewen, your basic fault as a preacher is that you use the wrong kind of language. You use eye language, instead of ear language. Eye language is for Essays. It has no place in the pulpit. There we must always use ear language, for the ear abhors convoluted complicated sentences." What he said was so compellingly self-evident that I wondered why no one had told me this before. "Murdo Ewen, you must begin to learn a new style of language. That means hard work." At the end of six months, I entered his study one afternoon. He handed me back my sermon without any correction or comment. I knew my commando course in preaching was at an end.

After tea, he looked hard at me with the suspicion of a twinkle in his eye. "Now Murdo Ewen we'll start on your prayers." "Oh my God" I said under my breath. Knowing as I did the importance D. M. attached to well-ordered service and his painstaking preparation of prayers, I experienced a shiver of apprehension.

The course on the preparation of prayers was if anything tougher than that on preaching. He abhorred extemporaneous prayers because they were so repetitive and cliche-ridden. If he detected any trace of sentimentality, he was merciless. Purple passages were anathema to him. There was one piece of advice I have never forgotten. "Let your first prayer be short. If it is long and boring, the congregation will switch off. If that happens, how can you expect to recapture their attention during the rest of the service?"

When Donald Baillie died in St. Mary's Hospital, Dundee, he was universally mourned. Two days before the end, his brother John, also a world-class Theologian, visited him. As he was leaving, D. M. said, "John, you remember the bronze plaque with the Gaelic inscription on my desk in the study. I would like to leave it to Murdo Ewen." I regard it as a very precious possession. This is the inscription in Gaelic: "Thig crioch air an t-saoghal, ach mairidh Gaol is Ceol" (The world will come to an end but Love and Music will endure). It stands in a prominent position in my study.

I have rarely known two brothers who were so close. In physique very different, spiritually and intellectually they were twins. John was disappointed by Donald's official obituary which appeared in *The Scotsman*. It did not do justice to him. He rang me up and asked me to write another. Fortunately the Editor of *The Scotsman*, Alastair Dunnet, was a friend of mine. He assured me that if I handed in the new obituary not later than 2 a.m. it would be included in the morning edition. This is an excerpt from the tribute I paid my brilliant Professor and great friend: "From the beginning we realized he was a giant and so great was our awe of him that we were in danger of regarding him as an Olympian who dwelt apart. We soon learned he was the simplest and friendliest of men, the most hospitable of hosts, a born story teller and a genius with children. As the months passed into years, we discovered something else. He was a saint in whose transparent humility we saw reflected the beauty of holiness."

There was an umbilical cord between St. Mary's and the University Chapel. Morning prayers at 9 a.m. in the Chapel were conducted by the six professors, assisted by the four town ministers. There was no chaplain in those days. This came much later. During my six years in St. Andrews, I never missed. I also attended on Sunday mornings, sitting under preachers, invited literally from all over Britain, irrespective of denomination. Sunday evenings I went to Hope Park church of which I was a member.

I vividly recall a very comic incident in the University Chapel. In a religious context, the absurd becomes much more absurd. The preacher on this particular morning was an English Bishop who could be described as an authentic eccentric. He preached for twelve minutes, rather short from a presbyterian perspective. In the sermon, he kept referring to the Alcoholic Fathers. The congregation, mostly academic, looked at one another in baffled amazement. The drill was always the same. The preacher, once he finished, came down from the pulpit and sat at the prayer desk on the right of the chancel. This the Bishop correctly did. During the taking up of the offering we witnessed an unusual spectacle. The Bishop stood up and solemnly made his way to the pulpit once again. After the prayer of dedication, the Bishop coughed and said, "For every time I used 'Alcoholic Fathers' please substitute 'Apostolic Fathers'." Great was the laughter thereof. The English produce more eccentrics per square yard than any country under the sun.

The University in a supportive way gave its benediction to the Byre Theatre in Abbey Street, diagonally across from my lodgings. If I remember correctly, it was in my last year at St. Andrews that the students staged a special show at the Byre. All professors and lecturers were pressurised to attend, which they surprisingly did. There was a short play followed by bagpipes, violin and concertina performances. They all received a vociferous reception. Then the surprise! I came on to impersonate ten of my university teachers. Let me be honest. To achieve a level of competence in this meticulous art, I had to work harder than I did in winning many first-class certificates and a number of class medals.

The curtains opened and I stepped on to the stage, feeling very nervous. I did Professor Stout demolishing Bertrand Russell. I did Professor Morrison on Plato's "Republic". I did Professor Rose, returning our Greek proses. I did Professor George S. Duncan lecturing on the Epistle to the Philippians. I did Professor Blyth Webster, championing Hamlet not as an intellectual dilettante but as a man of action. I did Professor Forrester in his Preaching seminar saying to a certain student, "Mr X the next time you preach that sermon you can cut out one half and it doesn't matter which half."

Of all my impersonations that night the one that received the warmest response was that of Reginald Jackson. He was a lecturer in logic and years later became professor of logic at Oxford. Regi, as we affectionately called him, was totally incomprehensible but strangely popular. He always took a roll call. When we heard our names, we answered in Latin 'Adsum', which I suppose means 'I am present.' If a friend did not make the class, as was often the case, we developed the habit of shouting 'Adsum' for him. If Regi suspected, he never let on. I remember him lecturing on sense data, reminding us of how misleading they could be. Under water an oar looks bent but we know it isn't. That particular day the class was woefully thin, roughly a third of its proper size. Yet when the register was called there was a full complement of 'Adsums'. As he was putting away the register, Regi looked at us and remarked, "It would appear that the auditory sense data do not correspond with the visual sense data." Difficult to understand he was, but not difficult to like.

There were critics who claimed that while St. Mary's was a centre of academic excellence, it sold students short on practical training. To be sure, with only four congregations in the town, students could not be placed in assistantships as they were in the much larger centres of Glasgow, Edinburgh and Aberdeen. Nevertheless, the College took practical training seriously. It ran a mission in the village of Grange, some two miles from the centre of the city. This mission was supervised by two students, nicknamed Bishop and Dean. In my time I was both. The Bishop and Dean organised Sunday services, various social activities and a certain amount of pastoral visitation. All St. Mary's students had to preach and conduct worship in the tiny church in Grange. One of the professors was always present to monitor their progress.

Gaelic speaking students had another outlet for practical training. During the long summer vacation, we were sent out to assist ministers in the West Highlands and Islands. As a rule, we were expected to preach in two languages. This was a marvellous experience. We mixed with ordinary people. This humanised us. What we must not forget is that we are human before we are scientists, before we are theologians, before we are ministers.

My first assignment was to the Isle of Lewis, a student assistant to the Rev. Murdo MacLennan of the parish of Carloway. He was by far the best at extemporaneous public prayer I have ever heard. The day I arrived, he took off for a month's holiday to his native Uig and left me to preach morning and evening for a whole month. As I had hardly any practice in preaching Gaelic, my first Sunday was sheer purgatory. I had lunch with a nice sympathetic elder, who told me I looked tired. He suggested that I ask one of the elders to lead in prayer at the evening service. I thought this was a good idea. "Which one"? I asked. "Oh! The senior elder, 'Iain Ruadh' (Red headed John)", he answered. My host did not tell me that red headed John was a bit of a snob. He preferred to be addressed as Mr MacLeod than as Iain ruadh. Ignorant of this I innocently asked, "Iain Ruadh will you lead us in prayer?" There was no response. I repeated the invitation. Still no response. Becoming more insistent I said "Time is passing Iain Ruadh, will you please lead us in prayer?" and he answered "No! Definitely not. I ate potatoes and herring for my lunch and there is too much wind within my stomach." I nearly passed out. I appealed to another elder, who leapt up like a Russian sputnik and prayed for thirty minutes.

My next assignment was in Kilchoan, Ardnamurchan, where I assisted that charming man, the Rev. Neil Gillies Macdonald. An excellent preacher in English and in Gaelic, he also had an outrageous sense of humour. He and his wife made me one of the family.

The day after I reported to him, he took me on a tour of the parish. Approaching a thatched cottage, he suddenly stopped the car and said, "Murdo Ewen, we are about to meet Ceit Mhor (Big Kate), the most compulsive swearer in the county of Argyle. If she mouths a few unparliamentary adjectives, I hope you won't be shocked." "Not at all Sir," I said. "I have played for the first eleven in St. Andrews, and where bad language is concerned I am unshockable."

Big Kate gave us an exuberant welcome. The Rev. Neil introduced me as the young student assistant. She looked at me and in Gaelic said, "A ghaol tha thu coimhead cho og" (My dear you look so young). She insisted on afternoon tea. After it was over the Rev. Neil said, "Kate, would you mind if the student assistant offered a word of prayer?" And she replied, "It would be myself that would be the disappointed one if you were to leave my house without putting up a word of prayer." I said to myself, "The Rev Neil has a wicked sense of humour. He is pulling my leg. This is a God-fearing pious woman."

Kate placed three towels on the floor as we knelt for prayer. My position was by the open door. Before I began to address the Almighty, I saw the cockerel striding in as if he was pursuing something with fell intent. On the table next to me was a naked loaf of bread. I had hardly finished the first sentence of my prayer when I felt the wind off the cockerel's wings as he ascended the table and got stuck into the loaf. There was an imperious tap on my shoulder and Kate whispered into my left ear, "Dean air do shochair a ghaoil gus a faigh mi "Mac na Galladh" a mach as an tigh". (Just a minute my dear till I get the son of a bitch out of the house). Never was a prayer brought to a speedier conclusion. After such an incident, how can one ever again be pompous?

I am inordinately glad I went to St. Andrews. It provided an atmosphere admirably congenial for study. I could not possibly improve on the words of Sir D'Arcy Thomson: "This is but a little town and our lives are somewhat narrow who dwell therein; but its traditions are not lost nor the lessons of its long history thrown away . . . the stones cry out to us as we pass, and tell us the story of our land, the chronicles of popes and kings, the history of the Old Church and the New."

CHAPTER 7
MY FIRST PARISH

WHEN I was called to Portree in 1939 the congregation was in the category known as Gaelic Essential. That meant that no candidate could be considered unless he was able to speak and preach in Gaelic. Now it has been reduced to the category of Gaelic Desirable. This is so despite the fact that its present minister is an excellent preacher in Gaelic and English. It is but another reminder of the relentless erosion of an ancient and beautiful language.

I was still a student in St. Andrews when I was approached by Portree in November 1938. How they ever heard of me still puzzles me. They made it clear the congregation wanted me to be the next minister. When I pointed out that I was taking a Bachelor of Divinity degree and that the final examinations wouldn't be over till the end of May 1939, they said, "That's all right, we'll wait for you." And so they did. I was inducted to the Parish of Portree in June and shortly afterwards I had to return to St. Andrews for my B.D. graduation.

In the interval between my promise to Portree in November and the completion of my studies in May, something totally unexpected had taken place. I was awarded the Petttigrew scholarship as the student with the highest aggregate of marks over the three years. Generous for these days this scholarship enabled a student to pursue post-graduate studies at Cambridge University. The Principal of St. Mary's, George S. Duncan, himself a product of Cambridge, wanted me to go there to study for a Ph.D. in Systematic Theology. After all it was my best subject and I was awarded a distinction in it. Professor Donald Baillie was also enormously keen on the Cambridge idea.

On the other hand, the Portree congregation had patiently waited for five months, dropping all the other candidates. I had given my word. And Portree parish was attractive. Scenically it was one of the most beautiful in the world. In Aesop's famous fable, the ass stood motionless between two equally tempting bundles of hay. It couldn't make up its mind. That precisely was my predicament. The two prospects beckoning me seemed equally attractive.

For two weeks I wrestled with the decision. Further studies in

Systematic Theology, my best subject, attracted me strongly. But I also felt a gravitational pull in the direction of the parish ministry. And after all I had given them my promise. When at length I made up my mind to go to Portree, a great sense of peace flooded my being.

Portree, the capital of Skye, is a charming little town. A tourists' delight, it is built round a lovely bay that provides a sheltered anchorage. The old name was Kiltaraglen. In 1540 it was changed to Port an Righ — the King's Harbour. In that year King James the Fifth anchored in the bay with a fleet of twelve ships. There the warring chiefs were summoned to pay homage. So impressed were they by the pomp and panoply that from that day the small straggling village was called after the King (Gaelic: Righ).

In June 1939, when I was inducted as minister of the parish, there were four denominations in the town. There was the Church of Scotland in Somerled Square at the very centre of the town. The Free Presbyterian Church and the Scottish Episcopal Church were only a few yards away. The Free Church stood near the Royal Hotel, overlooking the bay.

There was an excellent High School. In terms of the numbers it sent to universities and colleges of education this school had few equals in Britain, including the famous Public Schools. The pupils at this school came from every corner of Skye and from the Outer Hebrides, Harris, North Uist, Benbecula, South Uist and Barra. It had an outstanding academic record. Among many scholars, it produced Somhairle MacLean, one of the greatest of contemporary British poets, according to some critics one of the foremost in Europe.

On the whole, the different denominations got on tolerably well together. Early on I struck up a friendship with Donald MacKinnon, the Free Church minister. A good historian and a humble man, he embodied the traditional Scottish blend of piety and scholarship. A Roman Catholic priest, who paid a monthly visit, was an unforgettable character. A Russian by birth and upbringing, who loved the Western Highlands, he so mastered Gaelic, that he composed a dictionary in the language. The link between my congregation and the Episcopalian Church I valued. When my organist was on holiday, Dame Flora MacLeod of Dunvegan Castle, Chief of the MacLeods, used to drive over and play for me. She was a very attractive and gracious lady.

In 1929 the Established Church and the United Free Church united to form the Church of Scotland. Despite this the two congregations continued to worship separately. My predecessor, John MacKay, a robust Christian, agreed to a compromise which was unacceptable to me. Worship would be conducted in each church alternatively. In practice this was tantamount to being a minister of two different congregations.

With more zeal than wisdom, I was determined to put an end to this dubious arrangement. I persuaded the Kirk Session to appoint an architect to examine the two buildings and submit a report. On the basis of this report we would choose the building which was the better one structurally as the permanent place of worship. The report unambiguously favoured the building in Somerled Square.

Next Sunday at the end of a lot of sundry intimations I announced that two weeks from this day worship would take place permanently in this building. The reaction was explosive.

I must have been very innocent in not anticipating the backlash. In the course of visiting, doors were slammed in my face. More than once, I was stopped in the street and given dog's abuse. On market day in the town square thronged with men, women, children and animals, I was challenged to a fight. One of the most colourful and irascible characters of the community took off his jacket, rolled up his sleeves and put his fists up. "Put your jacket back on," I said, "I don't like taking funerals."

The Very Rev. Dr. Norman MacLean, a retired minister and a former Moderator, was a member of the congregation. Born within the bounds of the parish he was baptized in the church I was responsible for closing. The announcement from the pulpit the previous Sunday outraged him. He hated my guts. A superb preacher in English and Gaelic, a brilliant writer and skilful Ecclesiastic, I could not have chosen a more formidable opponent. The Apostle Paul must have collided with someone similar. We find him writing to his protege, Timothy, "Alexander the coppersmith did me much harm."

Dr. MacLean got up a petition and sent his henchmen round the parish. The idea was to set in reverse the unanimous decision of the Kirk Session. In addition he spread rumours to the effect that I had no theology and did not know how to construct a sermon. But nemesis was sniffing at Dr. Norman's heels. The miracle happened as if some

"Deus ex machina" (God outside the machine) had suddenly started pulling strings. To my utter amazement I had become a popular preacher. The church began to fill up and the increase in the evening service was dramatic. The gallery had to be opened and after it was full, chairs were borrowed from nearby houses. Christian liberality was also on the increase. By the time I left Portree it had trebled. All this put paid to Dr. MacLean's petition.

I found the Headmaster of the school equally unco-operative. His subject was English Literature and he resented that in my sermons I quoted from Shakespeare, Tolstoy, Dostoevsky, modern poets and modern novelists. He regarded English as his preserve and how dare I trespass? The pupils, especially the bigger boys and girls, were keen to come to the evening service. He forbade them, making the time the service lasted 'a prep period.'

I went to see him and argued with him as pleasantly and persuasively as I knew how. He didn't budge an inch. I reported him to the Presbytery Clerk, Dr. Hector MacLean, powerful in physique and personality. He was also a prominent member of the County Council. He had a chat with the Director of Education and the Headmaster of Portree received an almighty rocket. The pupils started coming to the evening service to add to our seating embarrassment.

To discover one is a popular preacher is in a sense a pleasing sensation. In another sense it is deeply disturbing. The gnawing fear that success would prove a mere flash in the pan began to haunt me. On Sunday nights I went off my sleep. At three, four, sometimes five in the morning, I was still tossing and turning.

I decided to confide in Donald MacKinnon, the local doctor. An alcoholic, he was without doubt about the most selfless person I have ever known. He reminded me of the alcoholic priest in Graham Green's novel, *The Power and the Glory*. The priest who, despite his weakness, in the end died a saintly martyr's death. After listening to me patiently, Donald told me not to worry. He explained to me what was happening. During the week I had wound myself up. The tension reached its height at the crowded evening service. I had to unwind and he suggested two ways of doing so. One was to talk and relax with my friends over supper. The other was to take a novel or a "Who done it?" with me to bed. And keep on reading until eventually I fell asleep. Sound advice. It worked like a charm.

The parish of Portree stretched far beyond the boundaries of the little town. It extended from Borve in the north to the village of Sconser some twelve miles to the south. It included the villages of Penifiler and Braes, where the battle with the police took place in 1882.

One of the oldest sites in the whole parish is the Royal Hotel with a commanding view of Portree Bay. It was there in MacNab's Inn, as it was then called, that Prince Charles said farewell to Flora Macdonald. And it was there, nearly twenty-five years later, that Boswell and Johnson dined on salted mutton, washed down by porter and port. The gossip, passed down the succeeding generations, tells of how the proprietrix approached the table of the two celebrities. "How do you like Skye mutton?" she asked. Johnson, the most aggressive of all literary hooligans, answered, "It is only fit for hogs." She smiled sweetly at him and riposted, "In which case, Doctor, you will be after a second helping."

By a week or two I missed the annual payment of my ministerial salary. For the next eight months or so, I was without any material means of support.

Fortunately, as my wife Betty says more times than I can number, "Murdo Ewen, you have always landed on your feet and you always will." Betty is right.

The treasurer of the congregation was also the manager of the Bank of Scotland in Portree. He combined a pragmatic no-nonsense shrewdness with humour and compassion. "Mr Macdonald," he said, "I'll advance you all the money you want till your salary comes to town." And so he did.

I was not able to live in the manse as I had no money to furnish it. Once again I landed on my feet. A very popular couple, John and Chrissie Lynn, invited me to put up with them. John was the principal Maths teacher in the High School. His wife, Chrissie, a native of Lewis, was not only highly intelligent but also very charming. When I told them I had no money till the annual cheque made its appearance, they answered jocularly, "When your big cheque arrives we'll take full advantage of it and book a holiday to Majorca."

At last the great day arrived. I got my cheque. After supper, in the living-room, sitting in front of a blazing peat fire, I waved my long awaited cheque triumphantly and said, "This is the day of reckoning.

You can now begin to organise your safari to Majorca! They both looked embarrassed. John turned to Chrissie and said, "Dear, on all matters domestic you are the boss." Chrissie looked at me and said, "Murdo Ewen, John and I haven't got a family. You are the nearest we'll ever get to having a son. We love you dearly and we are not taking a penny." I protested vehemently but it was to no avail.

Portree produced a rich crop of eccentrics. By common consent by far the most colourful character in the community was Mrs Thomson, known throughout the Island as "Ma." A native of Lewis, she married a Skyeman. She was a widow long before I arrived on the scene. Greatly loved by the Skye people she had the unchallenged reputation of being the best baker on the Island. I can speak with authority when I say I sampled her oatcakes, scones and crowdie every Sunday between the English and Gaelic services.

I remember being dragged against my will to a concert in the village hall. It was very heavy Celtic twilight stuff. Half way through, a woman with a harp between her knees was playing softly a soulful melody. The appreciative audience was visibly shocked when "Ma's" stentorian whisper was heard, "And I use no cream of tartar."

In addition to her exceptional baking skills, "Ma", when the occasion demanded it, had a blistering turn of phrase. Duncan Macaskill was the Postmaster in Portree. A bachelor, he lodged with "Ma." Whether he was serious or not, he always claimed he was an atheist, much to "Ma's" disgust. One evening, when I was at "Ma's" house for supper, Duncan was parading his pseudo-atheism in a characteristic aggressive manner. Suddenly "Ma" turned on him and shouted, "Shut up Duncan Macaskill, you are the stupidest man God ever put trousers on." I have known and indeed liked many unbelievers. Their sincerity as a rule I do not question. But "Ma's" demolition of a bogus uninformed atheist is the most devastating I have so far heard.

I had my troubles with the Very Rev Dr Norman MacLean, and Ian Murray the Headmaster, but with the vast majority of my parishioners I enjoyed a good relationship. Despite my brashness and inexperience they accepted me, warts and all. I made many friends.

There was Mrs Macdonald of Viewfield. She could be described as a dignified member of the Island squirearchy. All her children went to elitist fee-paying schools. Her two daughters, while coming from a privileged background, had a highly developed social conscience.

They were immersed in the welfare of the entire community. Her son, Colonel Jock as he was widely known, was a product of Fettes College and was a Scottish Rugby Internationalist. An outrageous, lovable, humorous character, he was conservative in his politics and all embracing in his humanity.

On my first visit to Mrs Macdonald of Viewfield, she laid down the law very firmly. "Minister," she said, "We are both native Gaelic speakers. Let us always speak to one another in our own language, not in the foreign tongue we call English." Her grandson, Johnny, went to Rugby. Suspicious of the standard of education dispensed at that very expensive institution, she insisted on my giving him lessons in Latin when he came home on holiday.

There were other dear friends. The Macdonalds of Seafield. They adopted me. So did the MacPherson family, all of them exceptionally good-looking. So did the MacCallums in their lovely house at Scorrybreac down by the sea. And Lindsay Hamilton, an Edinburgh man, employed by the Board of Agriculture in Skye. A great Elder, he always deputised for me in English when I was out of my own pulpit.

I am grateful I went to a good university but however excellent the education it provided, it fell short of preparing one for every possible contingency. This I learned to my cost while officiating at my first funeral. One day shortly after my induction to the congregation, a woman stopped me in the main street. "You are the new Parish Minister?" she asked. "Yes," I answered. "Is there anything I can do?" "I would like you to visit my father. He has been bed-ridden for years and he is not a member of any Church." I told her I would be delighted. From the very first visit, Alex MacLeod and I got on well together. So well, that before the end, he made it clear to his family that he wanted me to bury him. Of course I agreed. I did not realise Alex was a mason and I don't mean a stone mason, till I became involved in the funeral arrangements. It was then I learned his fellow-masons were determined to come to the grave dressed in full regalia to pay their last respects.

The service at the house, attended by his family and close friends went smoothly enough. Then I walked to the cemetery at the edge of the town looking across the bay to the lovely village of Penifiler. I took up my position at the end of the grave in which the coffin had already been lowered. The Church of Scotland Book of Common Order was firmly clutched in my right hand. I could hardly believe my eyes. Approaching me was a procession trying to walk in a straight line, but not succeeding all that well. I knew with clairvoyant certainty that Alex's friends had been to the Masonic Lodge and had imbibed rather liberally. They were dressed in aprons. They held sprigs of holly high above their heads as they drew near in a serpentine manner. Leading them was the Master of the Lodge, holding an enormous mace in front of him. The spectacle reminded me of the scene from 'Macbeth', Birnam wood coming to Dunsinane Hill. D. K., the mace bearer, was gloriously drunk and he had the fixed stare which all drunks adopt on ritualistic occasions. He walked, or rather staggered, on. Ignoring the edge of the grave, he fell on top of the coffin with a resounding clatter. In the deathly silence that followed, a voice from the bottom of the grave was heard asking, "What the hell am I doing down here?" The mourners standing around pulled out their handkerchiefs and snorted into them loudly to hide their embarrassment. I didn't know what to do. Then one of the very devout elders stepped forward. He leant over the side of the grave and said, "D. K. give me your hand." D. K. did precisely that and pulled hard. The elder executed a neat parabola and he too fell into the grave. My knees shaking, I recall communing with my anguished soul. "Somewhere in the New Testament there is a verse which promises the help of the Holy Spirit in times of critical emergency." In the dire situation, the only light I had was that this was not the time to intone the words of committal, "Dust to dust and ashes to ashes." I forget how we managed to haul the two of them to the surface, but I remember being very angry. Why was my first funeral marred by such bizarre happenings? Neither P. G. Wodehouse nor Compton Mackenzie at the height of creative genius could have imagined anything so comically improbable. As I walked home, the sheer grotesque absurdity of it all seized me. I found myself laughing till I was sore.

It was in the parish of Portree that the famous battle of the Braes took place. The Braes crofters used Ben Lee as a common pasture. Lord Macdonald terminated this practice when he reorganised his estate. The crofters petitioned him to restore Ben Lee as of right. When their petition was rejected they refused to pay rent.

The Sheriff Officer who walked the five miles from Portree to serve summonses was assaulted and his summonses were burned.

Whereupon fifty policemen, mostly from Glasgow, marched to Braes to arrest five ring leaders who had engineered this mass defiance of the law. They had to draw their batons and charge a crowd of men and women, surrounding them and pelting them with stones. Several policemen were seriously injured and at least five crofters suffered severe head cuts. Afterwards, the Braes crofters put their cows and sheep back on the old grazings on Ben Lee. Lord Macdonald was persuaded to accept this to avoid troops being sent in.

The Battle of the Braes sparked off a number of other law breaking actions on Skye, on the Mainland and in the Outer Hebrides. These combined to persuade an unwilling Government to appoint in 1883 a Royal Commission under the chairmanship of Lord Napier. Its remit was to investigate the problems of the crofting areas. As a result, the Crofting Act became law in 1886, granting crofters security of tenure. No longer was it possible for an arrogant greedy landlord to evict people without a penny of compensation.

Human nature is a baffling equation. Man can be more cruel than any animal. This is true, but at the same time there lurks in the deep recesses of our being a spirit of rebellion which defies injustice and oppression whatever the odds. This is our only ground for optimism regarding the future. This is why we dare believe that we are created in the Divine image in face of much evidence to the contrary.

In my twenty-fourth year, I was inducted to the parish church of Portree. This I have never regretted. All my predecessors were held in the highest esteem and I am sure this redounded to my benefit.

The same is true of my distinguished successors. My immediate successor, Alasdair John MacLeod, combined great height with sound scholarship and artistic sensitivity. He was responsible for transforming the interior of the church with its chancel side pulpit and stained glass windows. To him goes the credit. His successor, Donald MacLeod, was with me in Kingussie School. He was a good preacher, especially in Gaelic, in my opinion the best Gaelic preacher in Scotland. Donald was followed by Gilleasbuig MacMillan, who is now minister of St. Giles Cathedral, Edinburgh. Controversial he is in the very best sense of that term. Nobody, not even his critics can ever question his ability. Endowed, along with his father and uncle, with an outrageous sense of humour, he is also a superb pastor to those in real need. As a preacher, he has a well deserved international reputation. This is recognised by his appointment as the Warrack Lecturer in preaching. I remember sitting beside him at a dinner in Edinburgh. Opposite us was a formidable lady with a top drawer accent, bulging with self-confidence, monopolising the conversation. In a commanding voice she barked at Gilleasbuig across the table. "Mr MacMillan, coming from a small country parish in the Isle of Skye to St. Giles Cathedral must have been a very difficult transition." Gilleasbuig, summoning his most wicked facial expression answered, "Yes, it was difficult. I had to simplify all my sermons."

Jim Matheson succeeded Gilleasbuig. Ordained a minister of the Free Church, after the War he moved over into the Church of Scotland and to his great credit became Moderator of the General Assembly, a remarkable achievement.

The present incumbent of the parish of Portree is John Ferguson, a former student of mine in Trinity College, Glasgow University. According to all reports, he has nobly overcome that handicap. A good student with a lovely sense of humour, he is a born preacher. He was awarded the McKean memorial preaching prize which is not a church but a university award.

Portree was an ideal first parish. It was here my ministry began and my mountain climbing career took off. Despite my brash youthful enthusiasm, the Kirk Session was astonishingly loyal to me. The members, adherents and worshippers from other denominations were solidly behind me. I look back on my first parish with a warm and lasting affection.

CHAPTER 8

THE ARMY

MY introduction to His Majesty's armed forces could not be described as pleasant. In April 1940 I was commissioned Chaplain 4th Class (rank of Captain) and ordered to report to the Depot, the headquarters of the Queen's Own Cameron Highlanders in Inverness. I felt like Abraham of old leaving Ur of the Chaldees to face an uncertain future. When I reached the barracks built on a hill a mile or so from the centre of the town, I made several discreet enquiries. I was told to report to the Adjutant, always a very important person.

I knocked timidly on his door. There was no reply. When I knocked more loudly, there was an abrasive bark, "Come in". I entered. Sitting behind a very large desk was a Major in splendiferous Highland dress, the epitome of sartorial excellence. With appropriate modesty I informed him I was the new chaplain. He remained seated which I thought was exceedingly rude. Eyeing me from top to toe, with supercilious disdain, he snapped, "Padre, your suit has not been pressed since you bought it God knows how many years ago. Your clerical collar is dirty. You haven't been to a barber for months and you look like a Highland stirk." I swallowed my rising bile. Then he snarled, "Remove yourself from here, get a hair-cut and purchase an officer's uniform appropriate to your rank." "Yes Sir," I said meekly and moved towards the door. As I was about to open it another abrasive bark stopped me in my tracks, "You are not yet in uniform, so I would not expect you to salute me, but when you were speaking to me you should have stood to attention. After all I am a superior officer." I did not open the door. I turned round and walked slowly back to the Adjutant's desk. I looked him in the eye for nearly a minute. As he was beginning to squirm, I said, "You are an ill-mannered, over-dressed, mindless twirp and if you ever address me like that again, I'll knock hell out of you." He dropped his monocle and I left him sitting open mouthed beside his oversized desk.

Believe it or not, the Adjutant and I over the next two months became the firmest of friends. His nickname, and deservedly so, was the 'Pansy Highlander'. In his official capacity Major Rutherford was a pompous ass.

Underneath the blustering bully-boy exterior he was rather nice. Even more surprising he had a self-mocking sense of humour. When in July 1940 I went overseas with the newly formed 4th Battalion, we lost contact. I really felt sad.

The commanding officer, known throughout the whole Division as 'Smokey Stewart', was the very antithesis. Non-pompous, non-abrasive, non-authoritarian, he personified what we mean by an officer and a gentleman. He got his nickname from the fact that he was a compulsive chain-smoker. Anyone entering his office, to begin with, could not see him. He and his desk were enveloped in a thick cloud of tobacco smoke. A Scot, educated at an expensive English Public School, the moment he opened his mouth one would take him for the prototype, elitist, upper class Englishman. Like so many, educated at these posh schools, he was more aggressively Scottish than I was. Where the therapeutic values of sport were concerned, he was a thorough going fundamentalist. He really believed that the Battle of Waterloo was won on the playing fields of Eton. He assumed that all officers and non-commissioned officers were fellow apostles.

Though our social and educational backgrounds could not be more different, 'Smokey Stewart' and my proletariat self clicked marvellously from the moment we met. He approved of my participation in route marches, in football and gymnastics. When he discovered I was a keen mountain climber, he beamed total approval.

Our burgeoning friendship reached a climax when the Camerons and Seaforths met in the finals of the inter-battalion boxing championships at Invergordon. Two days before the great event, Corporal Morrison, the Cameron middle weight contender, went down with appendicitis. Frantically Colonel 'Smokey Stewart' tried to get a suitable substitute. He drew a blank. The finals were to take place in the evening at Invergordon. That very afternoon I dropped in on the Colonel to discuss a problem that had nothing to do with boxing. As I was leaving he asked me if I knew of anyone who could take Corporal Morrison's place in the finals at Invergordon. I answered, "Sir, I know the battalion well, honestly I can't think of anyone." Then casually through the thick pall of smoke he asked, "Padre, have you ever boxed yourself?" Completely off guard I replied, "Yes Sir, I was once a welter-weight champion, but that was a long time ago." 'Smokey

Stewart' leapt to his feet and shouted, "Padre you're boxing at Invergordon tonight." "But, Sir!" He dismissed all my protests with an unanswerable Olympian loftiness. I boxed in Invergordon that night and, to my own surprise and that of many others, I won. The Camerons got the championship.

From then on, I was 'Smokey Stewart's' blue-eyed boy. I could do no wrong. If he had been a Pope invested with magisterial power, he would have canonised me. He dragged me to every cocktail and sherry party in town. At the time I was a dedicated total abstainer, but the good Colonel forgave me that major defect. Embarrassingly at these alcoholic gatherings he would introduce me thus: "Meet the holy terror, my padre."

'Smokey Stewart' was a superlatively nice man. He embodied the very best qualities in the Public School sporting tradition.

During my stay in Inverness, socially I led a busy life. I preached in many of the churches in the town and in the process made a number of good friends. I became particularly friendly with two families. Dr John Mitchell and his sister, Jane, heard me preach one Sunday and invited me to dinner. For the rest of my stay in Inverness, I had dinner with them every Sunday evening.

The other friendship had a rather odd beginning. I was visiting one of the soldiers' canteens one night, when one of the women volunteer helpers came over to the table at which I was sitting. "You are the Rev. Murdo Ewen Macdonald, minister of Portree, Isle of Skye," she said. "Yes I am," I answered. "Well let me tell you this, my father hates your guts." "And who is your father?" I asked somewhat bewildered. "The Rev. Ewen MacQueen who was born and brought up in your parish, you have heard of him" she added with a twinkle in her eye, "You must, who hasn't?" "Oh yes," I answered. "Your father is a famous character. But tell me," I went on, "How can he possibly hate my guts when we have never met?" She smiled at me and said, "That's easy. He has heard that you climb mountains, play football, and that you were seen wearing your clerical collar at a Margaret Kennedy Fraser concert." At this point we both laughed. "Well!" I said: "Please convey my best wishes to your father and tell him I would like to meet him some day."

The very next night in the same canteen, the moment I came through the door, she streaked over to me and said, "My father wants you to come to supper on Saturday night. I hope you're free." And so one of the most enriching friendships of my life began.

Ewen MacQueen was a paradoxically attractive character. He was a minister of the Free Presbyterian Church which, despite its theological narrowness, has a knack of producing nice and brilliant people. Our Lord Chancellor is the prime example.

Rigidly Calvinistic and narrow in his theology, Ewen was gloriously human. His sense of humour was enormous. A born wit, when it came to the devastating mot and the demolishing retort, he was the equal, I am convinced, of Oscar Wilde and Lord Birkenhead. The following story in some small measure at least may illustrate what I mean.

In the First War, Ewen MacQueen was commissioned a chaplain to the Forces. The military dress in those days included breeches and spats. Ewen conformed without demur. But he refused to wear the military cap. Instead he wore a top hat.

It was in such a strange garb that he appeared at Passchendale where the casualties were astronomical. The Brigadier who greeted him was, to put it mildly, taken aback by this sartorial apparition. Looking at him in astonishment, he blurted, "Padre, why did you bring that top hat with you?" MacQueen looked at the Brigadier witheringly and replied, "Brigadier, I have brought it with me against the contingency of a funeral."

Later in the officers' mess the Brigadier was doling out drinks. He looked at MacQueen and barked, "Padre, which would you rather have, whisky or a lime juice?" This time MacQueen looked at the Brigadier even more witheringly and answered, "Brigadier, I have never yet ventured upon a lime juice."

A great character, I developed a genuine fondness for him. When I left Inverness as the chaplain of the new 4th Camerons, he insisted on coming to the station to see the battalion off. I introduced him to my new Colonel whom I hardly knew. I was very touched by what Ewen said to the Colonel: "Take care of Murdo Ewen. His theology is suspect, but I love him all the same."

I had a good relationship with Colonel 'Smokey Stewart'. With my next Colonel, Colin Barber, I had an even better one. In July 1940 I became the chaplain of the newly formed 4th Cameron Highlanders. My new commanding officer looked down at me from a towering height. Six feet seven and three quarters inches in height, he was predictably known as 'Tiny'. Over tea, we discussed my role as chaplain at some length. As I was leaving, 'Tiny' casually remarked, "By the way Padre, you are captain of the boxing team." "But Sir," I began to protest. He grinned at me and said, " 'Smokey Stewart' has told me all about you."

From Inverness the newly formed 4th Camerons entrained to Liverpool and boarded the *Empress of Australia*. We sailed under sealed orders and were a few days at sea before we had any idea of our destination. Then we learned our first stop was to be at Halifax in Nova Scotia, then Bermuda, then Jamaica and finally we were to disembark on the island of Aruba in the Carribean. There we had to guard the American Esso refinery, at that time the biggest in the world, and the much smaller British Eagle refinery.

On disembarking, we got a rousing welcome from the British, Americans and the native Aruban population. Aruba was a Dutch island, so we had to cultivate a delicate diplomatic relationship with those in power.

The battalion was very popular and on the whole well behaved. There were occasional clashes with the Dutch Police in pubs on Saturday nights. We organised boxing contests, football matches and other athletic events with the Americans, the Dutch and the Arubans. Apart from a few minor infrequent lapses we proved ourselves good ambassadors for Britain.

Bill Barrett, the minister of the Methodist Black Church in St. Nicholas, was a saint if ever I've met one. A bachelor absolutely devoted to his congregation, he hadn't taken a holiday for twelve years. He helped us immensely in organising a soldiers' canteen in the town, especially in procuring voluntary workers. I felt strongly he should go on holiday. Tiny Barber, the Colonel, who by now was a good friend, agreed. We had to change the time of the church parade to enable me to preach morning and evening in the Methodist Black Church. We sent Bill away on holiday for a month.

These black Carribean Methodists were wonderful people. Generous, hospitable, lovable, their humour was irrepressible. It could erupt in the middle of the most solemn religious service. They insisted on calling me Colonel. This greatly amused the whole Battalion. When I apologised to Tiny, my friend and Commanding Officer, he just laughed and said, "Not at all, Murdo, I rather like it. But the moment they start calling you Brigadier, I'll protest. You see I would have to salute you then."

I persuaded Tiny to put an end to the compulsory church parade. I argued that this institution made more atheists than all the H. G. Wells and Bertrand Russells of the world ever accomplished. Hesitant to begin with, in time he overcame his misgivings and co-operated magnificently. It was a great success. Making the service voluntary made no difference to the attendance. This was the first time it was done. Tiny and I regarded it as an important breakthrough.

In a year's time Tiny was promoted to the rank of Brigadier and called home. He commanded the 51st Highland Division at the crossing of the Rhine. He ended up as Lieut. General Sir Colin Barber, D.S.O. Greatly loved by all who served under him, I counted him as one of my very best friends. After I was taken prisoner, he wrote to me regularly to Stalag Luft 3. He ended each letter thus: "Cheer up, see you soon. Tiny." This must have thoroughly confused the Germans.

It was in the Island of Aruba that I met Betty Russell, my wife for the last fifty years. Within a few days of arriving in the Island I met her parents, Liza and Tommy, who were employed by the Standard Oil Esso Refinery. Liza practically ran the soldiers' canteen and was a great success.

Of course they talked a great deal about their two children Donald and Betty, both at College in the U.S.A. Betty was at Mount Holyoke College in Massachussetts, the kind of elitist establishment I am not particularly fond of. I was a whole year in Aruba before I met her when she came home for her summer holidays. She turned out to be a good-looking, charming extrovert. The inevitable happened. We became engaged before she returned to College. And on my way home to Britain in February 1942, we got married in New York.

When the United States entered the war in December 1941, they took over the guarding of the Carribean refineries and we were ordered home. After we embarked on a troop ship, we nearly bought it. There must have been a spy or two in Aruba during our sojourn there. The Germans knew of our departure. A cluster of submarines were lying in wait for the troop ships, off the island. Providentially, we eluded them by being diverted to take on water in the Island of

Curacao. Baulked by their failure to intercept, the submarines moved in and surfaced. They shelled the Esso Refinery and a number of oil tankers with a tragic loss of life.

We landed in New Orleans and travelled by train through the States, ending up at Halifax once again. There were stops at various places, including Chatanooga in Tenessee and Fort Slocum in New York. The Battalion in full Highland dress, with their fine Pipe Band, got a tumultuous welcome. The reception it got in Times Square, New York, was most moving. We were the first British troops on American soil since the war of 1812. The Americans are sometimes critical of us and rightly so, but underneath, I believe they are unambiguously pro-British.

We embarked from Halifax on the *Empress of Canada*, landed at Liverpool, then proceeded to Darlington. From there we put up at various places for short periods, Alnwick, Wooler and Bamburgh. I was impressed by its ancient castle and its lovely sea coast.

It was in Bamburgh, in the park underneath the castle, that the Brigade sports were held. I represented the 4th Camerons at throwing the hammer. To the astonishment of all the spectators and the chagrin of my bigger fellow contestants, I got first prize. It amounted to a ten shilling note.

Round about this time there was a national appeal for volunteers to form the 1st Parachute Regiment. I was immediately attracted. If I were to indulge in self-analysis, I reckon this is the reason. I had a sense of guilt that while the Battle of Britain was being waged I lived in luxury in a tropical climate, swimming in warm lagoons many miles away from danger.

Much to the displeasure of my commanding officer, Colonel Ian Begg, I volunteered for the Paratroopers. To leave the 4th Camerons was a painful wrench. I was very fond of the battalion and surprisingly they were fond of me. I joined the Paras at Hardwick Hall in Derbyshire, where the ground training took place.

The training was gruelling in the extreme. We were made to run distances ranging from two to ten miles. There were assault courses which could only be described as cruel. We had to scale walls at least twelve feet high. We had to wade through moats, the water up to our armpits, holding our rifles above our heads. We had to crawl on our bellies under coils of barbed wire with live bullets zinging over our heads. There were a few fatal casualties. Utterly exhausted, the final test was to pick up a rifle and aim at a target. To qualify one had to hit at least the magpie.

In addition, one platoon was selected for a tough rock-climbing course. As happened in Inverness, my unguarded tongue got me into trouble. One day I was sitting beside a Brigadier at lunch. "What do you think of the rock climbing course we are starting?" he asked. I told him I thought it was an excellent idea. "Have you done any rock climbing yourself, Padre?" he asked. "A little, Sir," I answered in all innocence. "Where?" he demanded. "In the Cuillin mountains of Skye," I confessed. The Brigadier leapt to his feet and, prodding me in the chest, boomed, "Padre you are the No. 1 rope in the rock climbing platoon."

Moreover, we were all subjected to parachute jumping aptitude tests. This included a visit to a psychiatrist. I was left with the impression that there was a ruthless deliberate policy to eliminate all who were vulnerable either physically or psychologically. Like Lawrence of Arabia who vowed he would beat the Arabs at their own game, I was highly motivated and very competitive. In the final assessment I got a surprisingly high commendation from the Judges.

From Hardwick Hall those of us who passed the severe, perhaps more accurately savage, test were sent to Ringway Airport, Manchester. There we were trained to jump. Those of us who were commissioned shared the R.A.F. officers' quarters.

Aldous Huxley once claimed that there were three stages of Evolution — animal, military and human. Somewhat unfair I think. I have come across much humanity among soldiers. If a sense of humour is part and parcel of our humanity, belonging to the Divine Image within us, I would argue that the average soldier is liberally endowed with it.

My first night in the Officers' Mess at Ringway Aerodrome, I was shown a mural which covered an entire wall. It depicted a Parachutist who was dropped behind the enemy lines on a frightfully important mission. Thoroughly briefed, he was given three parachutes. He was told a motorbike would be waiting for him at a crossroads just a few yards away from the landing spot. His mentors assured him that the first parachute was 99.99% safe. If perchance it failed, the second parachute was 100% reliable. The third parachute was not really necessary. It was a morale booster.

The mural showed the parachutist confidently stepping out through the open door of an aeroplane. He pulled the rip-cord of the first parachute. It didn't open. He pulled the rip-cord of the second. Ditto. At which point a smile of sublime confidence spread over his face. "Why worry, I have a third parachute." He pulled the rip-cord and nothing happened. As he sped towards earth with ever increasing velocity, you could see these words streaming out of his mouth. "I bet you the damn motor-bike isn't there either." Such is the genius of humour (see Arthur Koestler's 'Act of Creation') that the mural, far from sinking, actually uplifted our spirits.

At Ringway, our first two jumps were made in the early morning when most hangings take place. They were made from a balloon, hydraulically levered to a height of 800 feet. I recall sitting on the edge of a basket slung beneath the underbelly of this obscene contraption. As with mounting terror I looked down, all the minor anxieties of my life evaporated into the thin morning air. Only one anxiety, all dominating and overwhelming remained. Would I have the guts to jump the moment I heard the order "Go". I looked at the Jump Instructor standing on the grass below, megaphone tilted upwards. After what seemed an eternity, the order came, peremptory and unambiguous, "Go." With all my might I shouted "Go" and despairingly leapt into empty space. Not surprisingly most of the refusals took place at this stage.

After successfully completing two balloon jumps, we moved on to jump from a Whitley bomber, an experience only slightly less terrifying. This continued till the C47 Dakotas became available in the autumn of 1942.

We had to jump through a hole in the floor of the aeroplane. This was a tricky business. The hole was only three feet in diameter. One of the hazards of exiting was that as the parachutist's feet left the aircraft, the top of his body was automatically thrown forward. Consequently the jumper was in constant danger of butting his face on the opposite edge of the hole. This was known as "ringing the bell." Few got through unscathed. I was one of the lucky ones.

On the completion of five jumps from the Whitley bomber, we graduated to fully fledged parachutists. At a simple ceremony, we were issued with the much-coveted parachute wings. They were sewn on to our sleeve, near the top of our right shoulder. Apparently, Royal Air Force desk bureaucrats objected to the wings being pinned on our chest. Petty and small-minded. Proud that we had come through a very tough test, we waited impatiently for posting to a Battalion.

I got a short "jumping" leave which I spent in Portree, Isle of Skye. At the end of five days it was interrupted by a telegram ordering me to join the 2nd Parachute Battalion at Bulford. There I learned to jump from C47s by walking out through a door, instead of through a hole in the floor.

We made a single night jump. One "stick" landed unintentionally in a cemetery. Considering the density of tombstones in the grave-yard, casualties were miraculously few. In the dark I landed in a ditch and sank up to my waist.

In early November, the Parachute Brigade, 1st, 2nd and 3rd Battalions, entrained to Liverpool. Once again, from that busy sea-port, we set sail into the unknown. This time it turned out to be North Africa.

I found parachuting both frightening and exhilarating. A few years ago I watched Prince Charles being interviewed on American TV by a woman journalist. After many questions, some of them blasphemous or banal, she suddenly asked, "Prince, what is the most frightening experience of your life?" Without any hesitation he answered "My first parachute jump." I agree.

The unremitting tension was now and again relieved by the odd comic incident.

If I remember rightly, Major Pine-Coffin was B Company Commander in the 1st Battalion. Well over six feet in height, he sported an enormous walrus moustache. I had struck up a friendship with the Adjutant of B Company and at least once a week used to drop into his office for a chat and a cup of tea.

This particular afternoon as my friend and I were exchanging rude remarks, the phone rang. It was Major Pine-Coffin clamouring for a batman. Covering the mouth of the instrument with his hand, Jock, my rude friend, said, "Murdo, as you are absolutely idle till next Sunday, look up the battalion list and suggest a suitable batman for Major Pine-Coffin." This I did and to my astonishment I came across the name of Private Undertaker, "Oh this is terrific," I shouted. The

Adjutant put down the phone and asked, "Pray tell me what is terrific?" "Listen Jock," I said. "I've got the perfect batman for Major Pine-Coffin. His name is Private Undertaker." In all my experience as a preacher, I have never had a more enthusiastic and ecstatic response. Wielding all the clout of his office, the Adjutant despatched a runner to summon Private Undertaker into his presence.

In no time, a compactly built, bandy-legged, private soldier appeared and saluted the Adjutant with impressive panache. "Sir" he asked, "What have I done wrong?" "Nothing", answered the Adjutant. "On the contrary, I want to make life more comforting and more interesting for you, Undertaker. Would you be prepared to become a batman to the Commander of B Company?" Then, more persuasively than Dale Carnegie in his best-seller, *How to win Friends and Influence People*, the Adjutant sold him the job — exemption from Sunday chores and parades, etc.

The following morning before breakfast, Private Undertaker reported to Major Pine-Coffin. The Major was still in bed when his batman brought him a mug of tea. He yawned. "You're my new batman. What's your name?" "Undertaker, Sir," was the answer. To begin with Pine-Coffin refused to believe it, but later he adjusted to reality.

General Browning, who commanded the 1st Airborne Division, imaginatively grasped the propaganda advantages of this amusing relationship between Major Pine-Coffin and Private Undertaker. In the 1st Airborne Division's Newsletter there were some arresting headlines. "Pine-Coffin and Undertaker land in North Africa." "Pine-Coffin and Undertaker dropped in Sicily." "Pine-Coffin and Undertaker establish a bridge-head on the toe of Italy." However absurd the Pine-Coffin Undertaker camaraderie, in its own comic way it helped morale.

Inextricably entangled with the comic is the tragic side of life. Shakespeare understood this and projected it more sensitively and more dramatically than anyone else. According to him the comic and the tragic are inseparable, indistinguishable, if you like indivisible.

It happened at Ringway. His name was Jimmy Thorpe. He was so small that in boxing parlance he could be described as a light-weight. He was mercilessly teased. "Jimmy you don't need to worry if the chute doesn't open. You'll float down and land softly like a feather." And of course all of us, including Jimmy, laughed loudly at this corny funny. It was Jimmy's fifth jump and his parachute failed to open. We picked up his pulverised remains on an army blanket and carried him to a corner of the field on which he had dropped. Nobody laughed. We buried him with full military honours. Three volleys over his grave. The 'Last Post,' the most poignant of all farewells. Nobody laughed.

As we stood at attention, we knew we were in the presence of the Last Enemy, the basic irrationality, the ultimate incongruity, the final totalitarian contradiction.

CHAPTER 9

BEHIND THE LINES

IN November 1942, the 1st Parachute Brigade, made up of the 1st, 2nd and 3rd Battalions, went by train to Liverpool. There we embarked and this time there was no uncertainty as to our destination. We knew we were going to North Africa to join up with the 1st Army.

I remember passing through the Straits of Gibraltar at night under very faint moonlight. It was a large convoy heavily protected by cruisers and speedy destroyers. We landed at Algiers and on the way in were bombed by German and Italian planes. A close friend of mine, Dr. Ian MacLeod, was badly wounded in one of the attacks.

The first few days the 2nd Paras did not fare too well. As there was no suitable accommodation, we were put up in an empty zoo. Judging from the smell, the monkeys and their fellow-creatures had been hastily evacuated. To make matters worse, the ship carrying our rations was torpedoed, and for weeks on end we lived on tinned marmalade puddings. A bit much to have them for breakfast, lunch and supper.

Suddenly, deliverance came. We were moved to Maison Blanche, an airport just outside Algiers. In ridiculous contrast to the stinky zoo, we were billeted in a posh girls' school which had the most comfortable beds I have ever slept in. Though constantly bombed at night, for a couple of weeks we lived in comparative comfort, now that our rations had caught up with us.

At the zoo in Algiers, we had adopted a monkey and made him the batallion mascot. We nicknamed him Monty, because with his sharp features he looked uncommonly like Field-Marshall Montgomery. When he chattered, as he often did, he sounded like the great Monty addressing the troops, "I say, chaps." We taught Monty to jump and devised a special parachute for him. Unfortunately one night, during a bombing raid, Monty was badly wounded. When a few days later we jumped behind the enemy lines, we had to leave him behind.

In a series of operations, each parachute battalion was given a special task. The most difficult and, as it turned out, the most disastrous was given to the 2nd. Dropped at Depienne, approximately twenty-five miles from Tunis, their mission was to capture the airfield there, then proceed to Oudna on the very outskirts of Tunis. When the operation was completed, they were to join up with the 1st Army at St. Cypriere.

From the beginning, things seemed destined to go wrong. We had to jump on rough uneven terrain and the battalion was widely scattered across many ravines and gullies. There was one fatality, a sapper, at the very spot where he had fallen to his death.

When we assembled, and that took time, at midnight, we had to make a forced march to Oudna. When in an exhausted state we reached it, to our dismay we discovered the so-called airfield was only a landing strip. It was empty of the planes we were sent to destroy. Worse still, the 1st Army's drive towards Tunis had been halted. So the 2nd Paras found themselves virtually surrounded, more than fifty miles behind enemy lines.

Within an hour, we were attacked by five German heavy tanks and machine gunned by an ever increasing number of Messerschmidt fighters. At least a dozen Stuka dive bombers with their siren sounds came at us, but our parachute smocks made excellent camouflage. We were also pounded by column upon column of motorised infantry. At one point, we were completely surrounded. As we were running short of ammunition, any chance of extricating ourselves looked hopelessly bleak.

It was mid-afternoon. During a lull in the incessant bombardment, we decided to have a go and break through. Naturally our commanding officer, Lt. Co. John Frost, led. By chance I happened to be just behind him. We didn't know that a German machine gunner was covering us from one of the hills above. Fortunately he missed the Colonel, but got me and two others just behind him. The bullet struck me in the left biceps, nicking the bone on its way out. It spun me round and I found myself lying on my back. My Colonel stopped in his tracks. He knelt beside me and in a voice laden with anxiety asked, "Murdo, my dear boy, are you dead?" I opened my eyes and grinned at him, "No, Sir, I am not dead. I have a lot of damage to do yet."

It took courage to stop when a hidden machine gunner was

wreaking indiscriminate havoc. This spontaneous gesture on the part of the legendary Johnny Frost was characteristic of the man. It demonstrated his unfailing care for all those who served under him. Major General John D Frost, as he now is (retired), was a very correct professional and at the same time an unconventional swashbuckling hero. Take the Bruneval raid on the coast of North West France in February 1942. It was the kind of brilliantly successful attack on the giant Wursling Radar Station that appeals to the imagination. At the time, Johnny Frost was a Major commanding C company. After that epic it looked as if he was destined for great things.

And what about Arnhem? The fact that the Dutch renamed the Arnhem Bridge the Johnny Frost Bridge speaks volumes. He has richly deserved all his decorations, M.C., D.S.O. (Bar). I am proud to have served under him.

The second wound I got as we attempted to make another break through at dusk. It was not a bullet this time, but shrapnel that left a gaping hole in my right hand. A medical orderly helped me back to a shallow trench where the wounded were treated. Ronnie Gordon, the Battalion M.O., staunched the blood and bandaged my hand. The 2nd Paras were fortunate to have as their medical officers men of the outstanding character and calibre of Ronnie Gordon and Jim MacGavin.

By now, it had become very clear that if the survivors of the numerous German attacks had any hope of reaching the Allied lines, the wounded had to be left behind. After much soul searching, Colonel Frost detailed a rear party under the command of Lieut. Playford to stay behind with the wounded.

There were all sorts of ghastly possibilities. From Intelligence sources we were aware of Hitler's attitude to British commandos and paratroopers. They were to be killed. The Geneva Convention code did not apply to them.

No mercy must be shown. In addition, there were the marauding Arabs, who could be unbelievably cruel. They had a habit of mutilating prisoners, cutting their throats and leaving them to bleed to death. The decision Johnny Frost made to leave Lieutenant Playford and his platoon behind to guard the wounded was not easy, but it was the right one.

With incredible courage and tenacity, what was left of the battalion fought their way back to the Allied lines, through many German assaults and ambushes. On the 3rd of December, they made contact with an American column. That evening, 180 exhausted men marched into Medzee el Bete. Only a quarter of the number who had set off in such high spirits four days before.

My good and gallant friend, Dick Spender, (nephew of poet Stephen Spender), who was killed a few months later, wrote of that withdrawal:

Today some silent valley of Tunisia
Shall tremble at their strike from sky unsheathed
And, with the night, perhaps some God looking down
With dull, cold eyes, by the near stars, will see
One lonely, grim battalion cut its way
Through agony and death to fame's high crown
And wondering the friendless strength
Of little men, who die that the great truths shall live.

It was a frightful waste of expensively trained fighting men, above all of life. Much later, General Frost was to write that in North Africa the British Army had little or no clue as how to use the new airborne capability. It is a valid criticism.

As I have already said, only one quarter of the Battalion that flew from Maison Blanche made it. Three quarters, the dead and the wounded were left behind. Before those who could walk moved off, they came to say good-bye to me as I lay bleeding in a shallow trench. No stiff upper lip. Officers, non-commissioned officers and men warmly embraced me and all called me by my first name: "Murdo, the very best! Remember we love you."

As they disappeared into the gathering dusk, there was a lump in my throat. I knew I had won the admiration and affection of probably the toughest soldiers in the world.

The wounded were scattered on the side of a hill shrouded in mist. We had dropped without overcoats and in December Tunisia can be very cold. All through the long miserable night I listened to the incessant clicking of teeth and the moans of the badly wounded and the dying. My own wounds were hurting badly, but I did my best to console those in the last extremity. Looking back, I believe most of those who perished that night died of hypothermia. Was it not

Churchill who once said, "I am over eighty years old and I have never heard of Cambodia."? Well at that time I had never heard of hypothermia. Now everybody knows what it means.

Conversant with Hitler's orders regarding British commandos and paratroopers, I expected the worst once we were discovered. I prayed for courage to die well when the final test came. I did not want to disgrace the 2nd Paras who meant so much to me. Above all, I did not want to betray the Church of which I was an ordained minister.

Shortly before 7 a.m. those of us who were conscious spied figures emerging out of the mist. They turned out to be Africa Corps soldiers. They approached slowly and stealthily, their rifles at the ready. They stopped half way up the slope. Taking in the pathetic scene, they dropped their guns and approached us defenceless. In good English the Captain in charge said, "You are very cold. We will help you." Whereupon they lit their Bunsen burners, boiled water and ground their chocolate bars into it. This they gave to all the wounded. When my turn came, they noticed my two arms were useless. I could not help myself. One soldier tilted my head backward. Another with thoughtful gentleness trickled the hot chocolate down my throat. In my frozen condition I could feel this elixir of life flowing down into my stomach. What an experience! It warmed the inner recesses of my being.

The badly wounded who could not stand were placed on stretchers and carried to the nearest road. The Germans are noted for their efficiency and I was not all that surprised when within an hour ten large trucks rolled up. Because I was an officer, they placed me beside the driver in the front truck.

Motoring along a bumpy dirt-track I saw my friend, Kenneth Morrison, lying on his back, dead, beyond the verge. "That's my friend," I said to the driver. "Do you want to bury him?" he asked. "Yes!" He switched off the engine, leapt out and imperiously held up the convoy. There was a short conversation in German which I did not follow. After a few staccato commands, soldiers leapt from trucks, carrying shovels. They dug a grave and very gently lowered Ken into it. I took up my position at the end of the grave. Two soldiers had to shore me up as I had lost a lot of blood and I had no food for three days.

I had no Bible and no Book of Common Order, but I managed. A minister is a well-trained professional. He or she should be able to celebrate Communion, conduct a marriage, take a funeral without any book. From memory, I intoned that magnificent passage from the Book of Revelation: "And I saw a new heaven and a new earth: for the first heaven and the first earth were passed away, and there was no more sea.

And I, John, saw the holy city, new Jerusalem, coming down from God out of heaven, prepared as a bride adorned for her husband. And I heard a great voice out of heaven saying, Behold the tabernacle of God is with men, and He will dwell with them, and they shall be His people, and God Himself shall be with them and be their God."

I went on to repeat the words we find in the Gospel according to St. John, chapter 14: "Let not your heart be troubled: ye believe in God, believe also in Me. In My Father's house are many mansions: if it were not so, I would have told you. I go to prepare a place for you."

Then I offered a prayer thanking God for Ken's courage, charm and integrity, remembering his parents, his fiancee and all those who loved him. This was followed by the words of committal: "Forasmuch as it hath pleased Almighty God to take unto Himself the soul of our brother here departed, we therefore commit his body to the ground, earth to earth, ashes to ashes, dust to dust, in sure and certain hope of the Resurrection from the dead, through our Lord Jesus Christ."

This was followed by three volleys over the grave by the German soldiers who had captured us. They led us back to the trucks from which we had staggered and crawled to the place where Lieut. Kenneth Morrison was buried with full military honours. I was helped up into the front seat of the first truck by two soldiers who were polite and helpful. The moment I sat down I fainted. I suppose it was the culmination of exposure, loss of blood, three days without food and the emotional strain of taking a dear friend's funeral.

The convoy of trucks soon arrived at the main hospital in Tunis. We were well received. To my astonishment, because I was an officer, I was put into a room on my own. I had to be operated on as soon as possible as my right thumb was half hanging off and there was the danger of tetanus. Afraid that the French surgeons would amputate my thumb, the simplest thing to do, I appealed to my friend, Dr. Jim MacGavin (who stayed behind with us). "Jim, I'll fight for my thumb when I am conscious; you take over when I am under the anaesthetic." The operation took place at 2 a.m. I came to round about twelve noon and my first thought was, "Have I got it?" There was no way of telling for my right hand was swathed in layer upon layer of bandages. Shortly afterwards Jim MacGavin entered, and one look at his smiling face convinced me that all was well. "Murdo, you've got your thumb, but I had to fight like hell," said Jim cheerfully.

The French nurses were incredibly good to me. With my two arms wounded and in addition suffering from amoebic dysentery I was as helpless as a baby.

They took me over completely. They bathed me, changed my bandages, sponged me, levered me out of bed, helped me to sit on the potty and then wiped my bottom. To begin with I found all this very embarrassing. Soon I came to accept it as a normal routine.

When I got stronger, and my appetite returned, they began to feed me with extra food surreptitiously. They lived out and from their homes they brought in "goodies" which they hid under the bed. They would post sentries at strategic points. One outside my room and two others down the long corridor. Inside, the blond blue-eyed nurse from Brittany fed me with eggs, white bread and all sorts of forbidden delicacies. When I told her I was a fellow Celt and a clergyman, her ministrations became increasingly maternal.

This oasis could not last. Each day casualties kept pouring in and the wards were filling up to capacity. We knew it was only a matter of time till the walking wounded would be pushed out. And so it happened. One morning, without any warning, those of us who could walk were moved to a nearby horse stable. Makeshift palliasses were placed on a manure-smelling stone floor.

The next seven days were the nearest to hell I have ever experienced. Dante's hell is pleasant in comparison. From every point of the compass we were attacked by Arab fleas. They are fundamentalist and therefore more vicious than any other kind of flea this side of the Planet Saturn. My two arms were in slings, so I was unable to scratch. They were insatiably blood-thirsty. So much so that if only they had been unanimous, they could easily have dragged us out of the stable. I was overjoyed when one morning, again without warning, we were escorted to Tunis Airport. Put aboard a big aeroplane J.U.52, we were told our destination was Naples.

On the 20th December 1942 about 3 p.m. the great German transport plane landed smoothly at Naples Airport. Taken prisoners three weeks before in Tunisia, Dr James MacGavin and myself were being escorted, under guard, to the main building. Suddenly there was a loud explosion. All heads turned and watched the big aeroplane go up in a spiral of flame and smoke.

The incendiary time-pencil, hidden in the sling of my wounded left arm, did its job immaculately. My friend Dr Jim had dropped it unobtrusively among blankets and petrol casks at the rear of the plane. It was the type you squeeze to initiate a process of delayed action. There were no fatalities. All the crew disembarked safely.

Pandemonium followed. The guards prodded their guns into our backs while they pushed us unceremoniously to the edge of the runway. The ominous silence was broken by the stamping of goose-stepping feet on the tarmac. What looked suspiciously like a firing squad marched nearer. There was a sharp command and it came to a halt a few yards in front of us.

There followed a prolonged period of consultation punctuated by a number of hysterical outbursts. The audible clicking of rifle bolts indicated that the firing squad was getting ready for action.

It was then the miracle happened. A British Baby Austin car (captured at Tobruk) came down the runway and screeched to a stop between us. A tall man in civilian clothes stepped out and barked at the officer in charge, "What's going on?" "We are about to execute two British saboteurs who blew up a plane," was the answer. "Did you get a confession from them? Do you know how they did it?" he shouted. "No", was the answer. My knowledge of German was poor, but I knew the firing squad and the commander were at the receiving end of a blistering dressing-down. Then the important-looking individual beckoned us forward, bundled us into the back of the Baby Austin and drove at great speed to German Air Headquarters.

There the ordeal commenced. We were stripped naked. Our clothes were examined for any incriminating evidence. The cross-examination was relentlessly thorough. They found only one thing - a piece of paper in one of Jim MacGavin's pockets. On it a German colonel had written in good English - "Dr James MacGavin has treated German wounded with commendable compassion and skill. Wherever he is imprisoned he should be given the utmost respect." Our mysterious Inquisitor, who had so dramatically intervened at the airport, had a sense of humour. He smiled and asked, "Is it cricket to execute a good Samaritan?"

There was one other thing. He noticed that my wounds had gone sceptic. "This is most uncivilized," he shouted. "Why did you not report this and why were you not given medical treatment?" I answered "Sir, I did report it a number of times and nobody paid any attention." At my various schools and from my experience in the army I learned that the frequent use of the word "Sir" does one no harm. It certainly did not on this occasion.

A number of staccato orders were issued. In no time a medical orderly appeared. He was carrying a tray with all sorts of sinister-looking instruments. Round the end of one shining steel rod he twisted a wad of cotton wool, dipped it into some liquid, then stuck it deep into my wounds, full of suppurating pus. It was an excruciatingly painful experience, but I managed to keep a stiff upper lip. I was not surprised when my wounds began to bleed again. It did occur to me, however, that this was a somewhat pointless exercise, seeing execution was still on the cards.

While this was going on, our Benefactor, our 'Deus ex machina', made a number of phone calls. At times he would shake his head vigorously and in between shout what sounded like a peremptory order. As the medical orderly was putting the finishing touches to my bandages, the mysterious one behind the desk put down the phone with a decisive bang. He grinned at us and said, "Execution cancelled, let's have tea."

All through the tea ritual, this extraordinary man, whoever he was, chatted amiably in excellent English. Then he stood up and announced authoritatively, "You are leaving by the next train. I'll drive you to the station and I will see that you are both locked in the guard's van. Isn't that what you English call it?" All through the interrogation he kept calling us English. I felt, however, this was neither the time nor the place to assert my outraged Scottishness.

True to his word he drove us to the station and supervised our being locked up in the guard's van. After a long interval, during which I vomited again and again, the train began to move. We both felt a sense of relief. We arrived in Rome round about 2 a.m. and were led away by armed guards. On the way out of the station we saw a crowd of women, composed of wives, mothers, girlfriends, tearfully saying goodbye to their loved ones on their way to the front. What struck me was their unbridled emotionalism. Very un-Scottish, I said to myself.

That night and the next we spent in a civilian jail. Our guards wanted to put us in separate cells. Big, blond Dr. Jim MacGavin would not hear of it. "My friend is very ill and needs constant attention," He argued. "I am his doctor and I have to dress his wounds." When the guards still insisted, Jim, normally very good-natured, lost his temper. He lashed them with blistering invective. It was the first time I heard him swear. His wrath, terrible to behold, was not put on. It was frighteningly genuine and in the end effective. The officer in charge suddenly relented. Jim was allowed to share my cell.

By this time, I was really ill and had developed a temperature. The wounds which had been so robustly treated in Naples were now bleeding profusely. I felt cold, due I suppose to the loss of blood and the vomiting started up again.

With great gentleness, Jim removed the sticky, bloody bandages. With a sleight of hand, worthy of the most skilful magician, he produced clean linen from somewhere. Even more impressive was the way he cajoled one of the guards to provide hot water at 4 a.m. After he had cleaned my wounds, he poured sulphanilamide powder into the raw gaping holes. He insisted on my taking the only bed. He himself slept on the stone floor using his haversack for a pillow.

Jim is one of the very finest characters I have ever met. Educated at Oxford, he was charmingly unconventional, socially and professionally. Immensely tough physically, his courage was breathtaking. Above all, he was a man of great compassion. Before I was wounded myself, I helped him in a very modest way when he was operating. He taught me to administer anaesthetics. I noticed that he showed every bit as much care and devotion to the German wounded as he did to our own. I have not come across anyone quite like him.

CHAPTER 10

BEHIND BARBED WIRE

IN Rome, in the company of that superb gentleman, Dr. James MacGavin, I spent two nights in jail. All the way from Tunis he had looked after me like a brother, indeed like a mother. We were put on a train that ended up in Frankfurt-on-Main, Germany. The moment we alighted, we were escorted, under guard, to the camp known as Dulag Luft. It was the interrogation centre and that very night I found myself in solitary confinement. This lasted nineteen days.

The following day a benign-looking man in civilian clothes entered my cell. Sporting a huge Red Cross arm band, he placed a blank sheet of paper in front of me. He said, "I am sure your family, especially your mother, are worried about you. Write down their name and address and we'll dispatch a letter immediately assuring them that you are safe. Also give us the name and location of your regiment. I am sure your commanding officer will be very pleased to learn you are alive."

It was not all that difficult to see through him. "I'll give you my name, number and rank and nothing more," I answered. As he argued he became more and more aggressive and insulting. Goaded beyond endurance, I said, "You are not a Red Cross agent. You belong to the Gestapo and you are a lowdown unprincipled ruffian. You are going to lose the war anyway. If I ever get back I'll see to it that you will be tried and severely sentenced. You'll spend the rest of your life in prison."

The caring image dissolved and he became a nasty, brutal thug. He pulled a hand gun from somewhere and pushed it into the pit of my stomach. "I am going to kill you, you Englander Schweinhund," he snarled. I answered, "If you are going to shoot, please call me a Schotlander Schweinhund." Having no sense of humour, he did not understand. "Anyhow," I continued, "I am the first paratroop officer in captivity. You are curious as to how our parachute and technique of exiting differ from yours. If you shoot me without this information, your superiors may send you to the Russian Front.

Sorry, they won't. You are such a narrow-chested scrawny edition of a man that no-one would take you for a soldier. They'll shoot you instead." Losing his nerve, he put his gun into his hip pocket and shambled out.

That very evening, I was subjected to the heat-and-cold treatment. Without warning the temperature began to shoot up and the room became unbearably hot. It was so hot that sweat oozed through every pore of my body. It flowed in rivulets down my back. As the heat continued inexorably, breathing became difficult. The pounding in my head I found frightening. When there seemed to be no end I knew the meaning of panic.

Then, all of a sudden, I sensed a change. The choking feeling eased up and I knew the temperature was dropping. It kept on dropping till it went well below zero. The shivering, which started mildly, increased in intensity until I was powerless to control it. The single blanket I wrapped round myself proved totally ineffective. Just as I had become convinced I would die of hypothermia (at the time I didn't know the word), the temperature began to rise with cruel, tantalising slowness. It crawled up and up, till once again I experienced the choking feeling and that terrible pounding in my head. This alternation went on for two whole days. Then suddenly it stopped. I was left wondering if worse was to come.

I wasn't left long. My inquisitors decided on a subtler method. In the morning they sent in the prototype sort of thug who shouted, threatened and bullied. In the evening, they sent in someone completely different. He was so smooth and syrupy that he could have been the author of *How to Win Friends and Influence People*. With what looked like genuine solicitude, he would ask about my health in general and my wounds in particular. He would philosophize at length about the madness and stupidity of war. Then with consummate skill he would ask an innocent-sounding question — in reality a cunning trap. Born and reared a Calvinist, believing in the perfidy and perversity of human nature, I had no difficulty in coping.

They tried one more approach. I was visited by a paratrooper, a major in rank. He spoke with an impeccable English public school accent. After the opening pleasantries, I asked, "Where did you pick up that accent?" He laughed good-naturedly and said, "You sound like the foreigner and I sound like the Englishman." I agreed. He was very charming and did not ask a single question. Before he left, he said, "You are suspicious and I don't blame you. I didn't ask you any questions because there is no point. We are going to lose the war. Any information you could supply is infinitely irrelevant. There is only one question. Is there anything I can do to make the rest of your stay in Dulag Luft more palatable? In short, are you hungry?" "Yes, very," I answered. A few hours later, he came with a bulky parcel of biscuits and chocolate. I was still suspicious, but I was wrong. He was genuine.

At the end of nineteen days, some of them exceedingly unpleasant, I was moved under guard to Overmassfeld hospital. It was run by British doctors, captured in North Africa and Crete. When I arrived, I was in considerable pain. I am not belittling my operation in Tunis hospital. Deliberately, the surgeon had left more than a hundred tiny pieces of steel in the joint of my thumb. If he had extracted them, the joint would have crumbled. They acted as cement holding it all together. Unfortunately, the nerve that made my thumb work had been severed. I could not lift a cup or a glass in my right hand.

My wife, Betty, keeps on saying that I always land on my feet. On the whole she is right. How fortunate I was that in the hospital was a brilliant Harley Street orthopaedic surgeon by the name of Bill Tucker. He examined my thumb and with a smile remarked, "Macdonald, you're a Scot, but you'll never be able to drink whisky with your right hand till we sew up that severed nerve of yours." I told him I was a total abstainer and so in that sense the operation was not necessary. Smiling more wickedly, Bill Tucker said, "Hoping that one of these days you'll fall from grace, I am going to proceed with the operation." It was a brilliant operation. He sewed the severed nerve and later on, with carefully controlled electrical charges, stimulated the dead nerve into life.

From Obermassfeld, I was taken to a convalescent hospital called Klausterine, where the blind and the amputated cases were congregated. There I became deeply indebted to an Australian surgeon named Barlow. With the help of the Principal of the Dunfermline College of physical education, he nursed me on a slow but progressive journey to fitness.

It was here I was offered repatriation. Through the agency of the Red Cross, the two sides infrequently made repatriation exchanges of wounded prisoners. This prospect I pondered deeply. I prayed about it. And my answer was a categorical no. However conceited this choice may sound, I felt that as a paratrooper and a minister of religion I was in a special position to exercise a pastoral ministry among prisoners of war.

In Klausterhine, I collided with a very tough fellow paratrooper, Sergeant Hut. His great ambition was to escape from the hospital. After many acrimonious arguments, I managed to dissuade him. I pointed out that any escape would be followed by reprisals against the blind and amputated. He agreed when I promised that we would both try to escape on the way to whatever camp we were about to be sent to.

The time came when we were both declared fit to travel. The guard who eventually escorted sergeant Hut and myself from Klausterine was a walking arsenal. He had a rifle, a pistol and a large haversack that we suspected was full of hand grenades. We only had a thermos flask of tea and an abundance of sleeping pills.

After a hundred miles or so, we offered the guard a cup of tea, which he accepted with alacrity. While pouring it from the flask, we surreptitiously deposited, with the sugar, a number of sleeping pills and stirred the unholy brew. In half an hour, our guard had sunk into a deep, untroubled sleep. This was sergeant Hut's chance. I helped him through the toilet window. He jumped while the train was still in motion. I haven't seen or heard of him since.

I returned to the compartment. Not only was the guard still asleep, but he was snoring. As I looked at his inert slumped body, the decision was born. I am going to escape too. Suddenly the train came to a grinding stop, as if Providence had come into the act. I opened the door and quietly lowered myself to the ground. I lay flat on my face and after five minutes or so I watched the train gathering steam and clattering out of sight.

I was poorly equipped. My means of escape consisted of a map and a sensitized button in the top of my battledress that served as a compass. With no overcoat, I had ten bars of chocolate stacked away in my various pockets. My plan was to make for Holland, appropriate (not steal) a boat, and make for England.

It didn't work. On my third day out I was caught. In the early morning, while crossing an autobahn, I heard the click of a rifle, followed by the command "Halt." Automatically I put up my hands. My captor, an autobahn policeman, was not a brutal Nazi. He turned out to be rather human. "You are very cold," he said. "I give you cup of tea." After I drank it, he said, "I have three choices. I hand you to the army. They treat you tough. I hand you to Luftwaffe. They treat you good. I hand you to Gestapo. They shoot you. Vat is your choice? I answered, "If it is all the same to you, hand me over to the Luftwaffe." And so, once again, I found myself in Dulag Luft, the dreaded interrogation centre.

This time it turned out to be very different. My friend the paratrooper major was still there and he gave me a warm welcome. After the first roll call, he took me aside and told me a letter had arrived for me. I was thrilled. The first contact with my people back home. It was from Chrissie Lynn in Portree. When she got my postcard, she phoned the little post office in the village of Drinishadder, manned by my cousin, Kenneth. He left the office, ran all the way to our house, opened the door and shouted, "Murdo Ewen is alive."

My stay, which lasted three weeks, was relatively pleasant. At the end of the second week, the major, now a good friend, said, "In Dulag Luft the food is better than anywhere else. I can extend your stay by another week. It will do you good and perhaps you'll get another letter." I accepted. My German fellow paratrooper was exceedingly good to me. Every day he secretly supplied me with extra food. He even invited me to his fiancee's birthday party in Frankfurt. This offer I politely refused. If I had gone, the traitor, Lord Haw Haw, would have reported it over the radio with relish. It was here I met Colonel Dick Kloko and Major Jerry Sage, who later were to become good friends.

At the end of the three weeks, I was put on a train that took me to Sagan, the town within shouting distance of Stalag Luft III, beyond any argument the most famous prison camp of World War II.

Stalag Luft III consisted of five compounds: north, south, east, west and centre. Four of the five were reserved for officers. When I arrived at the beginning of April, the brand-new north compound was conspicuously international. It housed British, Canadian, Australian, New Zealand, American and though far fewer, South African airmen. There too were free French, free Dutch, free Danish and free Norwegians. We got on famously. I was not once aware of any nationalistic aggro.

This spirit was demonstrated when the Americans in their own exuberant manner celebrated the Fourth of July and their independence from British colonial rule. The Yanks had planned well in advance. They had distilled an alcoholic brew, anticipating the great day. It was a basic art they had borrowed from the British. What came to be known as "Kriege Brew" was a rough form of raisin wine. It was very potent, bordering on the lethal.

At 6.00 a.m. the Americans invaded the British barracks. With bugles, trumpets and guitars they shouted in unison, "The rebels are coming. Arise." They pulled the senior officers — wing commanders and squadron leaders — out of their beds and dumped them in the firepool at the centre of the camp.

At precisely 8.00 a.m. the British staged a counterattack. Raiding the American quarters, they captured most of the senior officers — colonels and majors — and carried them and bodily threw them into the same firepool.

The evening celebrations were even more hilarious. The scenario was the British attack on Washington in the War of 1812. Wing Commander John Day borrowed a large tub from the Germans. Along with Wing Commander Hyde, they paddled their way across the firepool, with one fell intent, to burn the White House. Defending that historic bastion on the farther side of the pool, were three stalwart Americans, Colonels Goodrich, Kloko and Stillman. They stood at attention until the two Wing Commanders had reached the half way line. Then they dived and overturned the tub, spilling the two Englishmen into the water. After a furious mock fight of splashing and ducking, the French umpire declared it a draw.

The next scene was in the realm of the tragi comic. Somebody spotted a body lying on its back at the bottom of the firepool. Three or four, representing the British Empire and the United States, dived in and hauled the inert body to the surface. On the edge of the pool, they turned him over on his face, thumped him on the back to get the water out of his lungs. Then rolling him over on his back, in turn they gave him the kiss of life. Suddenly the Englishman opened his eyes and, looking up into the evening sky, he said in an impeccable Oxford accent, "I know I am not the Messiah; I can't walk on the water."

The crazy capers left the Germans absolutely bemused. They had anticipated aggro on the Fourth of July, perhaps hoped for it. What they could not remotely understand was that the British celebrated this day of independence even more boisterously than the Americans.

At the end of the day, sitting around the firepool, in the warm Silesian twilight, RAF and American Air Force officers sang uproariously together. What was left of the Red Cross parcels they shared in a spontaneous, good-natured, extravagant picnic. It was an absolutely unique Fourth of July.

Soon after my arrival in the North Compound, three tunnels were started. They were called Tom, Dick and Harry. The word "tunnel" was never used. Too many prowling, eavesdropping guards were around who understood English.

The escape organisation was known as X. Head of X was Squadron Leader Roger Bushell. A South African, he was educated at an English public school and had practised as a barrister at the English bar. A fighter pilot, he had been shot down over Dunkirk. Already he had escaped twice and had nearly made it to Switzerland. Superbly equipped, he was the controller and co-ordinator of all escape activities. Ruthlessly efficient, he commanded the admiration, if not the affection, of his fellow prisoners.

On a number of occasions, I opposed him in camp debates. One encounter vividly comes to mind. Roger eloquently extolled the virtues of freemarket capitalism. With less finesse but with perhaps greater passion, I advocated the saving merits of socialism. To my astonishment, I won, though Roger was a more accomplished debater. Looking back, I cannot help feeling that as early as autumn 1943 a new political mood was taking shape. This shift alone explains the incredible defeat of Churchill at the polls in 1945.

The tunnel technician-in-chief was a big, likeable Canadian, Wally Floody. In civilian life, he was a mining engineer. It is not possible to exaggerate the part Wally played in the incomparable escape achievements of Stalag Luft III.

The collective ingenuity harnessed in the North Compound was truly astonishing. All sorts of factories were at work. One turned out clothing that looked like Luftwaffe uniforms and disguises of all kinds. Another forged passes, papers, even letters of introduction. Still another, controlled by Flight Lieutenant Al Haig of Australia and Captain John Bennett of America, produced compasses and maps of remarkable accuracy. Those who spoke German cultivated the "Ferrets." These were the guards, always on the prowl, looking for evidence of digging activity. Every hour of the day one could see them crawling under blocks with torches and steel rods.

Those with no special skills but who were still interested in escaping were used as "Penguins" and "Stooges." Penguins were given the job of getting rid of the sand dug from the various tunnels. This assignment was far from easy and so cunning tactics had to be devised. A Penguin would hang a sausage-shaped sack full of sand inside each of his trouser legs. Then he would casually join scores of others walking round the perimeter. Hands in pockets, he would pull strings that freed pins at the bottom of the sacks.

The sand would trickle to the ground, where it was pounded under hundreds of stamping feet. Thus, under the very noses of the guards, tons of sand were disposed of.

Stooges, too, had a vital role. Their brief was to report on the whereabouts of all Ferrets inside the compound. The Ferret-in-chief and by far the most alert was Oberfeldwebel Hermann Glemnitz. Honourable, hard working, incorruptible, he was never bad to prisoners. The British and the Americans highly respected him.

Three-hundred Stooges worked in shifts. Their boss was big S, the head security officer. He was Albert P. Clark, ("Bub"), who combined mildness of manner with an iron will and a fine intellect. He is now a retired Lieutenant General in the American Air Force. I have often wondered what my learned professors at the university would have thought if they had seen me acting in the dual capacity of Penguin and Stooge.

The tunnel "Tom" was accidentally discovered when it was near completion. "Dick" had to be abandoned because the Germans were building a new compound at the very place where it was going to exit. That left "Harry."

Its entrance in Block 104 was a model of ingenuity. The stove in one of the rooms stood on a concrete base, roughly four feet square. The "Engineers" shifted the stone, removed the tiles and reset them in a concrete trapdoor. It was an exact replica of the original base.

Tunnelling was a hazardous business. To defeat the German sound detectors, it was necessary to sink a shaft thirty feet deep, no mean engineering feat. It was not possible to work at such depth without an adequate supply of air. The compound technicians set to and invented air pumps out of Klim tins. They joined them end to end as cylinders to form a long pipe. The air was forced through a big bellows made of kit bags, worked by relays of pumpers.

The electrical specialists accumulated odd bits of wiring. Two coils were actually stolen. Light bulbs were removed from the block's corridors.

Trolleys were constructed big enough to carry two sandbags or one man. They were fitted with "tyres" and ran on rails made from the barracks mouldings.

It was Arnold of Rugby who said, "An educated man can do anything." In this famous dictum, Arnold did not mean that education conferred omnipotence or omniscience. He meant versatility. His insight was brilliantly demonstrated in Stalag Luft III.

On Friday night, 24th March, 1944, "Harry" broke. The Great Escape was on its way. Seventy-six men made their way out. We expected tough reprisals, but not the brutal, barbaric crime of which, within a few days, we were appraised.

Of the seventy-six who escaped, full of hope, fifty were executed by the Gestapo. Among them was Roger Bushell, the brain behind it all; Tim Wiellinn, who ran the forgery factory; Charles Hall, the brilliant photographer; Al Haig, the inventive compass maker; and Jim Cattanach, from Melbourne, Australia. Jim was my closest friend in the camp.

The Great Escape now belongs to history. The film based on Paul Brickhell's book, often repeated, has received universal acclaim. Of the seventy-six who exited, three made it home. A Dutch pilot in the RAF reached England. A postcard from Sweden with two fictitious names showed that two Norwegian pilots, flying with the RAF had also made it.

This most famous of all Escapes is like something out of Greek tragedy. Brilliantly conceived and every bit as brilliantly executed, it turned out to be a disaster of the first magnitude. The fifty who were executed were intelligent, courageous, resourceful and very attractive. For more than a year, they were dedicated to engineering their own destruction.

I took part in the two memorial services in the North and South Compounds. The one held in the North Compound, where the escape took place, is completely erased from my memory. I have tried my best again and again to recall it but cannot. So horrendously traumatic was the experience that unconsciously I had buried it beyond reach, a perfect example of what Sigmund Freud meant by repression. On the other hand, the service held in the South Compound I can remember in vivid detail. To this day I can hear "Tex" Newton, that superb bugler, sounding the "Last Post" — surely the most poignant of all farewells.

If the execution of the fifty was intended as an act of intimidation, the Gestapo stupidly misread the British character. In no time, the X escape organisation was reformed and work began on "George," under the theatre. In every way "George" was as ambitious as "Harry." In January 1945, the breakout was about to happen, when, with only one hour's notice, we were hurriedly evacuated as the thunder of the Russian artillery sounded from only thirty miles away.

My stay in the North Compound, predominantly British, was short. It stretched from the beginning of April to the middle of September, less than six months. Brief though it was, the experience proved enriching and exhilarating. Though I had no official status, I preached fairly often. Padre Robertson, an Anglican, was the official Chaplain. A dull preacher, he was also a saint, which is infinitely more important. Free of any trace of jealousy, he welcomed me as a colleague. He actually rejoiced in the terrific response I got.

In addition to regular preaching, I conducted classes in philosophy, psychology and Gaelic, which were all well attended. Most important of all, in that camp, friendships were formed that transcended all social and national barriers. They have endured and deepened across more than forty years.

If I hadn't been sent to Stalag Luft III, I would not have met that fabulous character, Wing Commander Harry Day ("Wings"). He was an Elizabethan and was without compare the most celebrated escapologist World War II produced. A wild hell-raiser in some ways, he was also sensitive, disciplined and genuinely religious. He loved to read the Lessons at the Sunday morning services in the theatre. He was out on the Great Escape and miraculously survived. Before the end, he made a daring escape. Crossing the Alps, he reached the American lines in North Italy. Coming from very different backgrounds, Wings Day and Padre Mac developed a lasting friendship.

Major John Dodge was one of the very nicest human beings I have met. An American by birth, he was a nephew of Winston Churchill by marriage. At age eighteen, he joined the British Army in World War I and fought at Gallipoli. He was the first non-Britisher to be awarded the D.S.O. He became a British citizen and in speech sounded more "pukka" than any topdrawer Englishman. His nickname was "Artful Dodger," for he was a compulsive escaper. He got out in the Great Escape and, against all odds, managed to survive. Aware of the Churchill connection, the Germans always treated him with respect.

A wealthy man, Johnny Dodge was free of class consciousness. He met everyone on equal terms and his charm was contagious. I had the honour of conducting Johnny's memorial service in London. It was a glittering occasion. Present were aristocrats, cabinet ministers, members of parliament, bemedalled admirals, generals, air marshals and a cluster of war aces such as Wing Commander Tuck, Wings Day and Douglas Bader.

Robert Stanford Tuck was the leading fighter ace of all the Air Forces, including the Luftwaffe. Slim in build, nervous in manner, strikingly handsome, he spoke with clipped vowels and his conversation was larded with public school jargon. We had a polite, nodding acquaintance. One day, after a debate in which I had taken part in the theatre, Tuck came up to me and said, "Padre, let's pound the perimeter." This was the only way privacy was possible. Halfway round the first circuit, the most brilliant of all fighter aces stopped and said, "Padre, over the last three months I have listened to you preach, lecture and debate. Despite your outlandish accent, I have come to the conclusion you are a well educated man." I laughed. From that moment, we were pals.

And, of course, there were the Scots in the compound. Most of them joined my Gaelic class. These were Melville Carson, Hamish Falconer, Bertie Louden from Edinburgh, Fred MacWhirter and Jack Harrison from Glasgow.

Fred is dead, but I am still in touch with the rest. I am particularly close to Jack, who is a first-class scholar. My only criticism of him is that he is infuriatingly modest.

My departure from the North Compound in September 1943 was tinged with sadness. The friends I have mentioned, along with many others, meant a great deal to me. Parting from them was a sharp wrench. The comfort of warm, meaningful human relationships helped to compensate for the gnawing hunger and the suffocating over-crowding. Jean-Paul Sartre ends his play No Exit (a modern version of Hell) with these words: "Hell is other people." Having lived in over-crowded rooms and barracks behind barbed wire for two and a half years, I think I know what Sartre meant.

Making do on the bare necessities of living, prisoners of war lacked many things. The only commodity we had in abundance was friendship. That was one thing our lords and masters could not take from us. In Stalag Luft III, friendships leapt across the barriers of climate and culture and geography. A crofter's son from the Outer Hebrides of Scotland became a friend of products of the elite English public school system, of graduates of American ivy league colleges and universities, of Texans, Midwesterners and Californians and of the Germans who guarded us.

What happened there in that camp, in circumstances grim and inauspicious, is, I would like to think, a prophetic sign and a symbol of the shape of things to come. Long before Martin Luther King, Robert Burns had a dream of human brotherhood:

For a' that and a' that
It's coming yet for a' that,
That man to man the world o'er
Shall brothers be for a' that.

CHAPTER 11
MINISTRY TO THE YANKS

WHY the Germans moved American airmen to a new compound will ever remain a mystery. According to the Geneva Convention provisions, their action was, of course, technically correct. One of these states categorically that prisoners of war of different nationalities should be housed in separate camps or compounds. But we suspected that was not the real reason. The more compelling one was that, from the moment they arrived, the Americans became enthusiastically involved in escape activities, proving themselves to be brilliant tunnelers. Segregation may thus have been a ploy to inhibit or at least slow the digging machinations.

In the North Compound, mainly British, I became known to the American minority. They had heard me preach, lecture, and debate on numerous occasions and in their own generous manner took to me.

When the Germans delivered the ultimatum to move, Colonel Charles Goodrich, the American Senior Officer (S.A.O.), asked me to pound the perimeter. After a couple of circuits, the Colonel stopped, eyed me speculatively and said, "We Americans are about to go over to the South Compound. We have no Chaplain and a number of your admirers are pressuring me to ask you to go over with us. What do you think?" I stamped my right foot and, under the gaze of the German guards, saluted him in the best British style and said, "Sir, if you want me I'll come." And so, on 8th September, 1943, I marched with my new congregation out of the North to the South Compound.

I was given a single end room, normally a privilege reserved for officers of senior rank. It was my friend, William Barnes, a graduate of Yale University, who pleaded my case. He convinced the Colonel that counselling the psychologically disturbed and comforting those who had received distressing news from home demanded privacy. I could not believe my good fortune. Privacy was a much sought after luxury.

I ate with the occupants of the room next door. They included Bill Barnes, Frank Newton, Bob Kemp, Frank Ross, "Red" Lally, Dick Sheiflebusch, Dick Bentley, "Chuck" Williams, John Winant and a tragic character called Sconiers. One and all accepted the Hebridean Scot with the strange accent, unconditionally. There we forged a lasting friendship. Over the passing years, we meet each other regularly from time to time. Recently three of my room mates with their wives visited us in Glasgow. They insisted on going to the Isle of Harris. "We have to see the place that produced our unorthodox and outrageous chaplain."

The number one enemy was hunger. The rations were criminally inadequate, not just in quantity, but even more in quality. Had it not been for the more or less regularly delivered Red Cross parcels, most of us would not have made it home. After D-Day, 6th June, 1944, the distribution of parcels became more and more erratic. During the last six or seven months of captivity, prisoners of war in all camps eeked out an existence on what only can be described as a starvation diet.

In the South Compound, we had, to our good fortune, an excellent set of senior American officers. Most of them were graduates of West Point. They combined professional military discipline with a large measure of humanity. Always accessible, they were both tough and tender.

Colonel Charles Goodrich, the senior officer in the South Compound, was a quiet American of medium height and stocky build. He had wiry red hair and complexion to match. "Roho," as he was called, was a man for whom I had much admiration and considerable affection. He was a close friend of the legendary Wings Day.

Lt. Colonel "Bub" Clark was Goodrich's chief executive and administrative officer. He was also head of the X escape organisation. Intelligent, soft-spoken, he could, when the occasion demanded, be exceedingly tough. Those of us who knew him were not in the least surprised when, years later, he became superintendent of the new Air Force Academy.

Lt.. Colonel Dick Klocko was in charge of education in the compound. Dick and I overlapped in Dulag Luft and had formed a good relationship before we arrived at Stalag Luft III. We soon discovered we were both addicts of P. G. Wodehouse. That cemented our friendship. He was the first to take me to a Roman Catholic mass.

Lt. Colonel Robert Stillman, a staunch Presbyterian, was an exceptionally attractive person. A graduate of West Point, he was also an All-American footballer. With his guileless blue eyes he was transparently and disconcertingly honest. In his courage and integrity he was Cromwellian. Those of us who knew him were elated when he was appointed the first Commandant of the new Air Force Academy.

Lt. Colonel Jack Stevenson, also a West Pointer, was a close buddy of Dick Klocko. He shared an end room with him across the corridor from my own. Combining formidable intelligence with a warm, humorous personality, he rose to the rank of General. When, years later, I was being appointed Professor of Practical Theology, Trinity College, Glasgow, General Jack was one of my principal referees.

To begin with, in the South Compound, for want of suitable accommodation, on Sunday morning I had to preach in the open. When the cold increased, we used the long corridor of the block I lived in. Before winter closed in, with the bricks and wood provided by the Germans, we had completed building the theatre. It turned out to be a tremendous boon. Each compound in Stalag Luft III had a theatre. It was the focal point where everything happened. In Stalag Luft III, theatrical productions ranged from the crudely amateur to the polished professional. Most of the compounds produced Shakespearean plays, featuring excellent props and fine Elizabethan costumes procured from Berlin. According to our German commandant, Von Lindeiner, the costumes, armour and weapons for Macbeth, played in the British North Compound, cost the prisoners of war more than 2,000 R.M.

The Germans, even under Hitler, attached great importance to the arts. That alone explains how, when the British in the North Compound staged plays like Hamlet and King Lear, those of us in the South Compound were allowed to attend. It goes without saying that we were escorted back and forth under guard.

The Americans did not always appreciate British humour. I have a strong suspicion that the reverse was also true. But we got on amazingly well together. To wit, as a Scot, a Highlander, a Hebridean, I was totally accepted by the Yanks. It is not for me to judge, but according to many of my American friends, I was the most popular person in the South Compound. Like all human beings, the Americans are sinners. But they do have in abundance a capacity for acceptance and an appreciation for ability, whatever the country of its origin. They are the least class-conscious of all people and they are remarkably generous.

As in the North, so in the South Compound, tragedy and comedy were inextricably mixed up.

One of my room mates, already mentioned, by the name of Sconiers, had become an American national hero. A bombardier, he was on a mission over Germany when the plane was severely damaged. The pilot was killed and the rest of the crew all but one managed to bail out. Sconiers found himself alone in the Flying Fortress and he argued with himself thus: "This plane is still capable of flying. It has cost the American government a lot of money, and I am going to land it in England." And he did so. In one of his famous fireside chats, President Roosevelt said, "If the American people emulate the courageous behaviour of Bombardier Sconiers, we are going to win the war." Naturally Sconiers was highly decorated.

Human nature is a maddeningly complex bundle of contradictions. Sconiers, a nice, ordinary man, was also a war hero. But in prison camp, the pressures proved too much for him. He became a victim of the condition psychologists call barbed-wire psychosis.

When we realised he was deranged, we protected him even more tenderly than his own mother would have. Whenever a guard entered the block, we hid Sconiers under a bed. He developed a pathetic dependence on me and followed me everywhere. In the middle of the night he would shake me awake and scream, "The God-damned Germans are going to kill me."

One day I had to go to a cemetery many miles outside the camp to conduct the funeral of a corporal murdered by a guard. As I was leaving, I said to my room mates, "Take care of Sconiers while I am away." I returned in the late afternoon. My room mates were standing inside the gates with very glum faces. They didn't need to say anything. Sconiers had been taken away. Those who suffered a nervous or mental breakdown were not sent to a psychiatric hospital. They were removed from the compound and given a lethal injection. A few days later the Senior Officer was handed a death certificate with the legend, "Died of pneumonia." That is what happened to Sconiers. Four days later I buried him in a cemetery near Breslau and sent a letter to his wife.

Various levels of barbed-wire psychosis were recognisable. One of the mildest forms was increasing inability to concentrate or to read at any length. Another was a sudden eruption of temper over matters that were really unimportant. Men who were very close would quarrel violently. Later on they would admit that blowing their top was stupid, serving no purpose whatsoever. One of the commonest symptoms was an annoying compulsive fidgetiness: someone would stand up in the middle of a meal or during a group discussion of a theatre production. Some prisoners had a feeling of mental and physical exhaustion and loss of memory.

We had very few cases of actual insanity. When it did happen, it wrought havoc in a room, even in an entire block. When someone went round the bend, he inflicted his own suffering on others. If the slightest sign of abnormal behaviour was detected, the Block Commander and the Compound Senior Officer were immediately informed. And of course the chaplain.

That was the dark side of prison camp. To their great credit, all but a few prisoners in both the North and South Compounds behaved magnificently. Not only did they keep their sanity, but they kept their sense of humour. I suspect the two go together. Considering how little we had towards the end, the amount of sharing and co-operation was most impressive, especially on the Death March. The numerous acts of caring and courage I witnessed on that gruelling journey reconfirmed my belief that human nature is not universally selfish.

In the midst of boredom, hunger and tragedy, we found much comic relief. Some of my room mates shared a wicked sense of humour. When they played a clever trick on me involving vitamin pills, I fell for it hook, line and sinker. We got on well, with no quarrels or stand-up fights or sullen silences.

Captain Gallatovich, the Compound Officer, was both a nice man and a snob. He was desperately keen to learn English. Snob that he was, he wanted to speak it, not with an American, Canadian, Australian, New Zealand or Scottish accent, but with the Oxford accent. The English boys in the North Camp, some of them spawned by such schools as Rugby, Eton and Harrow, assured Galli (as we called him) that Padre Mac had the purest Oxford accent in the whole of Stalag Luft III. He believed them.

We got down to serious business. After a week or so, Galli came into the compound and said, "I hear Bible has very good English. Will you give me a Bible?" I did. It was the King James Authorised Version of 1611, spattered throughout with "Thees" and "Thous".

Galli got down to it with typical Teutonic thoroughness. Within a week he would come into the camp and address me, "Good morning Captain Macdonald. How art Thou today?" I would pull my most solemn face and answer, "Verily, I am well today." At the end of six months, Captain Gallatovich had accumulated a big vocabulary, but he was not speaking English with the Oxford accent. He sounded like a Cromwellian soldier brought up in the Outer Hebrides.

I am sure that all prison camps have produced a crop of colourful characters. The one of which I was chaplain certainly produced them in abundance.

Frank Newton from Texas, the British christened "Tex." He was a versatile musician and it is not possible to exaggerate what this warm-hearted Texan meant to British and American prisoners. After the war, he became a Baptist minister. He claims I influenced him in that direction.

Bill Barnes, a graduate of Yale, was also a great morale booster. He was the organiser of the popular programme, "Tonight at Eight," which packed the theatre. Years later, he became a professor at prestigious Harvard University. A very intelligent man, Bill is also a character.

Jack Bennett, from Colorado, was the "Admirable Crichton" of the compound. An all-around handyman, he could turn his hand to anything. Whatever the crisis, Jack remained his smiling, unruffled, courteous self.

Robert ("Judge") Brown was a practising lawyer before the war. A bomber pilot, he was shot down and eventually arrived in Stalag Luft III. No-one, including his charming wife, Corinne, would accuse Bob of being a compulsive church goer. If I remember rightly, he was known as the camp agnostic. He and I frequently clashed in debates. The two of us were the finalists in a mammoth camp Liar's Competition. Bob won by a short head. I congratulated him warmly, but couldn't help adding, "Bob started with a distinct advantage — he is a lawyer." To the astonishment of the compound the Padre and the alleged agnostic became good friends.

John Winant's innate modesty could not hide the truth that he was a very important person. Near the end of the war, along with a number of British VIPs, he was removed to Colditz Camp. His father was the Ambassador at the Court of St James in London. He was immensely popular. The British have never forgotten how much this American aristocrat helped them in the darkest hour of their history. Scotland showed its appreciation by conferring on the Ambassador the Freedom of the Cities of Edinburgh and Glasgow.

Jerry Sage, a paratroop Major, like myself was captured in North Africa. He was a thorn in the flesh of the Germans; I forget how many times he escaped. In the end Jerry made it. He arrived home in Spokane before the rest of us were liberated from Stalag VII A.

Speaking of escapes, the British in the North Compound seem to have had a better record than the Americans. I am a bit sceptical about this claim. I tend to agree with General Bub Clark's suspicions. Let me quote from Professor Arthur A. Durand's excellent book Stalag Luft III.

"Although Clark was never able to confirm his suspicions, he is convinced that Bushell was responsible, at least indirectly, for the Germans' precautions. Clark felt that, in an effort to divert the Germans' attention from the two tunnels still under construction in the North, Bushell secretly gave them the impression that the British were happy to see the Americans go, that they, not the British, were the fanatic tunnelers."

The Germans fell for it. The proof is that they sent Herman Glemnitz, their most successful anti-escape expert to the South. He was always on the prowl and so most escape attempts were unsuccessful. It should not be forgotten, however, that the Americans proved themselves to be excellent tunnelers in the North. Furthermore, by acting as decoys in the South, they helped to make the Great Escape possible. It is only right that they were symbolically represented in the person of Steve MacQueen in the well-known film, The Great Escape.

I share General Clark's opinion. Roger Bushell was a brilliant man who could turn on the charm with great ease. He understood the German psychology and, to achieve his objective, would not allow sentiment to stand in the way.

In addition to preaching, pastoral counselling and holding classes in philosophy and psychology, I also at times practised hypnosis. It began when I was counselling a fighter pilot called Mitchell. When he was being shot down, he had suffered a blackout and somehow or other convinced he had failed in the dogfight. To compensate for his imaginary cowardice, at least twice he attempted to escape over the wire in broad daylight. I put him under and, when he was in the deep cataleptic stage, got three fighter pilots to help me question him. He experienced what is known as an abreaction. After I woke him, the pilots assured him he had not funked anything. Mitchell stopped his suicidal sorties.

Employing sundry devious means, the Americans maintained close contact with the British in the North Compound. Among the devices they used, were semaphore signalling, tins with messages inside thrown over the barbed wire and coded conversations. The most effective one, perhaps, was Gaelic, my mother tongue. By the way, Gaelic is not a mere provincial dialect confined to the Inner and Outer Hebrides of Scotland. It is a language older than Latin.

Each day, the Gaelic speaker in the North Compound, Corporal Peter MacNeil, would come over to the wire at staggered times and give me a digest of the BBC News in Gaelic. Later on I would translate it into English for the Americans.

It was thus we heard the momentous news of D-Day, the Allied landing on the beaches of Normandy. At about 6.00 a.m. a fellow soldier shook me awake and shouted in my ear, "The Scotsman is at the wire. He is very excited and wants to speak to you." I pulled on my jersey and trousers and ran over to the wire. Peter shouted two words in Gaelic, "Thainig iad," translated, "They've come." I turned on my heels, woke the South Compound, and pandemonium erupted. Men leapt up into the air and, shouting and crying, rolled in wild abandon on the ground. They knew that victory was in sight and that deliverance was around the corner.

Over the years, I have used this incident to illustrate what the Christian message really is. Properly understood, it is neither a philosophy nor an ideology. It is not even a morality. Essentially the Christian message is good news. It tells us of something stupendous that has happened, the coming of God in Jesus Christ. An Event more momentous and far-reaching than D-Day in Normandy. The Greek word is kerugma. It can be translated as the proclamation of a world-shaking event. This is the meaning of preaching. .

In the month of January 1945, Colonel Goodrich, the SAO, burst into the theatre, where all sorts of groups were performing, and made a terse, staccato announcement. "We have to leave the Compound within an hour. Stop what you are doing and pack up." The Russian advance was closing in and already we could hear the muffled thunder of their artillery.

Within two hours of that dramatic announcement, we marched out of Stalag Luft III camp, carrying our meagre belongings on our backs. Some argue about whether the temperature was 10 degrees or 20 degrees below zero but that is purely academic. The only thing we knew with certainty was that the cold pierced to the marrow of our bones.

The event that in several books on Stalag Luft III is called the Death March, resulted in a number of fatal casualties. On the second night out, Lieut. Jenkins, an All-American football player, decided to die. I heard the summons passed along the straggling line, "Padre Mac, you're wanted." Retracing my footsteps, I found Jenkins lying on his back in the snow. He insisted on giving me what remained of his scanty rations. I stayed with him till he died, closed his eyes and ran to catch up with the main column some three miles away. The summons came again and again.

We had marched about sixty-two miles in appalling conditions when the Germans pushed us into box cars for the rest of the journey. This ride turned out to be even more appalling than the march. They put about seventy of us into one box car. We hadn't enough space to lie down and so we devised a survival strategy. We divided ourselves into three shifts. One shift stood up for an hour while the other two shifts sat down. Then we changed places. With no toilet facilities, no water and excrement all over, tempers snapped. A few POWs went berserk. Again, as on the Death March the summons was heard, "Padre Mac, you're wanted."

At last we arrived at Stalag VIIA near the town of Moosburg, twenty-five miles north of Munich. The camp was built to house about 14,000 prisoners. By the time I left, it held at least 100,000. In space, food, heat and hygiene, conditions were execrable. Near the end, typhoid broke out and we were hurriedly evacuated.

My stay in Stalag VIIA lasted a little more than three months. It was a dirty, damp, rat-infested, disease-ridden camp. On Sunday morning, 29th April, 1945, after the church service, we were liberated by the American Third Army. In the afternoon, the flamboyant General George S. Patton, Old Blood and Guts himself, paid us a visit.

When he saw the conditions under which we were living, he actually cried.

Shortly afterward, I was moved to one of the British Compounds in this huge camp, in order to be repatriated. The American officers I had served as Chaplain in the South Compound and whose suffering I had shared on the Death March, gave a moving farewell. They clapped their hands rhythmically and shouted in unison, "We love you Padre Mac." I was reduced to tears. For nearly two years they had adopted and accepted this Gaelic-speaking Scot. Betty, my wife, was not there, but she has attended a number of reunions. Judging from the response I get, she always says, "Murdo Ewen, that was your greatest ministry." It's not for me to say, but she may be right.

In the British Compound I ran into trouble straight away. The Commanding Officer was a Group Captain with cruel, pale blue eyes and a vicious nature. He was very unpopular. If he had been German, he would definitely have belonged to the SS or the Gestapo.

When typhoid broke out in the camp, we had to be evacuated to the nearest town, Landshut. A team was picked to serve summonses on German families to leave their homes. I was included in the team. In a moment of weakness I accepted. No doubt my ego was massaged because, as a newcomer, I was even considered.

When I returned to my rat and lice infested barracks, I began to think things over. With clairvoyant certainty I knew that if I participated in this inhuman ploy, I could not preach the Gospel of Jesus Christ ever again. I donned my red paratrooper beret and walked over to the Group Captain's quarters. I knocked and entered. He was seated behind a ramshackle table. I saluted him smartly and correctly and said, "Sir, I am withdrawing from the team that is going to Landshut to evict German families. I am a minister and if I did that I could never preach again." He stood up and went obscenely berserk. He was the most foul-mouthed lout I ever met, all the fouler in that his obscenities were voiced in a clipped English public school accent. He called me a four-letter poof, a four-letter ignoramus, a four-letter oatmeal savage and a four-letter coward. Then he screamed, his face contorted with rage, "I am going to see that you are court-martialled." "Yes Sir," I said, stamping my right foot and saluting him with exaggerated panache. I turned my back while he was still screaming obscenities and then something strange, if you like eerie, happened. As I was approaching the door I saw a key on the inside. I walked up to it, turned it in the lock, turned back and moved over to face the Group Captain across the table.

I knew what I was going to do. I said to him, "You're the nastiest specimen of humanity I have ever met, worse than the Gestapo. I am going to beat you up." He was bigger than me and he began to laugh. I leapt over the table and hit him with both fists in the chest. Before he hit the floor I had groined him viciously with my knee. At the same time I hit him with the flat of my right hand on both sides of his neck and again above his Adam's apple. He went out like a light. It took less than seven seconds. "My God," I said aloud, "I've killed him." I kept shaking him and patting him on both cheeks. After what seemed an eternity, he began to wheeze and roll his head from side to side.

After he recovered consciousness I helped him to his chair. Then I stood over him and gave him the verbal works. "Group Captain, because you went to an expensive school you think you are educated. Actually you are a very stupid man. The trouble with you is that in your snobbish abysmal ignorance you equate education with intonation. Let me tell you that I went to inexpensive schools and I am cosmically better educated than you. Let me explain to you the meaning of the word 'paradox.' You are supposed to be the professional man of war, the tough guy, and as a clergyman I am supposed to be the professional man of peace, the dog-collared sissy, but I took you to the cleaners within seven seconds. You have threatened me with court-martial. Go ahead. It will do your reputation and your prospects of promotion no good when it is noised abroad that a Scottish clergyman knocked hell out of a decorated so-called warrior within a few seconds."

Irony of ironies is what happened the following Sunday. On Saturday evening, the official Chaplain of the compound went down with galloping diarrhoea and at the very last moment I was called to replace him. To my embarrassment, the Group Captain, unaware of this change, sat in the front row. I preached a sermon lasting fifteen minutes on the text, "Be strong in the Lord and in the power of His might." He was not amused.

Next day, we were evacuated to the town of Landshut. By some extraordinary coincidence three of us were billeted in a house and soon discovered we were all called Murdo. Murdo Macrae was a qualified teacher who taught in Crieff Academy. Murdo Macaulay came from the Isle of Lewis and was a product of that excellent school in Stornoway, The Nicolson Institute. A prospective divinity student, who had mastered German and could read the theologian, Karl Barth in the original, he is now a retired Free Church minister. And myself, Murdo Ewen Macdonald, an ordained minister and a paratrooper.

The woman we were billeted with was a widow, whose husband had been killed on the Russian front. She looked frightened. There was hardly any food in the house and so the three Murdos appropriated tins of Spam, Klim, flour and processed cheese from the American food stores. The moment she realised we were out to help her, she confessed that she had hidden her two daughters in cupboards upstairs. When we assured her we had no designs on her daughters, that on the contrary we were prepared, if it was necessary, to protect them at all costs, the frightened look on her face disappeared. She rushed up the stairs and brought down two beautiful girls, one nineteen years of age, the other sixteen. The six of us struck up a spontaneous, instant friendship. Murdo Macaulay, so fluent in German, spelled out the division of labour: the women would take care of the cooking and the men would wash up and do the heavy chores. It worked.

Before we were airlifted home, we raided the American stores once again and stacked up their cupboards. Mother and two daughters accompanied us to the airstrip where the Lancaster bombers were waiting to take us home. They hugged us and kissed us and cried all over us. As we entered the big plane, we waved and blew kisses. I remember saying to myself, "War is a stupid obscenity."

However absurd it may sound, I actually enjoyed my prisoner-of-war experience, which lasted two and a half years. The first two months, suffering from a nasty wound, I knew the meaning of pain. Always hungry, day and night, I dreamed of ham and eggs, above all of crowdie and cream. I resented the suffocating overcrowdedness from which there was no escape. But despite the hell of it all, by the grace of God I reaped benefits that helped me in my ministries in Glasgow and Edinburgh.

I count myself fortunate. Nearly 100% of prisoners of war were deprived of the professions and trades for which they had been so expensively trained. In Stalag Luft III and later in Stalag VIIA as Chaplain I was privileged to do the job for which I was trained. What an opportunity! And what a marvellous laboratory! It would be egotistic of me to try to assess my ability in this tough and trying arena. Instead, let me quote the citation of the American Bronze Star awarded to me. It is the exact equivalent of the British Military Cross.

Citation for Bronze Star Medal — Captain Murdo E. Macdonald, British Army, rendered outstanding service as Chaplain to American prisoners of war in Stalag Luft III, Germany, from September 1943 to April 1945. A British Paratrooper but likewise an ordained minister, he volunteered for the duty in which he tended the needs of many depressed prisoners, during the long weary months of their captivity. He also conducted well attended classes in psychology and philosophy, and concerned himself with the mental health of the Compound. He was exceptionally effective in his counsel to individuals suffering from mental depression and deterioration, and in at least two cases was directly responsible for preserving the sanity of those who were mentally ill. Captain Macdonald's inspiring leadership and example has contributed materially to the betterment of individuals under his care and reflects great credit upon himself and the British armed forces.

CHAPTER 12

NO MAN'S LAND

THE experience of boarding the Lancaster bomber, at the edge of the town of Landshut, bordered on the mystical. I was elated despite the pilot's cheerful confession that he was recovering from a king-size hangover after the VE-day celebrations. I was on my way home to be reunited with my wife and my parents. It was all over — the brushes with death, the perpetual hunger, the absence of privacy, the interrogation by the Gestapo. As I sat with my fellow prisoners in the plane about to take off, I was aware of an all-pervasive sense of happiness.

For some reason I have never understood, the Lancaster, instead of flying us direct to England, landed in Rouen in France. There we waited till the afternoon of the next day. With no accommodation available, we had to doss down in a field adjacent to the airport. Though it was the month of May, the night was cold and sleep was difficult. I spent most of it stamping my feet and waving my arms about to keep the circulation going.

In the morning, we were given a piece of bread and a cup of coffee. Suddenly, the fellow shivering beside me on the grass said, "I'm Tim Weir. I come from Edinburgh and I have been a prisoner for nearly five years." And I replied, "I am Murdo Ewen Macdonald. I come from the Island of Harris. I have been a prisoner of war for two and a half years." As we munched our meagre breakfast, we talked and, as so often happens in war, friendship was formed. We sat next to each other on the plane all the way to England.

In mid afternoon, we landed at an RAF base in Surrey, not far from London. The welcome we got took us by surprise. It was overwhelming. A brass band played while we disembarked. It escorted us to the open door of a huge hangar, where we all came to a halt. A Brigadier and an Air Vice-Marshal addressed us, followed by a high official from the War Office. They assured us we had served King and country with courage and tenacity and that no other country had a better escape record. I didn't know whether to feel proud or guilty. I had escaped once, but had been recaptured forty-eight hours afterwards.

After these pleasantries, we were taken to a large delousing centre. We were stripped of our dirty, bug-ridden clothes. In utter nakedness, we were subjected to three showers. In the first, a copious amount of what I assume was anti-lice powder was used. When we had towelled ourselves dry, we were led to a spacious room. There were laid out, in alphabetical order, our names and ranks and underclothes, shirts, ties and uniforms.

When we had dressed we were led to the hangar. Row upon row of trestle tables, covered with white cloth, beckoned us. We were served by nice looking, soft-spoken WAAC and WAAF uniformed waitresses. We were treated to a double portion of bacon and eggs, the meal I had so often dreamed of in prison camp.

At the end of this warm and spontaneous reception, we were given rail tickets that would take us to our respective destinations. I had decided to take the first train from London and to proceed with a stop here and there to the Outer Hebrides. I had reckoned without my new friend, Tim. "Murdo, you are not travelling all night. Don't be daft. You and I are putting up at an hotel." "But Tim," I protested, "I have no money." "Don't worry," Tim said. "Before the war I was an actuary in London and I did the accounts for St. James' Hotel. I'll get two rooms on credit, with a bit of luck free. Actually he got a suite — free.

At about 8.00 p.m. we went down to the diningroom, looking forward to a good dinner, the first for many years. As we were entering, a waiter held up his hand and stopped us. "Battle-dress not allowed," he intoned. "Dress uniform required." Tim lost his temper. "My friend and I came out of prison camp this very afternoon. How can you expect us to appear in dress uniform? I demand to see the manager." In no time the harassed looking manager appeared. Before he could open his mouth, Tim waded in. "I am Tim Weir, the accountant who did your books before the war. After spending the best part of five years behind barbed wire, I expected a better reception." The poor manager, manifestly taken aback, bowed and scraped and led us to a table at which sat a solitary Englishman. In the packed diningroom conversation stopped and all heads were turned.

As we were scanning the menu, the Englishman, pretending he had not heard the altercation, asked, "Are you on leave?" "No" snapped Tim, "My friend and I have come out of prison camp this afternoon." The Englishman leapt to his feet and imperiously beckoned the nearest waiter. "This calls for a celebration," he shouted. "Bring a bottle of your best wine."

The three of us hit it off at once. When our new friend discovered I had emerged from Stalag Luft III, he asked, "Isn't that the camp where the Gestapo executed fifty prisoners who had escaped?" When he further learned I had played a modest part as Stooge and Penguin in the construction of the tunnel, he leapt to his feet once again and called for another bottle of wine.

That night, having dined and wined in one of the best hotels in London, I wallowed in comfort in a soft bed with clean sheets. I was too excited and exhilarated to go to sleep. Round about 3.00 a.m. I became aware of movements from Tim's room next door. Eventually they stopped, but I was still curious. Why was Tim moving the furniture around? Was he ill? I decided to investigate. I went through to Tim's room and found him sleeping on the floor with his haversack under his head. I didn't disturb him.

In the morning, I rang up the American Embassy. I wanted to know if they had any word of John Winant, son of the Ambassador, one of my room-mates in Stalag Luft III. To begin with, I had considerable difficulty in making contact. When I said I was a friend and fellow prisoner of war of John Winant, I was through in a second. The Ambassador himself was at the end of the line. "Sorry, Sir," I began. "I am sure your Embassy is bombarded by calls from all manner of cranks, but I happen to be a room-mate and friend of your son, John. I am known as Padre Mac." He interrupted me. "I know all about you Padre Mac. On behalf of American Air Force prisoners of war may I thank you for what you have done to strengthen their morale in captivity."

I thanked him and said, "I am sure you know that your son, John, was classified as a VIP and, along with a number of British Prominentes, was sent to Colditz Castle. I was the last to speak to him before he was removed from Moosberg Camp and I promised that the moment I reached Britain I would contact you."

The Ambassador answered, "John has not arrived, but from intelligence we possess, we are about 100 percent certain he is safe. By the way, where are you speaking from and what is your programme over the next twenty-four hours?" "I am ringing from St. James' Hotel and I have a ticket in my pocket that enables me to travel all the way to the Outer Hebrides." With ambassadorial authority he said, "A car will call for you within half an hour. We want to see you at the Embassy."

I had a very nice time at the Embassy. Next morning, I took a train to Edinburgh and from there to Kyle of Lachalsh. I crossed over to Skye and stayed for two nights with my friends, John and Chrissie Lynn, in Portree. The second night, during dinner, the phone rang. Chrissie answered it in the adjoining room. She returned, her face registering astonishment as she said, "The American Ambassador would like to speak to you." The exchange was brief. "Yes, John has been in touch. He is safe and in good health. We'll see him within the next two days." Typically thoughtful of a genuinely great man.

From Skye I moved back to the mainland, sailed on the *Loch Seaforth* to Stornoway, climbed aboard an ancient bus, and arrived at Tarbert, Harris, at 11.00 p.m. Waiting for me with a boat he himself had built was my cousin Angus. In pitch darkness he skilfully navigated the boat through a cluster of islands till we came to the village of Plockrapool. He secured the boat by a small, rough-hewn, pier and accompanied me to the house I was born in. They came down the rough footpath to meet us, my father and mother, my sister-in-law Mary and her two children.

The scene had a Biblical flavour. My father, a very strong man physically, embraced me. I thought my ribs were going to crack. He began to cry. "Murdo Ewen, for six months we believed you were dead. And now you are here, come back from the dead." My mother was much more restrained. She kept patting my cheeks and saying, "Murdo Ewen, you look so well. I expected to see a skeleton." I answered, "Yes mother, I am surprisingly well, but remember I have had many good meals since I was liberated on 29th April."

For the next two weeks my mother fussed over me and overfed me. She plied me with porridge, bacon and eggs, trout, haddock, herring, crowdie and cream. With herring, I came a cropper. My stomach, accustomed to a poor diet for the last three years, couldn't take it. I explained to my mother and, intelligent woman that she was, she understood.

One afternoon over tea, scones, oatcakes, crowdie and cream, she suddenly remarked, "Murdo Ewen, you don't hate the Germans." "No mother," I answered. "But they shot you," she said. "Yes, to be accurate, they shot me twice." "And you still don't hate them. Why?" This was my answer, "Because after they shot me they were good to me. They operated on me and treated me well in three of their hospitals." At this point the conversation ended. Two days afterwards, while giving me afternoon tea, my mother remarked, "Murdo Ewen you are quite right. The Germans are just like ourselves. There are good and bad people among them."

From the Isle of Harris, I had to report to Edinburgh to get a medical examination. It was extremely thorough. Two young doctors tested everything, heart, blood pressure, lungs, stomach, muscles, reflexes. I got an excellent report. They told me I was impressively fit but that my stomach had shrunk due to the meagreness of my prisoner of war diet. If I wanted my stomach back to its original size, they advised me to eat large meals for the next six months. On the other hand, they said if I contented myself with smaller meals, my health would not suffer in the slightest. Lying on the couch where they examined me, I made up my mind at once. No big meals for me. This decision I have never regretted.

One of the doctors who examined the gunshot wound in my right hand said; "You're applying for a pension, of course." "Oh no," I protested. "I am so lucky to be alive that it would not occur to me to apply for a pension."

He left the room without saying a word. After half an hour or so, he returned with a pension application form neatly filled up. "Append your signature here," he ordered. He added, "If you were a manual worker, your right hand would be virtually useless. I am a minister's son and I know that as a profession you are not all that well paid. In signing this form don't harbour any sense of guilt." I did as I was told. After an appearance before a medical tribunal, I was awarded a 20% military pension. It isn't much, but it helps.

The young doctor was right. Since then the wound in my right hand has given me much trouble. The wound was inflicted forty-seven years ago, but it is still painful, especially in cold and wet weather. There are over a hundred particles of steel imbedded in the joint of my thumb. They can't be removed. Now and again, one of these particles gets dislodged and it entraps the nerve. When this happens, I experience pain and I have difficulty in falling asleep. To this day, I have periodic twinges of guilt about my war pension. Betty, my wife, dismisses this as nonsense. She argues that, considering the number of operations I was subjected to and the pain I have suffered over the years, I deserve it.

When this was all over, I was ordered to report to a holding Batallion stationed in Strathpeffer. It was composed of a curious collection of odd bods impatiently awaiting demobilization.

The Commanding Officer was a most colourful character — Colonel Ronnie Meyers, M.C., D.S.O. These decorations he had won fighting Field Marshal Romell in North Africa. He belonged to a warrior tribe. His brother, Commander Meyers of the Royal Navy won the V.C. The Colonel was a big man with a macho moustache and a parade ground intimidating voice. He bullied and terrified the young officers. The moment I met him, I intuitively sensed he took a sadistic delight in pushing subordinates around. I recall saying to myself, "Meyers, I'll not go out of my way to pick a fight with you, but if ever you start pushing me around I'll give you the works in the name of the Father and of the Son and of the Holy Ghost."

The breakthrough came one night at a dinner in the Officers' Mess. A certain Lieutenant P. had joined us. He was a noisy self-congratulating extrovert. Half-way through the dinner he got the attention of the Mess. Enjoying every moment of it, he boasted of how he had shot dead an Italian station-master who had given him cheek in front of his platoon. No-one protested. I am ashamed to say I heard some sniggering. Trembling, I stood up and said, "Lieutenant P. I see you are sporting a military cross and I am sure you deserved it. But I resent anyone boasting about the murder of a defenceless civilian. If you were German your place would not be in the Wehrmacht or Luftwaffe but in the SS or the Gestapo." There was a deafening silence as I walked out.

I went straight to my room and limply sank into an easy chair feeling an awful chump. "Macdonald you have blown it," I said to myself. "Tomorrow morning big Colonel Meyers will tear you a strip and post you to some Godforsaken spot." How wrong I was! One by one, all the officers came into my room and shook my hand. Last of all came Colonel Meyers. I let him have my chair and I sat on the edge of the bed. "Padre," he said, "That was a courageous thing to do. I feel guilty I didn't beat you to it." "Thank you, Sir," I replied. "Most of the time I am a coward, but I have a capacity for moral indignation which now and again erupts into a kind of reckless pugnacity."

In November I entered Bangour Hospital to get the wound in my right hand attended to. The bullet wound in my left arm had healed beautifully and had never given me any trouble. But the mortar shell wound in my right hand was a nasty one. It nearly severed my right thumb and there were over three hundred pieces embedded in the surrounding tissues. It was also painful. On examination I was told the deep scar tissue had to be excised. The cavity left by its removal required not a skin but a muscle graft. Three or four operations were necessary. This meant hospitalization for at least three months.

Once again I landed on my feet. The surgeon who performed the muscle graft operation, A. B. Wallace, was the No. 1 plastic surgeon in Scotland, and arguably, after MacIndoe, the No. 2 in Britain. We became friends and between operations he insisted on my spending weekends with himself and his charming wife in his lovely home in Edinburgh. I owe a lot to this good man.

Bangour Hospital was a kind of Theatre. The Dramatis Personae were in a sense Shakespearean. The most formidable personality was Betty, the senior maid. She struck terror into the hearts of G.P.s, surgeons, sisters, nurses and patients. For some unaccountable reason she mothered me. She said, "I notice you are a sleepy head in the morning. The cup of tea which the nurse puts on your locker at 6 a.m. is stone cold when I enter your room at 8. From now on this is what will happen. I'll tell the nurse to leave you alone. At 8.00 a.m. I'll bring you a cup of tea. Drink it and go back to sleep. Get up when you like, wander down the corridor, give me a nod and I'll clean your room." Betty's conspiratorial friendship I valued highly.

There was one embarrassing incident. Sister G., an excellent nurse, popular with staff and patients, took a fancy to me. She knew my wife was still in the U.S.A. and likely to be for some time, due to transportation difficulties. One day, after removing my stitches, she suggested I should divorce Betty and marry her. Taken aback, I explained to her this was not remotely possible. I pointed out that I was a minister and that the moment I got well I would look for a congregation. Betty, through no fault of her own, could not get a passage. Once this was possible, she intended coming to Scotland to share in my ministry.

It says more for Sister G. than for me that we remained good friends. Years later, when I was minister of St. George's West, I got a letter from Sister G. which read, "Would you consider marrying me in your official capacity?" I did, and afterwards acted as master of ceremonies at the wedding reception.

After I left hospital, my energies were directed to getting Betty over to Scotland. The problem was that millions of soldiers had to be repatriated to their own countries and ship space for civilians was virtually non-existent. I explored every avenue without success. Then Betty's father came to the rescue. He arranged an invitation from the Community Church in the island of Aruba. With their Esso Standard Oil connection, transportation was arranged. I crossed the Atlantic in an oil tanker and met up with Betty in Philadelphia, where she taught school.

After a short visit to New York where we stayed with Dickie, Betty's room mate in Mount Holyoke College and with Bill Barnes, one of my room mates in prison camp, we flew via Miami and Cuba to Aruba. At the end of six weeks, we returned to the U.S.A. and met up with Betty's brother, Donald and his wife, Adele. In September, we sailed on the liner *Mauritania* and took the train to Glasgow. We stayed with my brother, Murdo and his wife, Sadie, in their manse. With them, and their two lovely children, Mary and Helen, we remained for the next four months.

CHAPTER 13

PARTICK PARISH

IN Prison Camp I had made a vow. If I ever made it back to Scotland, I would unconditionally accept the first church that showed any interest in me. It mattered not whether the waiting congregation existed in slum or suburb. Having survived against all the odds, I felt this was the proper attitude. So in the teeth of well-meaning advice from relatives and friends, I remained stubbornly true to the decision arrived at in Stalag Luft III.

My older brother, Murdo, minister of Milton Church, Cowcaddens, questioned the wisdom of what he called my naive utopian attitude. A shrewd practical man, he argued that the logic of things was heavily stacked against me. "Murdo Ewen," he would point out, "Your ministry in Portree, Isle of Skye, was very short through no fault of yours. For the best part of five years you have been out of the country. Most congregations in Scotland don't know you exist. You are virtually unknown. You better start scanning the newspapers and apply for vacancies that are advertised." His advice, sincere, well-intended and persuasively presented, I resisted.

Behind the scenes, Murdo got things going. He arranged for me to preach in various churches, his own included. He also let it be known that I was on the open market as it were, free for the call.

A number of congregations showed interest. The first that made an unequivocal approach was Old Partick, within a stone's throw of Glasgow University. Territorially it was a fascinating parish. Its boundary to the south was the River Clyde, the mecca of shipbuilding, in 1945 at its most prosperous. It also included within its bounds the Art Gallery, the Kelvin Hall, the Western Infirmary and half of Glasgow University.

In the best sense of the term, it was a mixed congregation. It included teachers, doctors, lawyers, foremen in shipyards and factories and many working-class people. In other words, it was a healthy cross-section of humanity.

I had two remarkable predecessors in very different ways. Dr. John Smith was a powerful character. His dominant interest centred round education. He was largely responsible for building Jordanhill College, where graduate and non-graduate teachers are trained to this day. It is perhaps not surprising that Old Partick came to be known as the Teachers' Church.

My immediate predecessor, John Anthony Macrae, was a unique human being. Privately educated, a graduate of Cambridge, Chief of the Macrae clan, he was minister of Old Partick parish for eighteen years.

John was not a good scholar, nor was he a good preacher, but was a great man in a much more important sense. To put it simply, he was a saint, arguably in his time the most outstanding in the Church of Scotland.

In his first parish in Dundee, John Macrae developed a special interest in tramps. He spent a considerable amount of his energy and money feeding them, clothing them, as well as arranging shelter during the cold winter months.

When he moved from Dundee to Glasgow, many tramps followed him. They were frequent visitors to the manse. His wife, like her husband, expensively educated, must have been endowed with the patience of Job. Apparently she never complained.

Every Saturday afternoon, John bought at least a dozen packets of cigarettes. Before he went to bed he prepared a large number of sandwiches. He got up at 6 a.m. After a modest breakfast, one could see him carrying a heavy hamper, walking in the direction of the Marine Police Station, off Dumbarton Road. He moved from cell to cell distributing the sandwiches and cigarettes, getting to know the prisoners and warmly asking about their families. At 11 a.m. he would stagger up the pulpit steps of Old Partick, looking exhausted, and preach a rather dull sermon.

After the evening service, he did not go back to the manse for a well-deserved rest. Instead, you could see John Anthony climbing on to a tramcar, carrying another heavy hamper of sandwiches. These he gave to tramps sleeping rough under the bridges and arches of the city. At about one or two a.m. on Monday morning, policemen would see a solitary familiar figure wending his way wearily to his manse in the west end.

Needless to say, John had his critics. Some of the more respectable members of his congregation complained of his obsessive preoccupation with the undeserving and the worthless. At the same time, he seemed to neglect his loyal regular supporters, the men and women who, Sunday by Sunday, listened to his boring sermons and voluntarily contributed enough money to pay his salary.

Up to a point, these criticisms are understandable. The saint, contravening most of our conventions can at times arouse cynicism and invite hostility. The saint condemns and comforts at one and the same time. He condemns in that his purity shows up our own petty and pusillanimous behaviour. He comforts in that it is in sinful human nature that God has wrought this miracle of grace. The saint hurts and heals. The effect he or she has upon us can be best described in the words Iago used of Cassio:

> **He hath a daily beauty in his life**
> **That makes me ugly.**

In terms of free market economics, John Anthony Macrae's ministry was not successful, but at the last judgment the saint of Partick will hear himself addressed, "Come ye blessed of my Father, inherit the Kingdom prepared for you from the foundation of the world . . . Inasmuch as ye have done it unto one of the least of these my brethren, ye have done it unto me."

No doubt there were times when the good congregation of Old Partick writhed under the ministry of a genuine saint. When John moved on, that I am sure explains why they decided on a real change. I suspect this is the reason why my call was so overwhelmingly unanimous.

Shortly after my induction, I was approached by a shipyard within the bounds of my parish. They wanted me to become their industrial chaplain. Having experienced, and in a strange way enjoyed, the world of the military for five years, I was curious to know what the world of Industry was like. With the very minimum of soul-searching, I accepted.

What I discovered shook me to the depths of my being. It did not take me long to grasp that Management and Labour were chronically and paranoically suspicious of one another. They hated each other's guts. They shouted at one another, but there was no communication on the level of mutual understanding.

One week I lunched with the Management. We met in a lovely oak-panelled, wall-to-wall carpeted dining-room. Bottles of whisky, sherry and brandy were provocatively displayed on a mahogany sidetable. The Directors were urbane, polite and effortlessly civilised. They were never condescending to me. A minister, a university graduate, an officer in the army, they accepted me as one of them and were quite nice to me.

The next week I lunched with dungaree-clad workers and foremen in a large sprawling canteen, where self-service stood in sharp contrast to the Directors' waiter service. In contrast to the genteel well-modulated accent of Management, the language in the canteen was rough, blasphemous, sometimes obscene. They never minced their words.

At these lunches, I deliberately played the role of devil's advocate. In the workers' canteen I would defend the Management. "After all," I would argue, "they have to procure the orders which will keep the Yard open and secure employment for years to come." "And remember," I would intone, "they have their headaches too."

Predictably my argument was met with howls of blasphemous protest. "You are a betrayer of your working-class origins," they would shout. "With your clerical collar, you have been ordained to bestow your benediction on middle-class values and prejudices. You are not interested in us. You are a stooge of the Establishment." These attacks hurt, because I was aware they contained a disturbing element of truth.

Next week, lunching with the Directors, I would doggedly defend the workers. "They are suspicious, at times truculently unco-operative. Why? Because, in the past, they have been treated as serfs, indeed as sub-human. Restore unto them the dignity which is their due. And when at length this message gets through, they will behave as responsible, law-abiding citizens," I would passionately argue.

As they sipped their wine, my arguments were met with well-bred, cynical, low-key laughter. "Chaplain," they would say, "For someone who has spent five years in the army you are so naive. You fail to understand that shipyard workers are a lazy, time-wasting, paranoically union conscious, irresponsible lot. What they need is not less, but more bullying." And so it went on. When nearly three years later I left Old Partick to go to Edinburgh, to my surprise, Directors and workers sent me on my way with a couple of parties and a handsome cheque.

I could not help thinking that, if the relationship between men and officers in the armed forces had been as bad as that between Management and Labour in the shipyard I was chaplain to, we would have come to grief. We would not have won the Battle of Britain, the Battle of the Atlantic, or for that matter any other battle.

Good human relationships are of paramount importance. In fact, it is the highest form of competence. There can be no efficiency without it. In the war, the best fighting units were those in which officers like Tiny Barber and Johnny Frost commanded esteem and affection.

In addition to my chaplaincy in the shipyard, I was appointed chaplain to the Western Infirmary. This of course was voluntary before the National Health Service came into existence. When this happened, salaried full-time chaplains were appointed.

This I genuinely enjoyed. In time, I got to know the entire staff, the superintendent, the matron, the doctors, the sisters, the trainee nurses and of course the porters, who were indispensable to the smooth running of a large hospital.

The Western Infirmary was a teaching hospital, physically adjacent and closely linked to Glasgow University. That meant that a number of medical professors and lecturers served on the staff. So, as well as being in touch with Industry in a shipyard, I was also in touch with the academic world.

My chaplaincy to the Western Infirmary was rewarding. Some of the doctors, sisters, nurses and members of the administration staff joined Old Partick Church just on the other side of the street. This very substantially strengthened the congregation. The week before my departure, the hospital laid on a mammoth party. The size of the cheque they gave me was truly staggering.

If by chance I have given the impression that my two chaplaincies absorbed too much of my time and energy, this is far from true. Old Partick Church was my first priority. My job was to conduct marriages, baptisms, funerals, not just within the congregation, but also within the much wider bounds of the parish, which territorially was much bigger than the congregation. On top of this, I undertook the systematic visitation of the sick in hospitals and nursing homes all over the city. With no car, this took time.

But what really drained my nervous and psychic energy was preaching. The preparation and delivery of two sermons and at least four prayers every Sunday is truly a Herculean task. It is difficult for the laity to grasp imaginatively how utterly impossible this is. I am absolutely certain that the drill of preaching two sermons a Sunday, until very recently the norm in Scotland, was not ordained of God.

The late Dr. Archie Craig, one of the best Scottish preachers of this century, describes an encounter with Principal Martin of New College. They met in Princes Street and shook hands. Archie had only been six months in his first parish. "How goes it, Craig?" asked his former Professor. Archie hesitated and answered, "Well, Sir, I am finding preaching difficult." Principal Martin, whose eyebrows were even more menacing than those of Denis Healey, barked, "Craig, preaching is not difficult, it's impossible." And so it is.

Thomas Chalmers, one of the very greatest 19th Century preachers in Scotland, once confessed that he could only preach a good sermon every six weeks. I suspect Chalmers was boasting. The high level of expectancy we find in every pew, bears no relation to reality. The anticipation of one or two superlatively good sermons every Sunday is grotesquely absurd — an impossible ideal.

I worked hard at my sermons and prayers. Preaching is important. So is the disciplined conduct of public worship. Ministers and lay people, who believe the Holy Spirit is guiding them when they indulge in non-written extemporaneous prayers, are deceiving themselves. The Holy Spirit does not bestow its benediction on laziness and verbose sloppiness. Anyhow, this attitude is so palpably un-Biblical. The Bible contains written prayers. Psalm 51 — prayer of confession — a classic. Psalm 103 - prayer of thanksgiving — another classic.

As I had little money, I could not afford to buy many books. Consequently, I spent most of my mornings in the Mitchell Library, one of the best in Europe. There I had access to a very wide variety of books, religious and secular. Help when needed was always available. The atmosphere was congenial and conducive to work.

The month of January 1947, when I was inducted to the congregation of Old Partick, was one of the coldest of the century. I tried hard to convince myself that the meagre attendances were due more to the severity of the weather than to the fact that my saintly predecessor was not exactly a crowd puller.

This continued with only a slight improvement till the end of March. Then, like the miracle of Spring, which has a habit of taking us by surprise, things began to happen. The morning service started to improve modestly. But the growth in the evening attendance was dramatic. By the end of 1947, downstairs was full. By the end of February 1948, we had to open the gallery. By the Spring of 1949, it was difficult to sit the congregation, especially in the evening. The night I preached my farewell sermon, worshippers were standing in the aisle from the door right down to the pulpit steps.

Then when I was on the crest of the wave, out of the blue, I got a phone call from Dr. Walton, the Interim-Moderator of St George's West Church in Edinburgh. To say I was surprised is a mis-use of the English language. Naturally I knew of its existence, of its history and of its reputation not only in Scotland but in the whole of the English speaking world. But surely such an important church could not be interested in me!

Immediately I rang up my brother Murdo in his manse in Pollokshields. I told him about the mysterious phone call. My shrewd and practical older brother did not beat about the bush. He said, "Murdo Ewen, St. George's West is known for its apostolic succession of popular preachers. They have done their homework. They have ascertained that you filled the Portree congregation and Old Partick. They want you to be their next minister." Then he went on to say, "Murdo Ewen, you better start thinking hard and maybe a prayer or two would not be amiss."

Why did I leave Partick? Why was my ministry there so short? Scarcely three years. Why was it that, when I was basking in success, I turned my back on a congregation that had so enthusiastically supported me?

I know that human motivation is a puzzling and complex equation. So complex that it defies the most honest attempts at analysis. I am not for one moment claiming that my acceptance of the surprising call from St. George's West was totally altruistic. It was not quite so straighforward.

To be sure I was flattered and elated that one of the most famous pulpits in the world should even consider me. I think I am honest in claiming the offer of the biggest ministerial salary in Scotland did not

influence me at all. I have many many faults, but "Yuppie" materialism is not one of them. To her friends, my wife, Betty, frequently says,
"Murdo Ewen is a moron where money is concerned."

One important component in a very difficult decision was Betty's
illness. In the winter of 1948 she suffered a nervous breakdown. By
the time I received the call from Edinburgh, she was well on the way
to recovery. I consulted Dr. Anderson, a good friend who looked after
us. He argued that a change to a new environment would speed up
recovery. Another close medical friend, Dr. Angus MacNiven, was
even more adamant. I spent a few sleepless nights wrestling with the
problem. At the end of it all, not free from misgivings, I agreed to
preach as sole nominee.

With hindsight, it is not surprising that Betty had a breakdown.
She was used to affluence and came to a country ravaged by a long
and cruel war. The meagreness of the rations shocked her. Our manse
was enormous in size. It had no central heating and we had to make
do with one bag of coal a week. In short, she had to adjust to a way
of life she had not been accustomed to.

An additional burden was the presidency of the Woman's Guild
within the congregation. Along with sundry other duties, this
involved chairing meetings and making speeches. She also kept open
house on Sunday evenings. The pressures proved too much for her
and to this day I have twinges of guilt that I was not more understanding.

It did not take us long to make friends, who proved very supportive, especially during Betty's illness. Among these, were the Rev.
John and Bunty Brown, George and Anne Kennedy, Jack and Jean
Harrison. Jack and I had become friends in Stalag Luft III and it was
marvellous to meet up with him again. Jean and Betty hit it off as
they were both musical.

My ministry in Old Partick was an exciting one, but it had its
lighter moments. I vividly recall my first visit to Mrs M., who enjoyed
the reputation of being one of the most formidable women in
Glasgow. Her son, a very distinguished Eye Surgeon, warned me that
she strongly disapproved of me. Though housebound, she had her
spies and informers. According to her son, my theology was suspect,
my politics even more so, and to make people laugh in Church was
anathema. The good doctor assured me that, if I had any chance of

survival, on my first visit a body-guard was necessary.

In fear and trembling one cold November afternoon, I arrived at an impressive mansion in the west end. I rang Mrs M.'s bell. The door opened and a uniformed maid led me into a spacious drawing-room whose walls were cluttered with what looked like expensive paintings.

Mrs M. was lying on a sofa, a pillow under her head and a shawl round her shoulders. As we shook hands, she looked at me severely and said, "You are the new minister." "Yes Mrs M.," I answered with appropriate meekness. "I understand you were wounded — is that so?" "Yes Mrs M., I was." "It must have been in a battle," she opined. "Yes it was in a battle," I conceded. "Was it the battle of the Somme?" she asked. "No," I replied, "It was the Siege of Mafeking." Her old, frail body shook with laughter.

It was at this point I knew she was pulling my leg. I decided to go on the offensive. "Mrs M.," I said, "You are a wicked woman. Ever since I came through that door you have been taking the mickey out of me and I have to give you absolution." She laughed even more uproariously and ordered me to sit in a chair directly opposite her. I stayed for two hours and thoroughly enjoyed myself. That night, she rang up her son and told him she approved of me.

Beyond anything I could dream of, things went well. We started a youth club which catered for the rougher elements in the parish. It was run by two university students, Archie MacVicar and Calum MacLeod. Between them they did a brilliant job and across the years we have remained good friends. The Youth Fellowship was outstanding not just in terms of numbers, but even more so in terms of ability. It produced Headmasters, Headmistresses, Directors of Education, Ministers of Religion, Doctors and Psychiatrists who in various countries are now contemplating retirement.

I owe an enormous debt to Old Partick Church. I happened to have become its minister at the right time and at the right age. The response I got during a short ministry exceeded my wildest expectations. It was here I became known on a national level. If I had not been there and had not been successful, the chances are St George's West would never have heard of me. And it was my ministry in that famous Church which opened the way to Trinity College and Glasgow University.

CHAPTER 14

PREMIER PULPIT

WHEN it became known that I was about to become the new minister of St. George's West, the national newspapers had headlines like this: "Crofter's Son Called To Scotland's Premier Pulpit." This may have been a piece of journalistic exaggeration, but beyond any doubt whatsoever I was called to a famous pulpit.

St. George's West came into being as a result of the Disruption, a significant happening in the religious and secular history of Scotland. This event with its far-reaching repercussions took place on the 18th May, 1843. Dr. Robert Candlish, accompanied by a substantial proportion of his congregation, walked out of St. George's Church in Charlotte Square, Edinburgh. Thus, what came to be known as Free St. George's was born.

The new congregation was soon to include among its members some of the leading lawyers, doctors, academics and businessmen of Edinburgh. It grew dramatically and its impact was felt throughout the whole of Scotland.

In 1900, when the Free and United Presbyterian Churches came together, Free St. George's changed its name. It became St. George's United Free Church. Later in 1929, after the Union of the United Free Church with the Established Church, it changed its name once again. From then on, it was called St. George's West.

I would submit that changing the name of a congregation so often within a few generations was a mistake psychologically. It thoroughly confused its numerous devotees not only in Scotland, but also throughout the whole of the English-speaking world. Is there any reason why the original name, "Free St. George's," should not have continued into the national reunited Church?

The present building in Shandwick Place at the West End of the incomparable Princes Street was opened in 1869. It is not what the visitor would call a beautiful church. One looks in vain for an awe-inspiring nave, a gorgeous chancel, or dim-lit vaults of ancient days. On the whole it is a plain functional building. According to experts, St. George's West has only two features of architectural distinction. It has a huge vestibule, perhaps the most spacious in Scotland. And there is an impressive Campanille with a clock bearing a striking resemblance to that of St. Mark's in Venice.

Time has proved how wise the congregation was in its choice of a place of worship. Transport-wise, St. George's West is the most accessible in the City of Edinburgh. It could be argued that, to a certain extent, that was one component in its popularity.

Beyond any question, it was Dr. Robert Candlish who made Free St. George's one of the best known congregations in the English-speaking world. A warmhearted man with strong convictions, he was regarded as an outstanding preacher. He combined evangelical zeal with sound scholarship. In mid-life, he was appointed Professor of Theology at New College and later its Principal.

It was to him that the doughty warrior, Thomas Chalmers, passed the torch. Candlish was not good looking. Short of stature, his arms were as long as Rob Roy's and his hair was shaggy and unkempt. His appearance may have been unprepossessing, but he could sway the most sophisticated audience to moods of compassion, alternating with those of moral indignation.

Dr. Candlish died in 1873, having put Free St. George's on the map. Only the Victorians could stage a death-bed scene like his. Knowing the end was near, he summoned Alexander Whyte, his ministerial colleague, and Professor Robert Rainy. He ordered them to kneel on either side of his bed. Placing his right hand on Whyte's head and his left on Rainy's, he pronounced in solemn tones: "To you, Whyte, I leave my church and to you, Rainy, I leave my college." Splendid stuff! Why were the Victorians so embarrassed about sex and so uninhibited about death?

In 1861, Oswald Dykes, a big man with a fine presence and a massive intellect, was called to be Candlish's colleague. After four years, during which he had made his mark as a preacher, his health broke and he felt he had to resign. He went to Australia where he fully recovered. Years later, he returned to become Principal of Westminster College, Cambridge.

It was not till 1870 that a suitable colleague was found for the redoubtable Dr. Candlish. Alexander Whyte was persuaded to leave a successful ministry in Glasgow to begin his incredibly illustrious ministry in Edinburgh. I have no desire to subtract from the stature of his predecessors or successors when I say he was the greatest minister that occupied that famous pulpit. Significantly, to this day, the pulpit in St. George's West is known as Alexander Whyte's pulpit.

He was an illegitimate child born in poverty in Kirriemuir. His mother, a peasant woman, worked hard to pay for his elementary education before the compulsory Education Act of 1872. For some time, he was apprenticed to a cobbler. There is a story told about him when he was at the very height of his eminence in Edinburgh. A society lady disdainfully remarked, "Dr. Whyte, I understand you were once a shoemaker." He answered, "No madam, you are misinformed. I was once a cobbler's apprentice."

By his mid-forties, the cobbler's apprentice was regarded as one of the best preachers in the English-speaking world. He was almost certainly the best-read minister of his time. Let's not beat about the bush, Whyte was more than an outstandingly successful minister, he was a man of genius. More than once I have heard the distinguished theologian, Professor John Baillie, say, "Whyte of Free St. George's was the most impressive man I have ever met."

Consider for a moment Whyte's track record. From 1870 to 1916 he reigned in his famous pulpit at the heart of Scotland's capital. His ministry spanned the Victorian and Edwardian eras and overstepped the First World War. According to his biographers and to those who knew him well, at the end of forty-six years the congregation was in better heart than it was when he took over. He received many invitations to the United States. He refused them all. When at length he was made a freeman of the City of Edinburgh, a journalist asked him "How do you account for your remarkable success?" Whyte answered gruffly, "I do the job I am paid for."

Alexander Whyte has been called the last of the Puritans. In his unwavering emphasis on the sinful, devious ambivalence of human nature, the description may be right. At the same time, he was not a narrow life-denying Fundamentalist. In the celebrated trial of Professor Robertson Smith, the most brilliant Oriental language scholar in Britain, Whyte showed courage and integrity. He was prepared to stand up and be counted. At the General Assembly of the Free Church, in a moving speech, he pleaded for "Christian charity and intellectual freedom."

Whyte was an omnivorous as well as a disciplined reader. His famous Bible Class on Sunday evenings proves this up to the hilt. Hundreds of university students attended and Whyte introduced them not only to the Bible, but also to the breadth and depth of English Literature. Sir George Adam Smith, the eminent Old Testament scholar, was brought up in Free St. George's. He pays this generous tribute. "Here was a man the like of whom we students had not heard or seen in a pulpit . . . His early sermons already showed how widely and how deeply he had studied the best literature of our language; and we Divinity students and young ministers felt ourselves bound over to read, read, read; but always and only of the best."

I am proud to possess Whyte's renowned inter-leaf Bible. His eldest son, Sir Frederick, presented it to me one evening when I dined with him and Lady Whyte at their lovely flat in Kensington, London. Sir Frederick in his day was a distinguished ambassador and he also wrote the constitution for India.

Over coffee, he asked me if I had heard of his father's famous Bible. "Heard of it, Sir Frederick," I answered, "I was metaphorically bludgeoned with it in my homiletic classes when I was a student in St. Andrews University." Without a word, Sir Frederick left the dining-room and came back holding a well-used, battered-looking Bible. Handing it over to me, he said, "It's yours." I protested, but to no avail. Whyte's unique inter-leaf Bible is one of my most treasured possessions. I have it specially insured.

A cursory glance at this inter-leaf Bible demonstrates the amazing range of Whyte's reading. On the blank page opposite the Gospel of St. John, Chapter 3, there are over eighty references to various authors. They include Seneca, Cicero, Thomas Aquinas, Abelard, Rutherford, Ruskin, Milton, Cardinal Newman and many more. A humbling experience. The only vestige of comfort I got from this impressive display of erudition was this. My famous predecessor's handwriting was even worse than my own.

Known as the last of the Puritans, there were those who wondered whether Alexander Whyte had a sense of humour. The answer I would argue is an unambiguous yes. Douglas Miller, a surgeon in St. George's West during my ministry told me what happened one Sunday morning. At the age of nine, he was sitting with his parents in a packed pew. He watched the Beadle (Church Officer) handing Dr. Whyte a piece of paper. There were very few telephones in those days. The great preacher stopped in full flow, read what was on it, then intoned, "Will Dr. Alexander Frazer proceed to No. 18 Northumberland Street, where one of his patients is seriously ill?" At this point, a smallish man stood up. Looking distinctly uncomfortable, stooping to make himself as inconspicuous as possible, he made his way to the nearest door. When he shut it hehind him as softly as possible, Dr. Whyte added in a mournful voice, "And may God have mercy on the patient."

The other story was told to me by an old doctor who remembered Whyte vividly. Free St. George's was very mission orientated. Long before I arrived on the scene, they had built at least five other churches in the City of Edinburgh. They also provided funds to build churches in the remotest Highlands and Islands.

One Gaelic-speaking minister came down from the Outer Hebrides to raise funds for another Free Church congregation. The drill was always the same. He made straight for Whyte's manse in Charlotte Square. He was handed a jotter. On the top of the first page was written: "Dr. Alexander Whyte, £5." Then he was sent round the most affluent members of the congregation, judges, Writers to the Signet, surgeons, doctors, professors, teachers and businessmen. He was instructed to present himself at the manse every night to report progress. This the Hebridean minister in question duly did. The second night he reported and Whyte asked, "How did you get on?" "Very well," the supplicant answered. "I have been promised a lot of money, but I am afraid I fell foul of a very important person." "Who was that?" asked Whyte. "A prominent surgeon by the name of Sir Robert Granger Stewart," answered the minister. "He was rude to me. I lost my temper and I said, 'Who do you think you are? You're only a hell deserving sinner like the rest of us.' " Alexander Whyte leapt from his chair, pulled out his pocket book and said, "Here's another five pound note. I wanted to tell Sir Robert exactly that for the last twenty years."

In the early nineties, the need for a colleague became urgent. Two eminent scholars, Principal Martin of New College and Professor George Adam Smith, were unsuccessfully approached. In the end, they called Hugh Black, the young flamboyant minister of Sherwood Church in Paisley. His style was very different from Whyte's. It was their unique contrasting combination of qualities that gave rise to the remark: "Whyte blackballed the saints in the morning and Black whitewashed the sinners in the evening."

Hugh Black was the popular preacher par excellence. Never within memory had Edinburgh seen a young minister achieve success so swift and so overwhelming. The crowds that flocked to hear him at seven o'clock in the evening were colossal. How exciting these Sunday evenings were! Pews packed, people standing against the walls, chairs in the aisles, pulpit steps crowded. At the end of ten brilliant years, he was appointed Professor of Preaching at the world-famous Union Theological Seminary, New York. He wrote at least two volumes of published sermons.

In 1907, Dr. John Kelman was called as colleague and successor to Dr. Whyte. Again very different from Whyte, he exercised a powerful ministry, especially among university students. In 1919 he followed Hugh Black across the Atlantic and became a minister of the very prestigious Fifth Avenue Church, New York. There he did not command the wide appeal he enjoyed in Edinburgh. Liberally-minded in everything including his theology, he fell foul of right wing, fire-eating Fundamentalists. At the time, they wielded considerable influence and relentlessly they hounded him. Eventually, he returned to Britain, a broken disillusioned man. After a short ministry in London, he retired to Edinburgh, where he died in 1929.

A good all-round scholar, John Kelman's special interest was English Literature. That probably explains why so many students were drawn to him. With all his manifold interests, as preacher, author, public figure, it would not have been surprising if he had gone easy on the pastoral ministry. This is denied by what he once said to a friend, "I can't preach under a thousand visits a year." While I disagree with him here, I can't help admiring his disciplined humanity. When I was a student and a young minister, I met many lawyers, doctors and teachers who took pride in calling themselves "Kelmanites."

In 1921 James Black, the brother of Professor Hugh Black, was called to be the sole minister. Handsome in appearance, dramatic in manner and speech, he was, I would think, the last of the histrionic preachers. From the beginning, he attracted huge congregations, especially in the evening. Along with his superb popular gifts, James Black was a good scholar. A graduate of Glasgow University, with a number of medals to his credit, he spent one or two years in Germany doing research work.

In the course of his ministry, he wrote three volumes of sermons. His Warrack Lectures were published under the excellent title, *The Mystery of Preaching*. According to many discerning critics, this is the best in the whole series. I am inclined to agree.

Then came the Second World War, wantonly disrupting so many of our hallowed traditions. During five years of "black-out," petrol rationing, transport difficulties and the departure of so many young men and women into the armed forces, the Evening Service suffererd grievously. If James Black had retired before September 1939, his would have been one of the most brilliant ministries in living memory in Scotland. Unwisely, he held on to near the end of 1947. This was very sad. Boyish in looks and spirit, popular with the young, he was known as the Peter Pan of the Scottish Pulpit.

This constellation of brilliant preachers must on no account blind us to the calibre of the laity, office-bearers and ordinary members. Without lay leadership, the history of the congregation would have been very different. The roll-call is very impressive. Prominent were judges of the Court of Sessions, university professors, surgeons, physicians, Writers to the Signet, solicitors, advocates, educationists, town councillors, businessmen and women. It is not possible to exaggerate how much these lay men and women contributed to the status of the congregation.

1897 was an important year in the history of the congregation. It was then, under the influence of Hugh Black, that the organ was installed. The Kirk Session must have been guided by the Holy Spirit. In their wisdom, they appointed Dr. Alfred Hollins, one of the finest organists in Britain. Blind from birth, he became universally recognised not only as a superb player, but also as a good organ-builder. Over the decades, Dr. Hollins became nearly as famous as the great Alexander Whyte himself. Certainly his popular recitals were as much part of the tradition of the congregation as were Whyte's celebrated Bible Classes. Indeed it was said that there were those who came to St. George's, not to hear Alexander Whyte and Hugh Black preach, but to enjoy Hollins at the organ.

Over the generations, the congregation was noted for its colourful and eccentric characters. Perhaps the most colourful was Joseph Bell,

Professor of Anatomy in Edinburgh University and an elder in Free St George's. Apparently he had uncanny powers of observation. A born exhibitionist, in front of his students in the Royal Infirmary, he would examine the hands of patients and tell them what trade or profession they belonged to. He would also examine the mud on the students' boots and deduce which part of the City they stayed in. Conon Doyle, as a medical student, studied under him and was mightily impressed. It was Professor Joseph Bell who inspired him to create the most popular of all detectives, Sherlock Holmes.

When I arrived in Edinburgh in 1949, Joseph Bell's niece, Lulu Bell, was still alive. She had a large photograph of her famous uncle on top of a grand piano in her drawing-room. The ritual never varied and fortunately for me I was meticulously briefed how to behave on my first visit. She led me across the drawing-room to the grand piano, pointed to the photograph and asked, "Do you know who that is?" Drawing a deep breath I answered, "None other than Sherlock Holmes himself." After that I could do no wrong.

In my time, the most lovable and outspoken eccentric was Sheriff Johnny Jamieson. He had a marvellous turn of phrase. One Communion Sunday, he was on duty at three services, morning, afternoon and evening. I met him on the way home. "You look tired, Sheriff," I said. "Yes," he retorted, "I am suffering from a debauchery of the means of grace." He hated boring sermons, so he always took a book with him to church. If the sermon was really dull, he would open the book and begin to read it in full view of the congregation. Then, forgetting himself, he would turn to the person sitting next to him and in a loud voice exclaim, "I'll lend you this book. It makes fascinating reading." The preacher did not know where to look.

The Sheriff was gloriously unique. A good linguist, he always read his New Testament in Greek. In his own odd way, I suppose he could be called an amateur New Testament scholar. He wrote a book on the Beatitudes under the title, *The Kingdom of Heaven*. What this book lacked in theological profundity, it more than made up for in readability and originality.

In his younger days, the Sheriff spent a few years in the House of Commons as an independent member. With his uninhibited and outrageous sense of humour, he must have enjoyed his sojourn to Westminster to the full. The funniest talk I ever heard was his "A

Member's Day in the House." Long before the end, the audience was crying with laughter. The first time I heard it my sides were sore. As one would expect, he was in great demand as an after-dinner speaker in the City and beyond.

Round about the mid-fifties, some of the leading citizens of Edinburgh put their heads together to plan the restoration of the crumbling Candlemaker's Hall. Instead of making a public appeal, they decided to stage a series of prestigious expensive dinners, addressed by a succession of the most entertaining speakers in Scotland. Unanimously they agreed Sheriff Jamieson should be the first.

They sent Lord Thomson, one of the judges of the Court of Session, to ask the Sheriff to give his very amusing talk, "A Member's Day in the House." He explained their plan to restore the ancient historic Hall, then added, "Johnny they want you to be the first speaker," and the Sheriff answered, "I am delighted to come. Tell your committee I'll address them on my recent book, *The Kingdom of Heaven*. Lord Thomson's face fell, but he was too nice a man to argue.

He reported to the committee, "The Sheriff is pleased to come, but before I got round to suggesting 'A Member's Day in the House,' he volunteered to give a talk on his recent book, *The Kingdom of Heaven*." Their collective face fell. After a confused discussion, they sent Lord Thomson back to get the Sheriff to change his mind. A tactful man, he argued, "Johnny, I am sure your talk on *The Kingdom of Heaven* is fascinating, but remember this is a festive occasion and we all feel that your brilliant talk on 'A Member's Day in the House' would be much more appropriate." The Sheriff glared at him and said, "Thomson, you go back and tell your committee that if they don't want my *Kingdom of Heaven* they can go to hell." And *The Kingdom of Heaven* they got.

A fascinating eccentric character. I loved the Sheriff very much. I buried him in the graveyard of Anwoth Church in Galloway, a few feet away from the mystic, Samuel Rutherford.

CHAPTER 15

TURBULENCE
AND TRANQUILITY

MY first two years in St. George's West could be described as turbulent. I introduced a number of changes which the conservative elements in the congregation resented and stoutly resisted. One of the Judges in the Kirk session was my toughest opponent. A powerful orator when defending the status quo, he could become vituperative.

To begin with, I altered the format of the communion service. Lord Blades was furious and moved that the Kirk session overrule me. I ruled him out of order, pointing out that I was in sole charge of the conduct of Public Worship and the celebration of communion.

Against the advice of my friend, Sir Randal Philip, who was session clerk and Procurator of the Church of Scotland, I urged the Kirk Session to discontinue the queue which came into existence during Hugh Black's ministry. In addition, I suggested that we scrap seat rents and replace them by the free will envelope and bonds of annuity systems. Though strenuously opposed at the beginning, in the end it won support and was adopted. The result was dramatic. Within a couple of years, in terms of Christian liberality, we were ahead of any church in Scotland.

After these battles and other sundry skirmishes, peace reigned and exciting things began to happen. As in Portree, Isle of Skye and Partick Glasgow, the church continued to fill up and Lord Blades and I developed a curious liking for one another. He became a good friend and was unfailingly nice to Betty and myself.

It was around this time that, with the enthusiastic support of the Kirk Session, we launched a number of experiments. When in 1947 my call to St. George's West was written up by *The Scotsman* and *The Glasgow Herald*, I received a very rude letter from George MacLeod (Lord George). It read. "Dear Murdo Ewen, I am deeply disappointed. You had a marvellous Church in Glasgow. You were a part-time chaplain in a shipyard within your parish and chaplain to a hospital, also within your parish. You have turned your back on it all and accepted a call from St. George's West which is a glorified preaching centre with no social conscience — no more than a middle class religious drawing room". I did not reply. I never do to rude letters of which I have received more than most. But George was not only a genuinely great man, he could also be disarmingly gracious. When years later he learned of our socially orientated experiments in St. George's West, he sent me one of the sweetest letters I have ever had. He apologised for his rudeness and wished me God's abundant blessing in my ministry.

The first venture was a weekly lunch for old age pensioners in straitened circumstances, living within the parish. Agnes Watt, one of our members, providentially was Alister Dunnet's (Editor of *The Scotsman*) secretary. She enthused about this project and Alister wrote a leader about it. That very day, the Lord Provost invited me to lunch with some of his colleagues at the City Chambers. He questioned me closely about our aim. At the end, he promised that the Corporation would subsidise us handsomely. And it did. We were able to give the pensioners a three course lunch at the cost of one shilling. We began with a modest coterie of about twelve. When I left St. George's West in December 1963, we catered for over seventy.

The next experiment could be described as a cultural one. I like T. S. Eliot's definition of culture. He was cynically opposed to equating culture with high brow philosophy, high brow music, high brow literature. This is how he defines it. "Culture must include all the characteristic activities and interests of a people. Derby Day, Henley Regatta, Cowes, the 12th of August, a Cup Final, the Dog Races, the dart board in the pub, Wensleydale cheese, boiled cabbages cut in sections, beetroot in vinegar, 19th Century Gothic Churches and the music of Elgar. In short, culture is co-extensive with the whole of life."

Every Wednesday, we had prominent speakers who projected culture in the T. S. Eliot comprehensive sense. Among them, Lord Strathclyde on the theme "A Christian in Politics", Sir Samuel Curran, the atomic scientist; Dr Winifred Rushforth the internationally renowned psycho-therapist, members of Parliament — Tory, Labour, Liberal; novelists; poets; newspaper editors; prison governors; football managers and the occasional theologian. This venture was a tremendous success.

Another experiment followed in quick succession. It's aim was the theological education of the congregation. I am implacably opposed to the sanctified assumption that theology is the preserve of ministers and academics. If in a predominantly secular world we are to take Christian mission seriously, lay men and lay women must theologically become more articulate.

Perhaps the most significant experiment was the one called Cephas. The idea behind it (aided and abetted by the Presbytery) was to have a meeting place in the west end of Edinburgh for young people who were chronic non Church goers, some of whom were in trouble with the police. It should be run by committed Christians on Sunday nights and week nights. And it should be ecumenical in its outreach.

The Kirk Session after a long discussion offered the crypt of the Church (formerly a furniture store), thus sacrificing a considerable annual income. It was estimated that the alterations to the basement including an emergency exit would cost a minimum of £2,000. We set up a ways and means committee whose remit was proposed methods of raising the money. After the meeting, a young elder, a lawyer, invited me out to coffee and to my utter amazement offered me the £2,000, on one condition, that it remained anonymous.

The Cephas experiment was an instant success. To be sure there were problems, moments of crisis and panic. The night the club opened, it was picketed by Bible brandishing Christians, carrying placards with messages in various colours, "No dancing, No billiards, No loud jazz music". I recall being called out late on a Saturday night to quell a fight. It had broken out between members of the club and a gang which had invaded the premises bent on vandalism.

What the critics did not understand was that Cephas was an experiment in Evangelism. There were those of us who felt very strongly that only in a non judgmental context like Cephas, can the contemporary de-churched teenager encounter an understandable Christian witness.

In addition to these experiments, the congregation committed itself to building a church in a new housing area in the east end of the city. This meant raising a sum of £30,000. The first collection was taken on May 13th 1956. In the last collection on November 13th

1960, we passed the target by several hundred pounds. We raised the money in less than half the time allotted to us. We also provided a set of assessor elders to help the new congregation get on its feet.

The Kirk Session of over a hundred elders was by any comparison distinguished. At least six of them became Judges of the Court of Session, three sheriffs as far as I remember. I forget how many advocates, Writers to the Signet and solicitors. There was also a generous sprinkling of doctors, academics, teachers and lecturers. There was one millionaire, who was generous to the congregation and even more generous to the university. On the whole, I enjoyed a good relationship with them. Intelligent, liberal, tolerant, they were amazingly supportive.   ·

The paid staff was wonderful. It included Janet Park, the Church secretary, Mary Millar, my own personal secretary and Jim Finlay, the Church Officer. Jim was a larger than life character. Resplendant in an evening suit and bow tie, he was an imposing figure. He and I commenced our ministries on the same Sunday in June 1949. Janet, Mary and Jim were great colleagues. With untiring good nature, they tolerated my eccentricities, frequent lapses of memory and above all my execrable handwriting. We were a happy team.

My two sons were born in Edinburgh. In personality they are quite different. Alasdair is an exuberant extrovert whose highly developed sense of humour was evident at an early age. A good musician, he is married and lives in Norway. His wife, Inger-Lise, is a teacher who speaks perfect English. They have a lovely daughter, Mairi, who has inherited her parents' musical capacity. I am afraid I spoil her. Cheryl, Inger-Lise's daughter by a previous marriage is studying at Stirling University. She is most attractive.

Alan could not be described as an extrovert. Somewhat shy and sensitive, he also has a good sense of humour. A late developer, he did well at college and got a good degree and a couple of diplomas. A social worker, he has specialised in mental health. A keen mountaineer, he has become a competent rock climber. Unmarried, he lives with Betty and myself in our flat in Hyndland, Glasgow.

In St. George's West I had a remarkable apostolic succession of assistants. The first, while still a student, was Ian Pitt-Watson. Even then, he combined a first class intellect with an exceptional preaching gift. At the moment, he is Professor of Homiletics at Fulton

Seminary, California. The next was David Smith. A good preacher, a diligent pastor, an able administrator, he enjoyed a succession of impressive ministries and in time was appointed Moderator of the General Assembly of the Church of Scotland. Following him was John Robertson from the Isle of Skye and a Gaelic speaker. In the Carl Jung sense, he was the prototype extrovert and was immensely popular with the congregation. With his engaging grin and infectious laugh, he could charm anybody.

Then, lo and behold, the congregation began to produce its own assistants (permissible at that time). The first was George Elliot with his powerful intellect, his self mocking humour, his superb pulpit and pastoral ability. He was a difficult act to follow. Succeeding him was David Kelman Robertson, who in his one ministry of thirty two years has shown that the preaching and pastoral ministries are inseparable and indivisible. At Polbeth, not too far from Edinburgh, David, along with his wife Anne, is exercising one of the most significant ministries in Scotland. Next in the production line was Bill Shaw. A lawyer and partner in a prestigious Edinburgh firm, he decided to study for the ministry. A superb squash player, he played so often for Scotland that he got into *The Book of Guinness Records*. He has recently retired as Professor of Divinity at St Andrews University. Even when he was a student, I made not the slightest effort to teach him anything about preaching and the conduct of Public Worship. There was no need. The last assistant the congregation produced in my time, was the inimitable Terence McCaughey. A lecturer in Celtic in Edinburgh University, he joined St. George's West and in due time decided to become a minister. A brilliant expository preacher, and in the art of public prayer, he could rival the great George MacLeod. The congregation loved him. When he left us to take up an appointment in Trinity College, Dublin, my son Alan, then a wee boy, was devastated.

There were others who sat under me and decided to become ministers. Dr Andrew Ross, a past Principal of New College, was one of the most colourful. Dr. Gillespie, external examiner in tropical medicine to the Universities of Oxford and Cambridge, also joined the ranks. So did David Lyal, now a lecturer in Practical Theology in Edinburgh and not least of a number who became excellent parish ministers: George Munro, Douglas Glover and James Blythe.

If I include those who joined St George's West while still pursuing their theological studies, I would have to name Calum Carmichael, Professor of Languages at the renowned Cornell University in America, James Weatherhead, the shrewd, laid back, humorous Principal Clerk to the General Assembly and Professor Alex Cheyne, who has just recently retired from the Chair of Ecclesiastical History at Edinburgh. It is the unanimous verdict of all his colleagues that Alex was the best lecturer in the four Scottish theological colleges. He is also an outstanding preacher.

The congregation was a gathered one, scattered all over the city of Edinburgh and beyond. I visited conscientiously district by district on at least two evenings a week. I never once had a cool reception. Edinburgh people are sometimes accused of being less than friendly. This has not been my experience. I have always found them warm hearted, hospitable and loyal.

We had an open house every Sunday night after the evening service. Students from all over the world met in the manse and got to know each other over tea, coffee, sandwiches and ice-cream. Ours was a students' congregation. I cannot claim the credit for this. Long before I was born, under the great Alexander Whyte it was a students' church, but I can claim a modicum of credit for wooing them back after the war. One of our elders, a lecturer in sociology at the university, carried out a poll. He concluded that approximately four hundred students worshipped in St. George's West every Sunday.

At these Sunday evening gatherings, Betty was the perfect hostess. A natural extrovert, being American, she had an open friendly approach to people, a quality so characteristic of her people and which the more restrained British find attractive.

This is illustrated by an incident which took place early in my Edinburgh ministry. While we were away for a short holiday, our house was burgled and all the medals I had won, at school, univeristy and college, were stolen. We reported this to the police. They promised to do their best to retrieve them.

Shortly after the burglary, I had to leave for Australia as the Turnbull Trust preacher, without any trace of the medals. A fortnight after my departure, two policemen came to the door and informed Betty that my medals had been found in a pawnbroker's shop. "Oh good," she said, "I'll go and get them this very minute". "But Mrs

Macdonald" interrupted the police, "We have an understanding with pawnbrokers that if they co-operate in tracking down criminals, they won't be out of pocket. You'll have to pay for them". And to the Sheriff Court Betty went.

After a number of cases were dealt with, the magistrate in charge came to the medals. Holding one up and dangling it before the court, he asked, "How do we know that this medal belongs to the minister of St. George's West?" Betty at the back of the Court shot up like a Russian sputnik and in her American accent shouted "Have you ever heard of a cat burglar winning a medal in Systematic Theology?" So loud and sustained was the laughter that the magistrate had to bang his gavel and insist on silence in the Court. There were two reporters present who scribbled like fury. Next day it was in the papers and Betty found herself a celebrity.

Leaving St. Georges West to become Professor of Practical Theology, Trinity College, Glasgow University, was a painful wrench. Betty was in tears. So was her very close friend Sheena Monteath. So was Bertie Martin, the Session Clerk, a real saint. So was Willie Ballantine, tough journalist and brilliant editor of the Church magazine. There were others who cried. Alasdair and Alan loved our house with its lovely long back garden. They hated leaving it.

Being the minister of this famous congregation for nearly fifteen years was an exhilarating experience. Intelligent, generous, their patience was really incredible. I intuitively sensed when it was wearing thin and would say "My great great grandfather died at the age of a hundred and ten. My grandfather was over ninety when he died, my father is fast approaching ninety and going very strong. If there are any wishful thinkers in this congregation, let them join St. Giles or St. Cuthberts". They laughed and forgave me for another six months. They were good to us and despite my controversial views, they were genuinely fond of me. This was a miracle of grace on their part. On the eve of our departure to Glasgow, they gave us a substantial sum of money towards buying our own home. I am proud that I was called to be the minister of the church which the world over was known as "Free St. George's".

CHAPTER 16

MY LOVE AFFAIR WITH THE MOUNTAINS

IT is very likely I would not have taken up climbing had I not gone to the Isle of Skye, as minister of Portree in the month of June 1939. Skye is the Mecca of British climbing and the Cuillin mountain range was literally within my parish. How singularly fortunate to become minister of a church within twenty miles of one of the most famous climbing ridges in the whole of Europe. Sgurr nan Gillean, one of the most attractive peaks of The Cuillin, was only a mere ten miles away. B. H. Humble, the experienced mountaineer and superb photographer, writes of The Cuillin, "They are the most notable mountains in Britain and have no equal in all the world."

It all began more or less accidentally. Billy Wood, the excise officer for the whole of Skye, lived in Portree. An excellent rock climber, his was an ideal build. Short of stature, compactly put together, broad shouldered, he had long arms and very strong fingers. His climbing companion, the local chemist, had gone away on holiday and Billy was loath to climb in the Cuillin on his own. He thought I was fairly fit, so he asked me to accompany him on a climb. In my innocence I agreed.

Billy drove a small red Ford car. I noticed there was a rope sprawling untidily in the back seat. This puzzled me a bit. Why the rope? Was it there to pull the car out of a ditch if he went over the edges of the narrow roads of Skye? When we arrived at Glen Brittle, my puzzlement increased. Billy removed the rope and began coiling it round his waist. Then, signalling me to follow, he led me to the foot of a towering pinnacle, its head shrouded in a fleecy kind of mist. Uncoiling the rope, he tied one end of it round my waist, the other end round his own. Pointing upward, he said, "I am going to climb thirty or forty feet. You stay put where you are. When I reach a suitable spot, I'll tie myself to a jutting piece of rock and I'll beckon you to come." At which point he added, "Murdo Ewen, in climbing parlance this is known as 'belaying'." Meekly I obeyed and when surprisingly I caught up with him, he tethered me to rock and shot off to ascend another forty feet or so. This ritual repeated itself a number of times. It was then I looked down and lost my nerve. I shouted, "Billy, I have had it, I can't go on." The born psychologist, Billy Wood, answered, "Murdo Ewen, look below you, it's much easier to go up." I did and I knew he was right. So to my stunning amazement against my better judgment, I conquered the Inaccessible Pinnacle, the only Munro in Britain it is not possible to climb without a rope.

Subsequently, in the company of Billy Wood and his friends, I climbed a few more peaks in the Cuillin ridge — Sgurr Alasdair, Sgurr Thormaid, Sgurr Thearlaich and Sgurr Mhic Choinnich. Not only did I grow in confidence, but soon I found myself strongly attracted to this somewhat dangerous hobby. Then came the War and for a time my climbing aspirations were rudely interrupted.

In July 1942, while I was undergoing the Paratroop ground training at Hardwick Hall, Derbyshire, I belonged to a platoon which specialised in rock climbing. The course was very thorough. An instructor gave us lectures and demonstrations on balance, how never to move our feet till we had secured two firm hand holds. I was detailed No. 1 on the rope and though I found the experience frightening at times I really enjoyed it.

After I came back from prison camp in 1945, I was stationed at Strathpeffer, Ross-shire, marking time for demobilization. The Colonel, Ronnie Meyer, D.S.O. (Bar), was a lovable character with a very distinguished war record behind him. Beneath the tough, belligerent exterior, he was a kindly man and we soon struck up a warm friendship.

At the conclusion of hostilities in Europe there were literally millions of soldiers and airmen in Britain - Americans, Canadians, Australians, New Zealanders — all waiting for transportation back home. The War Office was faced with the daunting problem of how to keep them happy. Why not send as many as possible to climb mountains in Scotland? This would keep them out of mischief and at the same time preserve the fitness they were in imminent danger of losing. My commanding officer, Col. Ronnie Meyer, was appointed Organiser in Chief of this scheme.

Knowing I had climbed in the Cuillin of Skye, the Colonel ordered me to be the guide and one evening after dinner in the officers' mess he solemnly inducted me to this high office. For the next five months I led hundreds and hundreds of overseas soldiers up mountains in the Grampians, Glencoe, Wester Ross, Knoydart and the Isle of Skye. I must have climbed over a hundred Munros before I went to Bangour Hospital at the end of October to have a muscle graft operation for one of my wounds.

After demobilization and a long visit to the United States, I settled in Glasgow in September 1946 and took up climbing once again. In no time I had made a number of climbing friends. I teamed up with Jack Harrison who was with me in prison camp and together we did the Crianlarich group and the Arrochar Alps. Another climber friend was Alick Mitchell, an engineer and a member of my congregation. A careful, skilful, experienced rock climber, he took me up the Crowberry ridge in Glencoe and the Tower ridge on Ben Nevis which I found more difficult than the Matterhorn.

Edinburgh, to which I moved when I became minister of St. George's West, is not as accessible to the mountains as Glasgow, but strangely enough my climbing activities actually increased. This is the explanation. Bill Shaw, a member of the congregation and an international squash player who captained Scotland for a record length of time, offered to give me lessons in squash. I agreed on one condition that he would join me in climbing. Being a good athlete, he took to it from the very beginning. When circumstances permitted, we set off after the evening service on Sunday night, put up at a Bed and Breakfast or at a modest hotel, climbed on Monday and returned that night. Thus, over a period of fourteen years or so, we piled up an impressive number of Munros.

In the summer holidays, we became more ambitious and moved further afield. In the tradition established by the great Alexander Whyte, the minister of St. George's West was given a two months' holiday. It was one tradition of St. George's West that I made not the slightest effort to change. So in the summer of 1958, Bill and I set off to climb the Matterhorn.

As the amount of money one could take abroad at that time was still limited, we decided to economise by tenting instead of putting up at a hotel. We pitched our tents on a green patch at the edge of the little town of Zermatt, lying under the shadow of the famous mountain. We took an instant liking to Zermatt. With its hotels, chalets, churches and rich profusion of flowers it has a special charm. It was bound to become a popular resort for it is surrounded by more four thousand metre mountains than any other village in Switzerland.

After we erected our tents and unpacked our spartan belongings, we walked up to one of the popular hotels at the front of which, on a long stone bench, weather-beaten guides sat smoking their pipes, waiting to be hired. At the end of some discreet enquiries, we hired a good one, who insisted we would not attempt the ascent unless the weather was perfect. We agreed.

While we were kicking our heels waiting for better weather, we were offered jobs as "extras" on a film called *The Third Man on the Mountain*. The principal actor was James Donald. We had the pleasure of meeting him later. Though the money offered us was tempting, we declined. We had come to Zermatt to climb the Matterhorn and we were determined not to be side tracked.

Once the guide gave us the signal, with our ice-axes, haversack and crampons we were on our way. We walked up to the Solway hut, built under the shoulder of the Matterhorn at a height of 13,000 feet and slept the night there. Sleep we found difficult, no doubt due to a mixture of excitement and the effect of altitude. In addition, the hut reeked of the smell of tobacco and strong beer. There were also many rollicking songs and much loud laughter. Bill and I were the only clergymen present and our behaviour, though friendly, was if anything low key. The odour of sanctity was not too obtrusive.

We began climbing while it was still dark and the guides carried lanterns. The three of us, Bill, myself and our excellent guide, were roped together from the very beginning. We proceeded at a steady unhurried pace.

To begin with the going was not all that tough, less so than some of our climbs in the Cuillin of Skye and Glencoe. As we ascended, however, we came face to face with ice and rock and it became progressively harder. We watched the sun rising over the Alps, throwing an incomparable constellation of high peaks into sharp silhouette. It was a breathtaking spectacle. By 7.30 a.m. we had reached the roof, a few yards from the Cross that stands at the summit. We had made it. We had conquered one of the most famous mountains in the world, 14,691 feet high.

Next day, we visited the climbers' cemetery in Zermatt, where the Matterhorn fatal casualties are buried. Better climbers than us lay there. It was a very humbling experience. After a short rest, we climbed the Mettelhorn and the Riffelhorn, then returned to Edinburgh.

Three years later, we returned to Zermatt and again, after hiring a guide, climbed the Zinalrothorn (13,848 feet.) First we had to traverse a glacier, shudderingly exposed. Then we had to cut steps up a perpendicular ice face and finally we had to negotiate a rather hairy rock ascent. We made it, but the descent was far from happy. I developed a quinsy throat and a raging temperature. Next day I had to go to hospital where I was given a massive injection of Penicillin. The miracle drug worked wonders.

I felt for Bill, who during this illness looked after me with great solicitude. In addition to the Zinalrothorn, we had intended to climb the Monte Rosa, the Breithorn and the Weisshorn, but it was not to be. The moment I recovered, we made tracks back to Scotland.

My next experience of climbing furth of Scotland, was in Kenya in 1973. I was lecturing at Limuru College, not far from Nairobi and during a week's break between two courses, I decided, in the company of a Dutchman and a German, both engineers, to climb Kilimanjaro. We hired sherpas, who deserted us 4,000 feet from the top because they genuinely believed demons dwelt there. On the way up, we slept in caves. Kilimanjaro presents few technical difficulties. There are no perpendicular ice walls or sinister rock faces. It is the sheer brutal height (19,360 feet) that is so enervating and so utterly exhausting.

For the first time in my life I had a headache. I got it round 17,000 feet and it really worried me. When I got back to Limuru College, I rang up an old friend, Jack Wilkinson, the epitome of versatility. A general practitioner, a gynaecologist, an orthopaedic surgeon, a dentist, he is also an ordained minister. "I'll drive over to the college and fetch you for dinner", he answered. And so he did. While his wife was busy in the kitchen, he took me to his surgery and made me lie on a couch. At the end of a thorough examination, as he was putting away his stethoscope, he remarked, "Murdo Ewen there is nothing wrong with you. Your heart is purring away like a well-contented cat."

There was one other mountain in Kenya I climbed in the company of a Finnish engineer. 13,000 feet high, it was in the Rift Valley and had a crater half a mile in diameter at the summit. I cannot recall its name, but I distinctly remember that in the evening my climbing companion, whose name I also forget, invited me to a marvellous dinner in the most expensive hotel in Nairobi.

In Scotland all mountains of 3,000 feet and over are called Munros. The Explanation! Sir Hugh Munro, a very Victorian character, was the first to classify the Scottish mountains in terms of height. Previously, it was generally believed that there were only thirty mountains in Scotland that attained the height of 3,000 feet. Travelling by train and bicycle, Sir Hugh dedicated himself to the task of arriving at a correct assessment.

Sadly Sir Hugh never completed climbing all the Munros he had so carefully listed. The first Munroist was a minister, the Rev. Archibald Aeneas Robertson. He completed them in 1901 and it took him ten years. Providentially his parish was strategically situated in Rannoch.

In the spring of 1976, having climbed most of the Munros in a disorderly fashion, I suddenly made up my mind to kill them off. My son, Alan, himself an aspiring Munroist, thought this was a good idea. Very critical of my map-reading abilities and my contempt for compass and altimeter, he volunteered not only to take care of the logistics, but also to accompany me in climbing the eleven or twelve that remained. This involved journeys into the far reaches of Wester Ross, Glen Lyon, Kinlochhourn and all sorts of remote places in every kind of weather.

We assumed the last one was the newly promoted Munro, Ruadh Stac Mor (3,014 feet) in Wester Ross. It was very inaccessible as we were to discover to our cost. Dr. Joe Houston, a University colleague and friend, drove us up in his Land Rover to the Dundonnel Hotel, owned and beautifully run by Flora and Selby Florence.

Next morning, we set off at 9.30 and had to walk a long distance across a bog-ridden moor before we commenced the actual climb. We made the top and began our long journey back. When we reached the Land Rover in an exhausted condition, it refused to start and we had to walk the last four miles in total darkness. Near midnight we celebrated what we thought was my last Munro with a splendid supper of soup, venison and a bottle of wine.

Unknown to me, Joe and Alan wrote to *The Scotsman* and *The*

Glasgow Herald congratulating me on climbing my last Munro. A few days later a letter appeared in the correspondence column of *The Scotsman*. It read, "Alas the Rev. Prof. M. E. Macdonald must climb one more peak to complete his Munros for since the publication of the 1974 edition of *The Munro Tables*, yet another Munro has appeared. The Ordnance Survey Metric map has elevated 'Sgurr nan Ceannaichean' to the peerage, so that there are now 280 Munros on the list. So far as human fallibility allows there will be no more fresh creations." Signed: J. C. Donaldson, Editor, *The Munro Tables*.

So, on the night of April 13, 1977, my son Alan and I put up at Achnasheen Station Hotel. Next morning, we started shortly after 8 a.m. This is Alan's account of the climb in his Munro Diary (Vol. 1). "Followed the stalkers path into Coire Toll Nam Bian. Struggled through a heavy snow shower which lasted about fifteen minutes. We began climbing the north shoulder of the mountain. About half way up the shoulder, an abominable sort of blizzard began and we took shelter behind a convenient rock until it passed over. Continued up the shoulder and just as we reached the top of it, an even worse snow shower began again. Fortunately there was a small cave in the rock outcrop which was large enough for two. After the blizzard had subsided, we made for the summit. When we attained the ridge, we could see the top roughly 300 feet above. The wind was incredibly strong. To make matters worse, another snow shower descended upon us. This time it really was a blizzard. Again we sheltered behind a rock. After fifteen minutes, the sky cleared. The wind was still gale force, however. We decided to push on. Struggling to keep our balance on the slippery snow slope against the wind, about five minutes later we reached the summit (3,004 feet). Conditions too extreme to take photographs. Tried to get down the mountain as fast as possible. Had to shelter in a cave from a blizzard on the way down. Reached Achnasheen Station Hotel at 1 p.m. This was my father's 280th Munro, having now completed all the Munros in Scotland."

It is possible that a very limited number of Munros may still be elevated to the peerage. In *The Scottish Mountaineering Club Journal 1987* this reference to myself appeared. "151: Murdo Ewen Macdonald who completed in 1977 has hunted down all the new Munros that have since been discovered. He apparently uses this as an excuse for a continuing series of celebratory parties."

In the same year, 1987, a Munroist Tie made its appearance. It takes the form of a stylised heraldic eagle's head encircled by branches of laurel and oak and subscribed by the magic number 3,000. The motif includes major features of the Arms of Sir Hugh Munro and has been approved by the Lord Lyon Court. In appearance, the tie is attractive: it is also exclusive, only available to those listed as "Complete Munroists".

Apart from the intrinsic pleasure of hill-walking, there are the by-product rewards of friendships forged over many years. In my own case, I can think of many. Billy Wood, Alick Mitchel, Bill Shaw, John MacKenzie, Ian Bride, Bertie Martin, Robert Rankine, Joe Houston and Derek MacIntyre. And there is my friendship with Hamish MacInnes, one of the foremost ice and rock climbers of our time.

It was the American Philosopher Professor Platinga's suggestion that I should nominate Hamish for a Doctorate from Glasgow University. The more I thought of it, the more excited I became. I submitted a memorandum listing Hamish's prolific publications, also his inventions including the MacInnes Box, used on Everest climbs, and the Terradactyl ice-axe used the world over. And of course, I made much of the fact that Hamish is one of the world's greatest mountain rescue experts.

With characteristic modesty Hamish was reluctant to let his name go forward, arguing that he was not an academic. Betty and I wore him down and in the end he gave his consent. As I had anticipated, the University Senate were absolutely unanimous. The reception he got at the graduation in the Bute Hall was overwhelming. No doctorate awarded by Glasgow University has proved more valuable on the practical level. Hamish assures me that his doctorate has speeded up his visas and permits for entry into such countries as Argentina, Peru, Nepal and Tibet.

I have climbed in other countries beyond Scotland — England, Wales, Ireland, Austria, Switzerland and Africa. There are Munros I have climbed at least ten times. All this has given me immense pleasure. I regret I have not climbed in Norway, a beautiful country of which I am very fond. I regret it all the more because my ties with the country are so close and intimate. My older son, Alasdair, is married to a Norwegian, Inger-Lise, who is an artist and deeply involved in helping backward children and adolescents. My Norwegian granddaughters, Cheryl and Mairi, are beautiful, but I admit I am biased. Alasdair, with his impressive physique and basic athleticism could have developed into a good climber if he had given the same dedication to mountains as he has to music. The Norwegian mountains are much higher than our Munros, but even at my advanced age I feel confident I could tackle them. If Providence smiles on me, and time permits, I would like to have a go.

CHAPTER 17

EXTRA MURAL MINISTRIES

JOHN WESLEY once said, "The world is my parish". In a much more modest sense I could make a similar claim. Born in a small croft in the Outer Hebrides, I have preached and lectured all over the world, France, Germany, Poland, Canada, U.S.A., Australia, Kenya, Bermuda, Jamaica and the South Caribbean. This would never have happened had I not become a minister of the Gospel.

My first ministry in the U.S.A. was at a very prestigious congregation, Fifth Avenue Church, New York, at the heart of the world's most powerful metropolis. John Sutherland Bonnell, the senior minister had gone on holiday to his beloved Nova Scotia and asked me to take over the pulpit for five weeks.

My accent, still strongly Hebridean, presented difficulties to begin with, but within a few weeks they had generously accepted me. So much so that when Dr. Bonnell retired I was approached to succeed him with an offer of a salary at least twice as much as the one I had in St. George's West. Flattered though I was, nevertheless I declined. I was too deeply involved with my congregation in Edinburgh.

My second last Sunday in Fifth Avenue, a strong deputation from the First Presbyterian Church, Pasadena, California, came to hear me. Afterwards they had me to lunch in the Waldorf Astoria and asked me to become their minister, offering me a staggering salary. I thought it over for a couple of weeks. The answer was a polite no. Things were beginning to happen in St. George's West.

It was during my last week in New York that I received an invitation to address a joint meeting of the Buffaloes and the Elks. Big Buffalo was in the Chair. With a glittering eye he looked like the Ancient Mariner, cornering his victims and said, "Tell me about yourself, I want to give a big introduce." This made me determined to give him the barest minimum information. "Where do you come from?" he queried. "From Scotland." I replied. "Where in Scotland?" "From the North of Scotland." "Which particular spot?" Like the ancient Picts, I found myself driven further north and further west. At the end I found myself swept clean off the mainland of Scotland. His introduction was memorable, to say the least. It went something like this. "Our speaker tonight is the Rev. Macdonald (a title I hate) and he comes from the furtherest, remotest north-westerly tip of the country we call Scotland." I addressed them for forty minutes. They had not heard an accent like that before. When I finished a big Elk in the front seat bellowed in a carrying voice, "Gee, I think he's an Eskimo."

My next visit to the United States was somewhat different. I was invited to lecture at all the American military colleges. Let me explain. Up to the mid-fifties, the American Air Force was part of their army. So impressed were the Americans by the Royal Air Force during and after the Battle of Britain, that they decided to have a separate Air Force. The first Commandant of the new Air Academy was Brigadier General Robert Stillman, a good soldier, who combined charm with toughness and integrity. In Stalag Luft III he was a Lieut. Colonel, and we became close friends.

West Point, the first American military college had a curious tradition. From its inception, the chaplain was always a civilian. The new Air Academy was keen to preserve that tradition. The Stalag Luft III Colonels, a goodly number of whom were now Generals, put their heads together and made it clear they wanted Padre Mac to be the first Chaplain of the new college. So keen were they, that they were prepared to lobby in Washington, hence the invitation to lecture at West Point (Army), Annapolis (Navy), the Air Force Academy (Colorado Springs), the Air University, Montgomery, Alabama and the National War College in Washington. The salary suggested was approximately two and a half times more than I was getting in Edinburgh. In addition I was offered a free car, family allowance and a guaranteed full expenses paid holiday to Scotland once a year. I asked my friend Bob Stillman to give me a month to decide. It was one of the most difficult decisions of my life. In the end, I opted to stay with St. George's West.

But I have not severed my close relationship with the American Air Force. Every three years or so, a reunion of American Stalag Luft III ex-prisoners takes place in various centres in the U.S.A. Betty and myself are always invited as guests. Our return fares across the Atlantic are always taken care of. When I brought this act of generosity to the attention of Bob Brown ("Judge" Brown in prison camp) he answered, "Mac, you acted as chaplain and morale booster to the American Air Force in prison camp for nearly two years without any recompense. The invitation to Betty and yourself is but a small gesture of appreciation".

The next American involvement was the Massanetta Springs Conference, which met annually in the lovely Shenandoah Valley in Virginia. Organised under the auspices of the Southern Presbyterian Church, from the very beginning it continued to be gloriously Ecumenical. I have shared the platform in the spacious Hudson auditorium with Lutherans, Episcopalians, Baptists, Methodists, Church of Christ, Mennonites and the Salvation Army.

Under the successive directorships of Ruth Campbell, Phil Roberts and Charles Tally, I have preached and lectured at this Conference at least nineteen summers. The experience was very stimulating but, even more important, were the friendships forged there. First and foremost were the most hospitable of all hosts and hostesses, Fred and Zoe Speakman. Their lovely cottage on the hill was always open. They had a genius for making people, whatever country they belonged to, feel absolutely at home. It was in Massanetta Springs that my friendship with Dr. Bill Wiseman, and his nice wife, Mavis, sprouted. (He is now Professor of Religion in Tulsa University.) It was there I really got to know Professor Hugh Anderson of Edinburgh University and the intelligent and humorous Gilleasbuig MacMillan of St. Giles Cathedral — two good ambassadors for Scotland. In those days, the proportion of Scottish preachers and lecturers was very high. Professor Alex Cheyne, Professor Robert Davidson, Professor Earnest Best, Professor Robin Barber, Professor Norman Hope, Professor Ian Pitt Watson and myself. Their name was legion. No wonder they called us the Scottish Mafia.

And there was the incomparable Carlyle Marney, from the mountains of Tennessee, big, blond and brilliant, one of the very best preachers in the English-speaking world. Strongly backed by my colleagues, Professor Robert Davidson and Professor Earnest Best, I asked the Senate of Glasgow University to confer on him the Doctor of Divinity. The response was enthusiastic. Marney and his attractive wife, Elizabeth, stayed with us during the celebrations. I was overjoyed that the Senate appointed him the principal speaker at the celebratory dinner.

Not least there was that irascible English genius, Professor Eric Routley. Incredibly versatile, a historian, a theologian, a superb musician, he was beyond any question the greatest Hymnologist of the twentieth century. In such a company, leaping across all provincial and national barriers, no wonder I found Massanetta Springs compulsively fascinating.

My first invitation to Canada came from Pinehill Theological Seminary in Halifax. It was to give the Pollock Lectures in Preaching. The titles of the five lectures were, Preaching and Contemporary Culture, Preaching and its Meaning, Preaching and its Emphasis, Preaching and Reading, Preaching and its Mechanics. I got a good reception and the hospitality I can never forget.

After this introduction to the Canadian academic world, other invitations followed. Years later I returned to Pinehill, but by this time it had become part of the Atlantic School of Theology. In the same premises, Episcopalians, Roman Catholics, Presbyterians, Methodists, taught theological students together in a spirit of exemplary harmony. At an Ecumenical evening service at which I was the preacher, I distinctly recall a Roman Catholic Bishop, an Episcopalian Canon, a Presbyterian Moderator, a Methodist Superintendent and a Salvation Army Captain participating. Why has Canada given the rest of the English-speaking world such an inspiring lead in Ecumenicism?

Two or three years later, Dr. Leonard Griffith, ex-minister of the City Temple, London, invited me to take over the pulpit of Deer Park Church, Toronto for a month. Betty, myself and the two boys flew over and to this day Alasdair and Alan use superlatives when relating the good time they had. The hospitality was simply overwhelming. As we were on our way home, Macmaster University in Hamilton invited me to give a five weeks course of Lectures in Homiletics and Pastoral Psychology. I accepted. Betty and I and the two boys flew back as the school opened towards the end of August.

During our month in Toronto, there was an extraordinary coincidence. Marion Wylie invited us up to her summer cottage on one of the beaches of Lake Huron. One afternoon she asked the Rev. Ian MacKay and his wife, Seonaid, holidaying in a nearby cottage, to afternoon tea. After we were introduced, Seonaid kept staring at me. She got there a fraction of a second before me. Leaping up she shouted, "You and I were at Kingussie School, Scotland, together." And so a great friendship began. I stayed with them in their manse the five weeks I lectured at Macmaster's. Seonaid, the most charming of women, died some years later, but the friendship has continued through her daughter, Margaret, now a lecturer at Edinburgh University, married to an architect, John Gerrard, and living near to us in Glasgow.

I lectured a number of times at Knox College and on one occasion delivered the convocation address. Socially I had a wonderful time. Some of my wartime Stalag Luft 3 friends, among whom were Wally Floody (the tunnels' chief engineer) and Donald Morrison, the leading Canadian fighter ace, got the boys together, put on a magnificent dinner and presented me with a lovely air travel suitcase.

I have left it to the last for it was a moving and memorable experience. In 1965, I was asked to give the convocation address at the centenary celebrations of the Presbyterian College in Montreal, now affiliated to MacGill University. This I did and to my utter amazement, they conferred on me the degree of Doctor of Divinity. I am the proud possessor of a gorgeous hood which from time to time I wear in pulpits throughout Scotland.

On two occasions, I conducted Holy Week services in St Paul's, Hamilton, Ontario. When the church became vacant, I received a call. A couple of years later St. Andrew's, Toronto, made a similar request. Though greatly pleased by the two approaches, I felt I could not leave Scotland.

Then followed the Lutheran experience. It all began at the St. Andrews American Institute of Theology. Dr. Wietske, Director of Theological Education in the Lutheran Seminaries and Universities, a robust and charismatic personality, asked me to deliver the Syme Lectures on theology and Preaching in six Luther Colleges and Universities in the U.S.A. Though I had little previous contact with Lutherans, I felt very much at home among them. The majority of Lutherans in the U.S.A. stem from German and Scandinavian origins. I came to the conclusion that despite ecclesiastical structural differences and Liturgical divergencies, the Church of Scotland and the Luther Church have a close kinship. They both attach great importance to Theology and Preaching.

In the Autumn of 1953, I received an invitation to become the Turnbull Trust Preacher in Melbourne, Australia. The terms of the

Trust were absolutely unambiguous. The person appointed had to preach for three months, morning and evening, in the Scots Church, Collins Street, but was relieved from all pastoral duties. The Trust had been established by a Scot called Turnbull who, as a teenager, had emigrated to Australia. Without formal education, but highly intelligent, he had become a millionaire. His two sons were killed at Gallipoli and the idea of the Trust was to perpetuate their memory. Every three years or so, a Scottish minister of some note was invited.

I went out by air, via Canada, San Francisco, Hawaii, Fiji and Sydney. I came back on a P. & O. liner that called at Perth (Australia), Ceylon, Bombay, Suez and Marseilles. It was an exhilarating experience and, after thirty-five years, I look back at it with fond memories.

On my way out, at San Francisco I met a certain Professor Menzies. An Englishman, his mission was to deliver a course of lectures on atomic physics to Australian universities. A born extrovert, in no time we became friends. Before leaving Scotland I was told I had to attend a Press Conference in Sydney. By sheer chance we touched down at Sydney airport the day the Americans had exploded the first Hydrogen Bomb. When the Australian journalists learned there was a real live atomic scientist aboard the plane, my stock plummeted to zero. When we came through Customs, they ignored me completely and swarmed round Professor Menzies, biro pens at the ready. Imperiously he informed them they had the wrong man. Pointing to me, he said, "That man you see carrying two suit cases is Professor Menzies, the greatest living British atomic scientist." They dropped him like a hot potato and galloped in my direction, while the real Professor Menzies disappeared and caught a taxi. "Professor, are you afraid of the Hydrogen Bomb?" was their first question. I told them, "You are the victims of the smoothest, slickest trick I have ever witnessed. Professor Menzies has escaped. I am a Scottish clergyman and my ignorance of the Hydrogen Bomb gives you a rough idea of what mathematicians think they mean by the infinite." "But, speaking as a clergyman, are you afraid of the H. Bomb?" "No", I answered, "The H. Bomb is neutral. It can't of its own volition press the fatal button. It's sinful suicidal human nature I'm afraid of."

I had a rendezvous with Professor Menzies for lunch the next day at the Windsor Hotel, Melbourne. He had booked a table and was there before me. As I wended my way across a crowded dining-room, this outrageous extrovert leapt up and waving a newspaper above his head, shouted, "Mac, you have made *The Sydney Evening News*." In horror I looked at the headlines, "Scottish clergyman takes a dim view of human nature."

In Melbourne, the newspapers' and radio covering were embarrassing. I could not possibly be such an important person. Frankly I was lionised. I lunched and dined with the most important persons on that vast continent, Robert Menzies, the Prime Minister, Sir Owen Dixon, reputedly the best legal brain in the English-speaking world. So successful was the evening service, the queues began to gather one hour before. The eminent Scot, Sir Alexander Stewart, was so impressed by the evening attendance that he literally took me over. While I was away on some engagement or other, he and his chauffeur arrived in a Rolls Royce at the modest hotel I was staying at and removed my belongings to the exclusive Melbourne Club, where I wallowed in comfort for the rest of my stay. I worked hard but I had a good time.

In 1980, Scots Church, Sydney (the oldest Presbyterian Church in Australia) invited me to occupy the pulpit for three months and to deliver the Ferrie Lectures on "Theology and Preaching". Betty, my wife, was included in the package. She adored Australia. Before we returned home, they presented her with a rather expensive beautiful painting which is prominently displayed in our study. It attracts a lot of attention. Rex Smart, the session clerk of the church and a leading Q.C. looked after us like a brother. So did Hector MacFarlane, Principal Clerk of the Presbyterian Church in New South Wales.

The Australians are a robust people and not just in the physical sense. They attach great importance to Education, the Arts and Culture in general. Spontaneously hospitable, they have a genius for making strangers feel at home.

And there was my Kenya ministry. In 1973 I was asked to deliver a course of lectures on Theology to ministers in Lumura College, some ten miles outside Nairobi. My fellow lecturer was an American, Donald Shriver, Professor of Social Ethics at Emery University, Atlanta, Georgia, now the successful President of Union Theological Seminary, New York. After a few weeks, Don's wife, Peggy, and their children arrived on the campus. Instantly I was adopted as one of the family and we have not lost touch.

Most of the ministers we lectured to were not highly educated, but they were intelligent, enthusiastic and very responsive. And they had an irrepressible sense of humour. Soon after I arrived on the college campus, I became friends with an Alsatian bitch that had been deserted by her owners. Her name was Ginger. She was appallingly thin and had become a compulsive scavenger. I procured food and gave her hospitality in the house which I occupied on the college grounds. The two of us became inseparable. She accompanied me to morning prayers at college chapel, where her behaviour was impeccable. She also accompanied me to the lectures, lying down beside me on the rostrum. For thirty minutes she would be absolutely still as if she was taking in every word. Then she would lift her head, look at me and yawn noisily and mightily. My class thought this was very funny. For ten minutes they would laugh uproariously. Ginger became very popular.

Writing of extra mural ministries, I cannot possibly omit my ministry to the American Institute of Theology in St. Andrews, Scotland. It meets for three weeks every summer and those attending come from every part of the United States. The university goes out of its way to give them the red carpet treatment. I have given four courses of lectures and over the years I have been made more or less permanent Chaplain to the Institute. This demands conducting worship every morning in the ancient, beautiful St Salvator's Chapel and preaching for approximately ten minutes — not an easy exercise. The Director is Dr. George Hall, an American adopted wholeheartedly by the Scots. A Senior Lecturer at the University of Systematic Theology, George stands in direct succession to the great Professor D. M. Baillie. Happily, I am still involved in this important ministry.

CHAPTER 18

TRINITY COLLEGE, GLASGOW UNIVERSITY

I WAS out visiting all evening. Turning the key in the lock at 10 o'clock, I heard the ringing of the phone. Leaving the door open, I ran and lifted it up. The voice at the other end I recognised at once. It was that of Ian Henderson, Professor of Systematic Theology, Glasgow University. He wasted no time on pleasantries. "Murdo Ewen, I want you to come over straight away to Glasgow. It's very important." Some years before, he had a serious illness and I thought he had a recurrence and needed pastoral help. I was his minister in Old Partick Parish Church, Glasgow. How wrong I was!

Intrigued and puzzled, I drove over to Campsie Glen where Ian lived in an attractive old manse. While Kay, his wife, was preparing dinner, Ian led me to his study and shut the door. He sat opposite me and came to the point at once. "The Chair of Practical Theology in Trinity College is vacant. Along with my colleagues, John Mauchline, the Principal of the College, Ronald Gregor Smith, Professor of Divinity, William Barclay, Professor of New Testament, I want you to be the next occupant in the vacant chair." He bowled me over. The thought of becoming an academic had never crossed my mind.

When I recovered I said, "Ian, you have taken my breath away. Do you really think I am intellectually able enough for an academic post.?" He shot out of his chair and stood over me and said. "You may not know that I was your external examiner in Systematic Theology when you sat your finals in St. Andrews. I awarded you a Distinction. What is more, I joined your church in Clasgow and for three years I sat under you at least once and sometimes twice a Sunday. Three things impressed me. You communicated theology through your sermons. You are widely read, especially in modern existentialist literature. And you are one of the few popular preachers in Scotland. The congregation was broken-hearted when you left. From the grape vine in Edinburgh I gather that history is repeating itself."

He went on to add that he had consulted two parish minister friends of his, well known in university circles, Johnstone MacKay and William Steven. They were every bit as enthusiastic as his academic colleagues. At this point I interrupted. "Ian, I can understand why most of those you named are so keen. They are friends of mine, but I find Professor Gregor Smith's support somewhat puzzling; we have never met." And Ian answered, "The explanation is simple. His brother-in-law, Hamish Falconer, a dashing spitfire pilot, was with you in prison camp and he gave Ronnie a glowing account of your ministry there." I was silent for a long time and then remarked, "Ian, it looks as if there is no escape." We both laughed. As we were going downstairs to dinner, he grasped my arm and looking at me with his hypnotic blue eyes said, "Murdo Ewen, the post has to be advertised. However much it goes against the grain you must apply formally."

Late at night I drove back to Edinburgh in a state of turmoil, and told Betty. Her first reaction was one of stunned shock. "But, Murdo Ewen," she expostulated, "we are so happy in Edinburgh and in St. George's West and we have such wonderful friends. Going to Glasgow would mean I would not see my friend Sheana every day. And what about our other close friends, Bill Shaw and his mother, Nansie; Alex and Mona Cheyne; Willie and Margaret Ballantine — to mention only a few."

The next day I took our two sons Alasdair and Alan into my confidence. Their response was far from enthusiastic. They were happy in their respective schools and they were loath to leave their friends behind.

I discussed the problem with my former colleague and friend, Bill Shaw, by this time a lecturer in Theology at Edinburgh University. I knew that his advice, whatever it was, would be intelligent and honest. He thought it over for a few days, then dropped into the manse one night and advised me to apply. He pointed out to Betty and myself that the strain of preaching to big congregations twice a Sunday, year after year, was utterly exhausting. After I wrote the letter of application, the two of us took a few days off to climb the Glen Affric mountains.

The day we returned, late in the afternoon, Johnstone R. MacKay, minister of Stevenson Memorial Church and a member of the appointing committee rang the manse bell. When I opened the door, he held out his hand and said, "Professor Macdonald, let me be the first to congratulate you." Johnstone was a very temperate drinker, but we persuaded him to have a sherry. Lifting up his glass, in a short delightful speech he wished Betty and myself and our two sons the very best on the eve of this challenging adventure.

The first person I told was my oldest brother Angus, the natural inheritor of the croft in Drinishadder, Isle of Harris. After a few pleasantries about the health of his family, cousins and friends in the community, I said I was the new Professor of Practical Theology at Trinity College, Glasgow University. There was a longer than usual silence at the end of which he stammered, "You are telling me, Murdo Ewen, you are a Professor," and I answered, "Angus, that's what I am telling you and I am not sure I am all that happy about it." He answered, "Wait till I tell father," who was ninety years old. On his way back to the phone, before he picked it up, I could hear him laughing "Do you know what father said when I broke the news to him? He removed the pipe from his mouth and said, "I am not at all surprised. Of my four sons, Murdo Ewen was by far the oddest."

When we arrived at Glasgow, Betty and I were given a warm welcome. John Mauchline, Professor of Old Testament, Language and Literature in the University and Principal of Trinity College (a church appointment) held a reception in his spacious house in the University Square. Sir Charles Wilson, Principal of the University, was present. So was Christian Fordyce, Professor of Humanity, Clerk of Senate, next to the Principal, the most powerful figure in the University. Miraculously, I managed to get on with him but he was by no means popular. Someone who knew him well composed this ditty:

I am the Clerk, I'm called Fordyce
I am not young, I am not nice
Christian my name, a parent's vanity
And I am Professor of Humanity.

Present were other representatives from the Faculties of Arts, Law, Medicine and Engineering. Half way through the tea party, something happened that took everybody by surprise. Mr Main, the Bidellus (Head Janitor), ex Regimental Sergeant Major, came in and stood at attention. In a parade square voice he bellowed, "Phone call for Professor Murdo Ewen Macdonald from Heidelburg, Germany." I murmured my apologies and as I left the room, I could feel my stock spiralling up to the ceiling. It was a phone call from General John Stevenson of the American Air Force. When I returned, Professor Gregor Smith sidled up to me and whispered, "That was perfect timing. Did you organise it?"

I had no difficulty in relating to my colleagues in Trinity College. They were congenial, easy to work with and immensely supportive. John Mauchline, Professor of Old Testament and Principal of the College was an able administrator, a kindly man and genuinely interested in students. Professor Gregor Smith was Professor of Divinity. A mischievous kind of Socratic gad-fly, he had an extraordinary ability for provoking controversial discussion. His book, *Secular Christianity*, won him international renown. His ability was never in doubt. While still a student at New College, Edinburgh, he translated Martin Buber into English under the gripping title, *I and Thou*. Ronnie and his German wife Katie adopted Betty and myself and could not have been more kind.

Ian Henderson, Professor of Systematic Theology, was quite different. Born in the Island of Tiree, he was savagely critical of what he called Anglican ecclesiastical arrogance. An original thinker and a brilliant polemicist, he was, I think, the first to introduce Bultmann to the English speaking public. A devout Churchman, he became a member of Partick congregation during my ministry. I remember Ian with affection.

William Barclay, Professor of New Testament Language and Literature, was unique. It could be claimed that he was the most popular theologian in Britain, indeed in the whole of the English speaking world. He was so unusual that all the apocryphal stories told about him are in a sense true. I have lost count of the number of books and commentaries he wrote. They provided an inexhaustible supply of sermonic illustrations to preachers the world over.

When Willie's royalties rocketed to such astronomical levels that, where income tax was concerned, he could no longer cope, he consulted a well-known accountancy firm in Glasgow. Dumping the demands for increased contributions on a spacious desk, Willie said, "Straightening my income tax is like groping my way through the thick undergrowth of the Burma Jungle. You take it over and I'll be glad to pay whatever you charge." After he left the two accountant partners closely examined the very impressive royalties. They were genuinely amazed that anyone could make so much money from writing books. On looking closer, they were even more amazed. The books on whose royalties they had to assess income tax were not preoccupied with sex or macho military adventures: they were positively religious. At which point one accountant turned to the other and remarked, "John, you and I should have worked harder at Sunday School too."

Willie had a widely acclaimed international reputation but essentially he remained a simple and very accessible person, as much at home with doorkeepers, waiters and waitresses as he was with important academics. Gloriously crumpled and dishevelled, his suit looked as if it had been made by a committee that had received an uncertain brief.

The Professor of Church History, William Friend, made history. An Anglican, he was the first layman to be appointed to a chair in Trinity College, Glasgow University. An indefatigable letter writer to *The Glasgow Herald* and *The London Times* he was also a self-appointed amateur archaeologist. Without rest or let-up, he claimed there was a Roman Fort buried near the Lake of Mentieth. Few took the professor seriously. Recently as a result of sophisticated aerial photographs the fort has been discovered exactly at the place Willie had so prophetically proclaimed.

Indubitably, the most eccentric Professor in Glasgow University was Mullo Weir, an inveterate bachelor whose housekeeper was a member of the Free Church and verbally examined him and his students in the shorter catechism. An incomprehensible Lecturer, he nevertheless produced a number of excellent scholars, Professor Willie MacKane, Professor Willie Johnston and Professor Hugh Anderson of Edinburgh. He was implacably opposed to women in the ministry. Half-way through my Professorship of Trinity College a pamphlet was circulated by the British Council of Churches, entitled, *The Shape of the Ministry*. The senate of Trinity College was asked to examine this document and report. At a special senate meeting, all of us Professors and Lecturers had our say. Mullo Weir remained as silent as the sphynx in the Egyptian desert. At the end, when we were pushing back our chairs, Mullo broke his silence, "One thing is certain. If women are allowed to enter the ministry, its shape will be changed."

The lecturers in the Old Testament department were Willie MacKane and Bill Johnstone. Later they became professors, one in St. Andrews, the other in Aberdeen. Till he left Glasgow, I regarded Willie as my closest friend. We regularly went to football matches together on Saturday afternoons.

They were succeeded by Alasdair Hunter and Robert Carroll. Alasdair was a fine mathematician before he switched to Theology. An excellent preacher, he had a good rapport with his students. Robert is rather unique and is a formidable scholar. He has a reputation for not suffering fools and fundamentalists gladly. Tough though he is, Bob has a generous side to his nature. Once after battling with a set of hard line fundamentalists on a television programme, I received a most appreciative letter from Bob.

The New Testament lecturers, Ainslie MacIntyre, Neil Alexander and John Riches, were an interesting lot. Neil, who served for a few years in a parish, was a brilliant pianist and a fine teacher. Ainslie was a good linguist, a good preacher and an amusing after dinner speaker. John, an Anglican clergyman, was an authority on Bultmann. I admire his strong commitment to the Church and his courageous involvement in social and political issues.

The Church History lecturers were impressive. There was Stewart Miechie, an ex parish minister and meticulous scholar. Later came Ian Muirhead, basically a philosopher. He had a wry pawky sense of humour. The department was definitely enriched by the advent of the Canadian Gavin Whyte with his blend of thorough scholarship and zany humour. Ian Hazlett from Northern Ireland made his own original contribution.

I could claim to have had a special relationship with the department of Divinity. My friendship with Ian Henderson and Ronnie Gregor Smith continued with their successors, Alan Galloway, George Newlands and Joe Houston. I preached at Joe's ordination; climbed mountains with Joe and walked the Outer Hebrides with Alan. When the Professor of Humanity, Christian Fordyce, heard of this venture, he asked us, "Who is Boswell and who is Johnson"? This question we discussed with the utmost solemnity. We knew that Boswell was a notorious womaniser and that Johnson was regarded as a glutton. By the time we approached the borders of Benbecula, we were suffering from a crisis of identity. Later Alan was appointed to the Chair of Divinity.

In time, a number of my colleagues either retired or died. They were succeeded by other colleagues equally congenial; Professor John Macdonald, Professor Robert Davidson and Professor Ernest (Paddy) Best. I cannot speak too highly of their warm friendship and unfailing support.

The students varied widely in ability and motivation. I liked them enormously. I was on the staff of Glasgow University for twenty-one years and I came across only one nasty student. Members of staff and fellow students were unanimous that he had a high coefficient of obnoxiousness. He didn't make the parish ministry, praise be to God.

Inevitably there was a goodly percentage of bright students, indeed an imposing list: Peter Thompson, John Harvey, Ian Whyte, Stewart Smith, Michael Mair, Andrew Munro, Stuart Ritchie, Colin McIntosh, John Sharp, Jim Millar, Robert Brown, Andrew McLellan, Robert Glover and others of honours and research calibre. But there were students who entered university on the non-degree slot, yet were exceptionally able. Roddie MacKinnon is a good example. A carpenter by trade, he was accepted for the Licentiate of Theology diploma. He turned out to be such a good student that Professors Ronnie Gregor Smith, Henderson Barclay, Galloway and myself unanimously agreed that if it depended on us, we would have awarded him a first class honours.

I am implacably opposed to fundamentalism. It assumes many shapes and forms. Biblical fundamentalism, political fundamentalism, behaviourist psychological fundamentalism, patheistic fundamentalism and not to be forgotten, structural fundamentalism. This was what the novelist, Kafka, was hitting out against in his condemnation of bureaucracy which he regarded as about the greatest evil. Surely academic structures should be sufficiently flexible, not only to allow but to encourage students of exceptional promise to move out of a rigid non-degree slot to one which does justice to their abilities.

In Trinity College I was appointed to what is called a Church Chair. That meant that the subjects I taught were not included within the Bachelor of Divinity degree. Very soon moves were set in train to integrate my department within the University structure. The senate was open to the idea provided a respectable corpus of knowledge and an acceptable curriculum were presented. With the help of my colleagues, this was duly done, so Practical Theology was recognised as a department of the university. This empowered it to teach and examine students on the levels of ordinary degrees, honours, Master of Theology and Doctor of Philosophy.

For a one-man department, this, however desirable, was in practice impossible. So, in their wisdom, the University senate agreed to the appointment of a Lecturer, David Millar, the University Chaplain. His field was Liturgy, sacramental theology, Church and Society. In addition he was responsible for students' placements and attachments. David's sound scholarship and shrewd perspicacity added considerable strength to the department. Over the years, he and his wife Jean have become close friends.

With David the department employed a number of outside part-time Lecturers. Dr. Arthur Shenkin, a distinguished Psychiatrist, taught Clinical Psychology. A brilliant communicator, there are many ministers in Scotland who feel deeply indebted to him. Dr Andrew Herron, Presbytery Clerk and a qualified, practising lawyer, taught Church Law. His legal expertise along with his pastoral experience, humour and wit, endeared him to the students. Religious Education was taken care of by a series of experts, Dr. Hutcheson, Dr. MacFarlane and Dr. Ian Gray, a good classical scholar and a dear friend of mine. Voice production was in the hands of two charming ladies, Anne Morrison and Dorothy Devine, both very popular with students. And there was the secretary of the department, the incomparable Jean Gardiner. What a superb secretary, none better in the university. She combined a high level of efficiency with a charming accessibility, qualities that do not always gel. It was a happy department.

In my second year at the university, I was invited to preach at the famous City Temple Church in London. After the morning service, a prestigious committee interviewed me and to my surprise asked me to be their next minister. I was flattered that they considered me worthy to succeed such great preachers as Dr. Joseph Parker, Dr. Leslie Weatherhead and Dr. Leonard Griffith.

In the course of discussion, there was an amusing incident. A large tweedy lady with an imperious top-drawer public school accent, eyed me severely and barked, "Professor Macdonald, if you accept our unanimous call are you prepared to modify your accent?" I answered, "On one condition: that you are prepared to modify yours." Good naturedly she joined in the laughter that followed.

They gave me two weeks to decide. Reluctantly I declined. I had been a popular preacher in the Isle of Skye, in the infantry, in prison camp, in Glasgow and Edinburgh and I knew what that cost in terms of mental and emotional energy. I decided to remain as Professor of Practical Theology at Trinity College, Glasgow University. This agonising decision may explain my fitness at an advanced age. Well over seventy years of age, I have not the slightest difficulty in climbing a Munro.

To my surprise I was appointed the first Director of the Selection School, set up by the General Assembly of the Church of Scotland. Its remit was to choose candidates for the Ministry in a more thorough and professional manner. I am certain I speak for all selectors when I say we are immensely indebted to Kenneth Murray, Chairman of the Civil Service Commission. We could not have got off the ground without him.

Candidates are examined in groups of six. There are three assessors allocated to each group. Two of them are Church assessors, drawn from the ranks of parish ministers, theological academics and Church elders. The third is a psychologist. There is also a staff officer who sees to the smooth running of the school. How fortunate we were in our succession of staff officers; Henry Sefton, Henry Shepherd and Ronald Blaikie. They may not have been infallible but they were superb. The Director, who acts as chairman, gives the introductory talk and during the two and a half days moves from group to group to try and ensure parity of standards.

There is no infallible selection procedure. Selectors, amateur or professional, are prone to error. On the other hand it could be modestly claimed that the system we adopted by virtue of its comprehensiveness and thoroughness did definitely reduce the margin of error.

Trinity College, a creation of the Disruption of 1843, came into existence in November 1856. It remained a Free Church seminary till after the union of the United Free Church and the Established Church in 1929. In 1935, in terms of a Minute of Agreement between the

University and the Church of Scotland, three Chairs from Trinity College, Systematic Theology, Old Testament Language and Literature and New Testament Language and Literature became University Chairs. Others were to follow.

It has sometimes been argued that theological education at seminaries is inferior to that provided by universities. This is by no means true. The record of the three Free Church seminaries, New College in Edinburgh, Christ's College in Aberdeen and Trinity College in Glasgow is indeed a glorious one. They produced theologians who had a world-wide reputation; William Robertson Smith, who was removed from his Chair on charges of heresy; Marcus Dods, also accused of heresy; A. B. Bruce and the great George Adam Smith, whose classroom and frayed gown I inherited when I came to Trinity College.

It is also true that Glasgow University which came into being in 1451 had, through the passing centuries, men of genius on its staff. In Philosophy there was Thomas Reid, founder of the "Common Sense" school of philosophy. The magnitude of Adam Smith's accomplishment as the founder of Modern Political Economy should not be allowed to obscure Adam Smith, the Moral Philosopher. There were others like James Watt, not the inventor but the perfector of the steam engine, Joseph Black, who must be counted among the immortals of Chemistry and Joseph Lister, who took Pasteur's discovery of the action of living microbes and applied it to wound sepsis, thus saving many lives.

There are those who maintain that Practical Theology is the sole responsibility of the Church, so they advocate the establishment of a Church College. Such a college would complement rather than replace university training. Parish ministers could be released by the Church for sabbatical terms. Thus, with an existentialist understanding they could more effectively communicate to students what is happening in urban and rural parishes. Let me make three comments.

The first comment is that these very proposals have been implemented for years in the four departments of Practical Theology. In Glasgow, within the terms of the Stanley Mair Lectureship, we have parish ministers holding seminars on Preaching, the Conduct of Public Worship, City Centre Challenge, Suburbia and the witness of the Church in the volatile pop culture of contemporary society.

The second comment is this: I am increasingly suspicious of the cult of the relevant and the demand for a non-theoretical pragmatism. Life in general and human nature in particular are maddeningly complex equations. Situations keep changing with bewildering rapidity. There is no pre-packaged answer to every problem. Better by far the cultivation of a flexible mind and the application of canons of critical analysis. The good minister is the kind of person who approaches human dissonance with a large measure of non dogmatic tolerance.

And the third comment: I am an ardent disciple of the Philosopher, the late Professor John MacMurray. No one has more freely attacked the heresy of divorcing theory and practice. In his Gifford Lectures, "The Self as Agent," this is how he puts it: "The self that reflects and the self that acts is the same self." MacMurray emphasises the primacy of the practical while insisting it must never be separated from the theoretical.

When first we came to Glasgow, we missed the social life we had so hugely enjoyed in Edinburgh. But not for long. Within a few months, we had made a host of friends. At the university we developed a warm relationship with members of the academic establishment. Professor Robert Rankine and his wife Mary, Dr. Dan Martin, Professor Derrick and Carol Thomson, Farquhar and Janet Gillanders, Dr. George Wylie and Sir Charles and Lady Wilson who were very kind to us.

When we bought a flat in Hyndland, within walking distance of the University, we truly landed on our feet. As if Providence had carefully arranged it, we found ourselves in close proximity to ideal neighbours, Ian and May Moreland, Pat and Hilary Shaw. Non-church goers that they were, they did not seem to mind when occasionally I wore my clerical collar. I may have failed to convert them to Churchianity, but I did brain-wash them to become dedicated followers of Celtic, the first British team to win the European Cup under the management of the soccer genius Jock Stein.

On every available Saturday afternoon, Ian and Pat and I attended football matches. I recall one exciting incident which took place at a Celtic/Rangers Cup Final. One of the Rangers' players fell flat on his face in Celtic's penalty box — as deliberate a dive as I have ever seen. The Rangers players began jostling the referee, clamouring for a penalty, which, the courageous man that he was, refused. Ian and Pat were so relieved that they demanded from me a suitable Biblical text to dignify the occasion. Without a second's hesitation I supplied it "Why do the heathen rage and the people imagine a vain thing? He that sitteth in the heavens shall laugh: He shall hold them in derision." Ian and Pat were impressed but on the way home they both accused me of making it up. I took them to my study, opened my King James Authorised Version Bible and pointed them to Psalm 2. They apologised handsomely after which Ian remarked, "But Murdo, you are still capable of making it up."

After settling in our flat in Hyndland, our two sons, Alasdair and Alan, went to the excellent local comprehensive school noted for the number of pupils it sent to colleges and universities. We joined Wellington Church, whose minister Stuart MacWilliam is one of the most outstanding preachers in the English speaking world. We missed him when he left, but we have not lost contact. Betty and myself regarded Stuart and his late wife Margot among our very closest friends.

When I retired in 1984, the students and staff gave us a terrific send off. There was a number of farewell parties. The departmental party was hilarious and was hosted by Jean Gardiner, the departmental secretary. She had leaked information about my absent-mindedness and the student who proposed the toast exploited the leak to the full. Before the party took place, they insisted on presenting me, in addition to the cheque, with something tangible by which I would always remember them. I thought it over and opted for a Hamish MacInnes ice-axe. The rascals leaked this request and I remember colliding with the Principal, Sir Alwyn Williams, a good friend, in the quadrangle. Highly amused, he remarked. "Murdo, this is the first time in the history of the ancient University of Glasgow that a professor, retiring at the age of seventy, regards an ice-axe as an absolute necessity."

The Faculty party was more formal, but thankfully not too much so. The Principal, Sir Alwyn, was not present, but his wife Lady Joan, a charming lady with a beautiful sense of humour, was. Professor Robert Davidson, Dean of the Faculty of Divinity, gave the first eulogistic speech. He started by claiming that the history of the Faculty of Divinity in Glasgow University could be divided into two distinct periods B.M. and A.M. Before Murdo and After Murdo. Then he proceeded to tell a few apocryphal stories about my absentmindedness. They were so witty and so brilliantly told that far from resenting them I found myself laughing more heartily than anybody present.

I forget how many farewell parties Betty and I had, but perhaps the most impressive was the one staged by the former students. The idea belonged to John Bell, a first class student and first class preacher (McKean Memorial Prize man) but it was implemented by Andrew MacLellan with the sort of secrecy that would have shamed the K.G.B. and MI5. The guest speaker was Professor Bill Shaw, my friend and ex colleague in St George's West. His theme was, "Murdo's vices, not his virtues. It was a brilliant performance. My wife Betty's speech, over which she agonised, was also brilliant. After a superb dinner and scintillating speeches, the former students and their spouses who came from all over Scotland and England presented us with a very handsome cheque. This was the first time such a thing had happened in the history of Trinity College, Glasgow. I would like to think that such a marvellous gesture indicated that my former students did not consider me a failure.

CHAPTER 19

EPILOGUE

IT was George Bernard Shaw, with characteristic percipience, who remarked, "You know what a person believes not from the creed he formally professes, but from the assumptions on which he habitually acts."

Throughout my life, I have had many concerns, but only a few dominant ones. These are passionate interests that gathered up my scattered unco-ordinated energies and have given them a sense of purposeful direction.

One of these dominant concerns is Politics. In the Hebridean community in which I was brought up, ordinary uneducated crofters were deeply interested in politics. At their Ceilidhs they could knowledgeably discuss the virtues and vices of the Prime Minister, the Chancellor of the Exchequer and the Home Secretary.

Among Christians there is a deep-seated aversion to mixing religion and politics. One reason is historical. In the past, the Church's involvement in politics was far from edifying. The historian, Professor Herbert Butterfield, himself a devout Christian claims that when the Church occupied the seat of power, she was every bit as ruthless as Communism. In the present the savagery of the Provisional I.R.A. and of the extremist elements of right wing Protestants in Northern Ireland illustrate what I mean.

Another reason is the tacit assumption among many Christians, that the proper sphere of religion is spiritual, while the proper sphere of politics is physical, the material needs of men and women; in sum the world here and now.

The divorce between the spiritual and the secular has its roots deep in antiquity. It goes back to the Manichaen heresy with which the great Augustine for a time flirted. It was the belief that the spirit was good and that the body was bad. Persian in origin, in due course it penetrated Christianity. It became so powerful and pervasive that some of the early Church Fathers were openly hostile to sex. Origen got himself castrated.

The Old Testament prophets did not recognize any spiritual

dichotomy. To them religion was an intensely personal business. Jehovah called each one of them by name. It was He who summoned them to leave the vines they were dressing and the herds they were tending to witness in the maelstrom of Middle East politics.

The privatisation of religion never once occurred to them. The God they proclaimed was Sovereign Lord of all History. The distinction so many Christians insist on drawing between individual and social salvation they would find utterly incomprehensible.

The Manichaen heresy, the exaltation of man's spirit and the denegration of his body is still with us. It sits in every pew in every church in the land. Right wing and Left wing governments are about equally hostile to clerics meddling in politics. This was true of Stalin and Hitler. It is also true of Mrs Margaret Thatcher.

By the time I was half way through my first degree at university, I knew I was a Socialist of some kind or other. Let me make it plain that I have never had any truck with the frenetic hard line Extremists on the right and on the left who are incapable of changing their minds however much the human situation changes. Victims of an arrested development, they have no place in politics.

Most preachers are careful never to get mixed up in politics. They take refuge in sonorous generalities and innocuous banalities. Worshippers in the pew haven't a clue which side they support. On the other hand a minister must not use the pulpit as a party political platform. The preacher who does this is guilty of grossly abusing his high office. Congregations have every right to resent it.

Nevertheless, a minister can with a good conscience pronounce on issues which transcend party politics. Issues like Health, Education, Apartheid and the Nuclear dimension. The preacher must do this intelligently and sensitively. There must be no attempt to gain any partisan ideological advantage.

On television, radio and public platforms I have condemned the piling up of nuclear weapons, the insanity of the overkill. I am not a conventional pacifist, but I am an atomic pacifist. Immensely indebted to Arthur Koestler, in sermons and lectures I have argued that we are living within the New Calendar. The Old Calendar came to an end on the 6th August, 1945. Let me explain. Before that day, mankind lived with the prospect of death as individuals. In the obscene carnages of the battles of the Somme, Passchendale and Stalingrad, each soldier died as an individual. But the moment the first atomic bomb outshone the sun, when it burst over Hiroshima, in a thousandth fraction of a second, we moved from the Old Calendar to the New Calendar. That means that mankind now lives with the prospect of death not as individuals but as a species.

Pro-nuclear advocates maintain the balance of terror is the sole guarantee of peace. A curious argument! I agree with Bertrand Russell. If there is going to be a nuclear war, it will probably come about as a result of accident, not design. At a circus we can reasonably expect an acrobat to be able to walk the tight-rope for five minutes, ten, perhaps twenty, but he can't go on doing it indefinitely. The Soviet Union and the United States can't possibly go on playing a game of Russian roulette ad infinitum.

Another dominant concern is Education. Above all others, this is the one which provoked criticism, sometimes amounting to vicious hostility. At university and later on in the army, I became more and more suspicious of an expensive elitist form of education. Of course the private sector produces highly articulate, brilliant students. It would be surprising if it didn't. It also produces nincompoops who, because they speak with correct upper class accents, occupy positions for which they are lamentably ill equipped. An influential section of the British public tend to equate intonation with education.

Right wing Victorians held that heredity was the sole determinant of intelligence. Marxists supported the opposite view. They claimed that all normal children were potentially equal in intelligence. According to them, environment, not heredity, was the only determinant.

My guess is that right wing Victorians and left wing Marxists were guilty of special pleading. I also suspect that the Elitists have persistently over-estimated the influence of heredity and played down the importance of environment. They have proceeded on the assumption that the educational race goes to the fittest and that an accommodating Providence ensures the fittest are as a rule found in the upper and middle classes.

The late Anthony Crosland drew what seems to me to be a valid distinction between the weak and strong definition of equal opportunity. The weak definition is that children of equal measured intelligence should have the same start in life. In Britain, even according to the weak definition, we have fallen far short of equal opportunity. No amount of propaganda can hide that ugly fact. The English Public Schools and their Scottish equivalents, to all intents and purposes, remain closed to the poorest children, however clever. Those who are able to buy private education have a distinct advantage in securing entrance to the two privileged citadels of learning — Oxford and Cambridge.

The strong definition of equal opportunity is that subject to differences in heredity, every child should have the same chance of acquiring measured intelligence as far as this can be controlled by social action. The implications of the strong definition of equal opportunity are radical in the extreme. Taken seriously, it would mean the creation of a new society where bad housing, bad incomes, badly educated parents are eliminated. The weak definition of equal opportunity invariably goes hand in hand with a laissez-faire market outlook.

In Edinburgh, perhaps the most educationally elitist city in the British Isles, my two sons, Alasdair and Alan, went to comprehensive state schools. The congregation of St. George's West was shocked, but, bless them, they remained loyal and supportive to the end. There was a good deal of sniping from friends and critics alike. "Isn't it your bounden duty to do the best for your children?", they would truculently ask me. My answer to this as a rule evoked blank incomprehension. "I am a preacher and every week I proclaim the most radical of all doctrines under the sun, 'The Fatherhood of God.' This implies I must implacably oppose educational segregation". Reinhold Niebuhr is right. The family is the most selfless and at the same time the most selfish of all human groups.

Reading, I would claim, is one of my most pleasant and rewarding concerns. It began at primary school and has continued ever since. According to American research, most university and college products give up serious reading within a few years of graduating. This is tragic. It spits in the face of the meaning of Education. A university and college education is only the aperitif, whetting our appetite for the main course. There comes a time when we can dispense with our tutors and take up the serious business of educating ourselves.

A preacher's reading must be as comprehensive as it is humanly possible. He or she must keep abreast of what is happening in Philosophy, Theology, Psychology and Science. We live in a world shaped, if not indeed dominated, by Science. As most ministers, with notable exceptions, are not trained in Science, they must rely to some extent on lucid expositors. It is my conviction that there is none better than the late Arthur Koestler. We shall learn much about astrophysics, psychology, neuro-physiology and politics if we read his *Ghost in the Machine, Janus, Act of Creation* and the greatest political novel of the 20th century, *Darkness at Noon*.

For the preacher, reading is not a luxury, it is a basic necessity. It is not possible to proclaim the Gospel, week after week, month after month, year after year, in any relevant sense unless we commune with the original thinkers and creative writers of our day. What is more, reading has considerable utilitarian value. In the business of preaching, it is grist to the mill, providing the preacher with an inexhaustible mine of illustrative material. John Milton described a good book as "the precious life blood of a man's spirit." Thomas Carlyle, the craggy sage, put it thus: "All that mankind has done, thought, gained or been, it is lying in magic preservation in the pages of books."

Fascination with the Paranormal I would also include among my concerns. I share this interest with my preacher journalist friend Stuart Lamont. My conversion from sceptical undergraduate arrogance to an unwavering allegiance to the study of the Paranormal was truly dramatic. While still a student at St. Andrews University, I spent the long summer holidays at home in the Isle of Harris. One lovely August afternoon, I was helping my father cut the corn, when Alasdair MacKinnon, a crofter who lived a mile or so away, on his way back from the village shop, stopped to speak to us. He invited me to a ceilidh in his home. Later on, after I had doffed my working clothes and washed, the two of us walked along a footpath on the edge of a beautiful loch.

Without warning, it happened. Alasdair stopped in his tracks. His face underwent an indescribable change. He began to shiver. Big globules of sweat stood out on his brow. He whispered in a kind of strange, strangled voice, "Calum is dead." I knew who he was referring to. Calum was his son who had emigrated to Canada some twelve years before. I grasped Alasdair by the elbow, steadied him and helped him home. For the rest of the evening he did not utter one word. Round about noon the next day, the postman called at our house and said to my mother, "Isn't it sad about Calum MacKinnon?" "What happened?" she asked. "He was killed yesterday in Montreal," was the answer. Later I calculated the time difference. Calum's death coincided uncannily with Alasdair's strange psychic experience.

More than once in Edinburgh, Stirling and Glasgow, I have had direct experience of Poltergeist phenomena, puzzling, sometimes frightening. On two occasions, accompanied by my friend, Professor Bill Shaw, I have taken part in services of exorcism which appeared to prove successful. I am not sure. The energy behind these inexplicable disturbances may have been on the point of petering out when Bill and I stepped in.

Since then, I have read many books on the Paranormal. They play sheer havoc with our traditional understanding of cause and effect. How do we explain Alasdair MacKinnon's awareness of his son's death? Was it telepathy, precognition or clairvoyance? Frankly I don't know, but of this I am absolutely certain, the perversity of modern physics and the evidence for psychic communication may not have a profound religious significance, but between them they have utterly discredited an old fashioned materialism and a Newtonian mechanistic universe.

All these interests I have found exciting, but by far the most compelling of all my concerns is the communication of the Christian Gospel.

Theology used to be accepted as the Queen of the Sciences. It may have lost a lot of its former prestige, but it is still a vital discipline. All our problems are, at bottom, theological ones. So was slavery. So is apartheid. So is every injustice that robs men and women of their God-given dignity.

The preacher must be hospitable to the insights of the great Theologians. He will listen attentively to Barth, Bultmann, Bonhoeffer, Baillie, Niebuhr, Tillich and Moltmann. His or her task is to take their insights, strip them of abstractions, clothe them in vivid imagery and idiom and communicate them persuasively from the pulpit. Not an easy task, but an exhilarating one!

A staunch ally of Theology is modern Existentialist Literature. Sartre, Camus, Millar, Golding and Ian Crichton Smith, Derick Thomson, Norman MacCaig and others may be agnostics, but one thing they have in common with the Theologians, they take the human predicament seriously. And some of them wrestle with it more robustly and more sensitively than many preachers.

On the whole, much of modern Evangelism depresses me. American millionaire Tele-Evangelists have sordidly devalued the Christian faith by harnessing it to a free-for-all profit-making capitalism. To very complex questions they deliberately and dishonestly give simplistic answers. Worst of all, many of them have sanctified their voracious acquisitiveness in the name of Jesus Christ.

I do not claim to be a born again Christian, though I fully accept that there are those who can genuinely make that claim. The nearest I have ever come to this enviable experience was in the Moral Philosophy classroom when that brilliant Philosopher, Reginald Jackson, was expounding the "Ethics" of the atheist, John Stuart Mill. One sentence in the book leapt out and hit me with sledge-hammer force, "I can only believe in a God who is better than myself." For me this proved a kind of Damascus road experience. On my way home to my lodgings I said goodbye to the neurotic, life-denying God, who is opposed to healthy sport, uplifting secular music and the ordination of women as elders and ministers.

There are ministers and lay people who claim that the outbreak of 'Aids' is a Divine Judgment. God lost his patience with a lascivious and promiscuous generation, so he sent this scourge worse than the Black Death to teach us a lesson. How can any decent, intelligent man or woman bow the knee to such a Cosmic, mindless sadist? I am not saying this monstrous Deity is proclaimed from all our pulpits, but he is from some of them.

If the Christian Church is to survive, we must preach a God who is better than ourselves, in sum, God the Father of our Lord Jesus Christ. He is infinitely more intelligent than the most brilliant among us, infinitely more compassionate than the purest of the saints, infinitely more involved in the human predicament than the most outrageous of all radicals. Isn't that the meaning of the Incarnation? If we are really serious about Evangelism, we must not preach a God who is morally inferior to ourselves.

If we are to communicate the Gospel meaningfully, we must take preaching seriously. Let us create a generation of preachers who will emulate Laurence Olivier with his incomparable skills as an actor. This calls for hard work, determination and great sensitivity. The preacher's task is not just demanding — it is frightening. He or she is called to proclaim in word and action the authentic marks of the Christian Faith.

One authentic mark is critical reflection, hence the importance of Theology. Critical enquiry belongs to the Divine Image within us. It is no respecter of persons. It recognises no sanctified precincts, no sacred niches, no holy of holies. Over our pretentions and posturings, it stands like a flaming angel. It is the sworn enemy of mushy sentimentality.

Another authentic mark is human compassion. The Apostle Paul is right. Love is the supreme gift. Compassion is not a disembodied theological abstraction. It is always incarnate and always costly. Love knows no bounds. It embraces the whole of humanity. The black man is neither my ward nor my case, he is the image of myself in which I experience the agony of belonging. The prostitute is neither my case nor my campaign. She is the incarnation of my sale of true selfhood. The saint is neither my idol nor my reproach. Kagawa of Japan and Mother Teresa are not my accusers, they are the challenge urging me to unearth the Divine Image buried deep within my nature.

Finally there is the authentic mark of a redeeming and reconciling community.

What is the number one threat to the survival of the human race upon this planet? Is it the Hydrogen Bomb? Certainly not! The Hydrogen Bomb is neutral. Of its own volition it can't press the fatal button. No! The real threat is the fact of proximity without community. Science has forced proximity upon us, whether we like it or not. We can have a breakfast in London, then step aboard the Concorde and have a second breakfast in New York, one hour before the one we consumed in London. That is proximity.

But Community! Dear God, it seems a million light years away. We can control objects orbiting in outer space, but we cannot control Northern Ireland. We can land men on the moon, but it took us about thirty years to cross a few yards from East to West Berlin. Yes! Without any shadow of doubt our most deadly enemy is the fact of proximity without community.

Margaret Thatcher, the longest serving Prime Minister of this century, has gone on record as saying, "There is no such thing as Society; it is made up of individuals." She is abysmally wrong. The truth is that Society is more than an aggregate of individuals. It is also made up of basic philosophies, unexamined assumptions, entrenched prejudices, which between them are capable of denying the Brotherhood of Man.

The God who has addressed us so unambiguously in Jesus Christ, will not allow self-appointed reactionaries to thwart His invincible purpose in history. Authentic religion is not a private, esoteric, individualistic affair. It is rooted in social solidarity. God acts through individual lives. Of course He does. He also acts through social and political structures. Christian commitment is first and foremost commitment to Christ, but commitment to Him carries with it an unyielding resolve to create a healing community transcending our mutual alienations and antagonisms.

ACKNOWLEDGEMENTS

I would like to record my sincere thanks to all who have helped in the making of this book.

Mary Millar, my former secretary, typed the first draft perfectly.

Mysteriously several errors appeared in the printed first edition, and I am indebted to friends and relations, Rhoda Macleod, John Angus Macleod, my niece, Catherine Macdonald, the Rev. Roderick Mackinnon, Professor D.W.D. Shaw, Iain Moreland and my wife, Betty, for helping to eliminate them from the second edition.

Paul Currie, Chris Sugden and my son, Alan, for their efforts in publicising the book.

I must not forget Isobel Macdonald and her late husband, Donald N. Macdonald, who introduced me to *The Stornoway Gazette*.

• •

COLLAGE ON THE BACK COVER

Top: The funeral of Bombardier Sconiers, an American war hero (See Page 112).

Centre: On 29th April, 1945, the day we were liberated, Bob Brown, bomber pilot and lawyer from Spokane, suggested that we celebrate this great event. With a *Heath Robinson* fishing tackle we walked down to the nearest river and caught a pike.

Bottom: The *block* in which we lived in Stalag Luft III taken one summer.